ESSENTIAL QUALITIES *of* THE PROFESSIONAL LAWYER

PAUL A. HASKINS, EDITOR

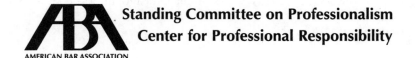

Standing Committee on Professionalism
Center for Professional Responsibility

Printed in the United States of America.

17 16 15 14 13   5 4 3 2 1

Library of Congress Cataloging-in-Publication Data is on file.

ISBN: 978-1-62722-052-1

Dedicated to the memory *of*

Jeanne P. Gray

Director, ABA Center for Professional Responsibility

Legal Ethics Pioneer, Inspirational Advocate,
True Professional

ABA STANDING COMMITTEE ON PROFESSIONALISM
2012–2013

FREDERIC S. URY, CHAIR
Fairfield, Connecticut

NATHAN D. ALDER
Salt Lake City, Utah

KELLY LYNN ANDERS
Omaha, Nebraska

LISA JILL DICKINSON
Spokane, Washington

BART L. GREENWALD
Louisville, Kentucky

DENNIS R. HONABACH
Highland Heights, Kentucky

ANTHONY C. MUSTO
Miami Gardens, Florida

JAYNE R. REARDON
Chicago, Illinois

PATRICIA A. SEXTON
Kansas City, Missouri

Liaison, Board of Governors
PAUL T. MOXLEY
Salt Lake City, Utah

*Liaison, Association of Professional
Reponsibility Lawyers*
JAN L. JACOBOWITZ
Coral Gables, Florida

Liaison, Business Law Section
ANN YVONNE WALKER
Palo Alto, California

*Liaison, National Organization of
Bar Counsel*
TRACY L. KEPLER
Chicago, Illinois

*Liaison, Tort Trial and Insurance
Practice Section*
JOHN W. ALLEN
Kalamazoo, Michigan

AMERICAN BAR ASSOCIATION
CENTER FOR PROFESSIONAL RESPONSIBILITY

Director
ARTHUR H. GARWIN

*Senior Counsel
Lead Counsel, Standing Committee on Professionalism*
PAUL A. HASKINS

CONTENTS
[CONCISE]

CONTENTS
[EXPANDED]

CHAPTER 15
eProfessionalism   189
Stephanie L. Kimbro

CHAPTER 16
Pro Bono and Public Service   207
Anthony C. Musto

FOREWORD

WILLIAM M. SULLIVAN

This is a moment when lawyers, especially new lawyers and law students, need resilience. This book speaks directly to that need. The authors provide tools and concepts that can successfully guide beginners in the law through an increasingly uncertain and challenging career landscape.

Today's new lawyers find themselves entering an American legal profession that is undergoing disruptive innovation in the way legal services are provided and law practices are organized. Under the impact of a severe economic downturn that has made all consumers of legal services more conscious of cost, advances in information technology are rapidly transforming legal work itself. Despite unmet needs for legal representation among many Americans, fewer law jobs are forecast. On all sides, demands that new lawyers be "practice ready" are growing. As established practices are swept away, expectations about what a legal career is and can provide have become less certain.

The challenge for beginners in the law is to develop a sense of direction and the competencies for navigating uncertainty. Despite the facile optimism that often attends talk of "creative destruction" and enhanced "flexibility," students of social change have long noted that adapting to disruptive changes is costly. To describe these problems, they have used terms such as anomie and demoralization, with the results often cynicism and opportunism. There has been important research into what makes some individuals and groups more resilient to such shocks than others. The clear message of this research is that resilience is a function of developing a sense of purpose that is rooted in strong commitments to values beyond the self. For lawyers, resilience requires identifying with the larger values of the profession, including justice and service to society.

How, then, can lawyers and law students set about developing a sense of purpose that will enhance their resiliency in the face of potentially disorienting change? Clearly, individuals need to achieve this in order to become "practice ready" for the long term. But doesn't legal education, both in law school and in subsequent early training in the profession, need to foster resilience? For law schools, this means guiding and nurturing students toward professional identities grounded in the defining purposes of the law and the legal profession.

In *Educating Lawyers*, the 2007 report of the Carnegie Foundation for the Advancement of Teaching, we criticized the current structure of legal education for neglecting to nurture resilience. We saw law school as placing most of its emphasis upon inducting students into learning legal reasoning through what we called the Cognitive or Academic Apprenticeship. By contrast, few schools gave much attention to preparation for practice, which we called the Second Apprenticeship of Practice. We found that schools typically gave least attention to what we called the Third Apprenticeship, that of professional identity and purpose—the very area in which resilience is cultivated. In response, we proposed a rethinking of law school and its educational practices to focus on the formation of identity and purpose as the overarching aim that should integrate all areas of legal education.

Since then, a survey of all U.S. and Canadian Anglophone law schools, conducted in 2011 by Educating Tomorrow's Lawyers, an organization promoting the principles of the Carnegie Report within a consortium of law schools, found that law schools have moved significantly in the direction outlined in *Educating Lawyers*. The teaching of lawyering through reflective engagement with problems of practice has expanded. More courses now give additional attention to understanding the impact of law and the legal profession on society, introducing students to the variety of roles lawyers play. Some schools now offer radically revised third-year curricula to prepare intensively for varied kinds of practice. Ethical issues are more pervasively taught in many curricula, and learning is being more adequately assessed.

However, while there has been progress, law schools still give insufficient attention to the formation and nurture of personal meaning and professional purpose. It is one thing to understand cognitively that resilience depends on developing professional purpose. It is quite another to develop a proactive stance toward achieving a satisfying form of professional commitment. That requires personal engagement with deeper questions such as what larger purposes one wants to accomplish in a legal career and the relative importance of service to clients and society in relation to the search for prestige and livelihood.

Becoming self-reflective and self-critical is essential to improving one's practice and developing a mature, professional identity. They are also keys to resilience. Many of the chapters presented in this volume outline a journey of discovery by engaging with such questions. They provide tools for thinking and self-discovery on the path to greater resilience and satisfaction as a developing lawyer. Those chapters are complemented by others focused more outwardly on usable resources, the importance of wellness in a professional's development, personal and professional development avenues, professionalism challenges in the global legal environment, the critical need for mentoring with identification of mentoring resources and guidance, and the opportunity and duty of pro bono and public service. All serve the larger goal of guiding new lawyers on the path of professional formation.

WILLIAM M. SULLIVAN is co-author of *Educating Lawyers: Preparation for the Profession of Law,* a 2007 report of the Carnegie Foundation for the Advancement of Teaching. He currently serves as Director of Educating Tomorrow's Lawyers at the Institute for the Advancement of the American Legal System.

INTRODUCTION

Background and Purpose

This book is intended to support, guide, and equip law students and young lawyers on the path to professional formation and a career of service. The title, *Essential Qualities of the Professional Lawyer*, uses the term "qualities" in a very broad sense. It should be read to encompass the qualities, traits, habits, duties, values, ideals, practices, and particular knowledge and convictions that together characterize a lawyer as a true professional.

The presence of "professional" before "lawyer" in the title would be unnecessary if all lawyers were professional, in the authentic sense of the word. It is known from disciplinary records and ordinary observation that many are not. Mothers and fathers will continue to proudly believe a professional has joined the family any time a son or daughter graduates law school or passes the bar—or marries a lawyer. But the field of lawyer professionalism and various professionalism codes developed from the premise that a quality of "being professional" cannot be assumed for lawyers, nor is the concept intuitive.

It is said that professionalism is something that even good, principled lawyers must continually aspire to and work on, and that some lawyers have difficulty ever attaining, if they even try. The qualities addressed in this book are the tools new lawyers will need in order to emerge as authentic *and* successful professionals, and all that encompasses, according to leading thinkers in the field.

The book is intended for use in law school professionalism courses. It is also meant to be read by new lawyers just starting their careers in a time of wrenching change in the legal profession. The approach and style of the book's content are intended to be accessible and engaging as both class material and as a casual read.

This volume reflects the vision and commitment of the Standing Committee on Professionalism of the American Bar Association. The committee's purpose is to preserve, protect, and advance the highest ideals of the profession. One part of its mission is to help reexamine and redefine lawyer professionalism in relevant ways as the practice of law evolves. Another part is to support legal education on professionalism. This book merges both of those elements of the committee's larger mission. While there is no consensus on the constituent pieces of professionalism— an amorphous concept—the book assumes agreement that certain core qualities, habits, values, etc., are essential and always present in lawyer professional formation and development, and takes it from there. Those self-evident elements inform many of the chapter topics of *Essential Qualities of the Professional Lawyer.*

Note that "qualities" has a broader intended meaning in the book title than in the definition Professor Neil Hamilton assigns to the term in Chapter 1.

In the preceding Foreword, William M. Sullivan views this book as an important new resource for confronting an acute need within legal education to focus more attention on both preparing for practice and, critically, on supporting the formation of professional identity and purpose. Mr. Sullivan, co-author of the groundbreaking 2007 report of the Carnegie Foundation for the Advancement of Teaching, *Educating Lawyers: Preparation for the Profession of Law*, refers to research concluding that for the emerging generation of lawyers to withstand continuing shocks to the profession, they must acquire "a sense of purpose rooted in strong commitments to values beyond the self. For lawyers, resilience requires identifying with the larger values of the profession, including justice and service to society."

Mr. Sullivan sees this volume as serving the legal profession's urgent interest in aligning lawyer education and training with new lawyers' actual professional development needs, as identified in that seminal Carnegie Foundation report.

Consistent with that report, a primary message of the book is that internalizing the highest values of the profession not only uplifts the profession and distinguishes the lawyer, it also provides a practical path to acceptance from peers and clients and thus, in the end, to a successful legal career.

Overview of Content

The book is anchored at the front by two chapters respectively (i) revealing core professional values and (ii) addressing the need for students not to lose touch with their true selves and their personal values and convictions in the process of becoming a lawyer. It is anchored at the back by a forward- and outward-looking examination of the transformative impact of globalization on legal practice, and of progress made, and yet to be made, in the acceptance of legal professionalism norms in an international practice environment.

In Chapter 1, *The Qualities of the Professional Lawyer*, Professor Neil W. Hamilton draws on original research in making the compelling case that a strong service ethic is at the core of professional formation and a contributor to professional success. The professional lawyer develops an internalized moral core characterized by a deep responsibility for others, particularly clients, Professor Hamilton reports. Empirical research by Hamilton and colleagues has established that legal employers recruiting new lawyers look beyond technical skills and consider qualities such as capacity for integrity, honesty, and trustworthiness, as well as evidence of good judgment and teamwork skills. Clients look for similar traits, Hamilton reports, as well as high commitment and responsiveness. Thus, a strong service ethic, encompassing client service and public service, not only informs the professionalism ideal, but also represents what colleagues and clients look for in a lawyer.

Chapter 2, by Professor Daisy Hurst Floyd, is *The Authentic Lawyer: Merging the Personal and the Professional*. Professor Floyd observes that, by its nature, the classic form of legal education introduces a risk that students will experience a damaging loss of self as they replace the identities they brought to law school with new professional identities. Gathering, explaining, and advancing scholarship on point, Professor Floyd examines the importance of remaining authentic as a law student and as a lawyer, identifies challenges to doing so, and offers strategies for remaining true to both the personal and the professional "self".

The book then shifts to an examination of that singular quality that goes to the heart of professionalism—civility—approaching the topic from two divergent but compatible perspectives. Chapter 3, *Civility as the Core of Professionalism*, is a classic and wide-ranging treatment of civility as highest ideal, surveying the term's meaning, its interplay with the ethics rules, what civility looks like in practice, and what many jurisdictions are doing to strengthen lawyer observance of civility. The chapter was written by Jayne R. Reardon, executive director of the Illinois Supreme Court Commission on Professionalism. Chapter 4 is the flip side of Chapter 3, making a persuasive case from the practitioner's perspective that a civil approach to representation is quite often the most successful approach as well, in terms of meeting client objectives and conserving resources. Chapter 4, *The Practical Case for Civility*, was contributed by Peter R. Jarvis and Katie M. Lachter of Hinshaw & Culbertson LLP.

In Chapter 5, Professor William D. Henderson, another pre-eminent figure in lawyer professional development scholarship, presents a frank and powerful thesis, backed by extensive empirical data, that the "cognitive markers" that have long driven law school admission and lawyer recruitment by top-ranked law schools and national firms, i.e., grades and scores, are not the best predictors of lawyer success. Professor Henderson's work reveals that factors not highly valued by the most selective schools and firms are more likely to correlate with professional effectiveness and success. Among the mass of evidence Henderson marshals is the observation that top-tier schools historically have not fared well against lower-tier competition in national trial advocacy competitions, which test a quintessential measure of lawyer ability—trial skills. (A notable exception to that rule among top-tier schools being the Northwestern University School of Law.) Professor Henderson urges an overhaul of legal education with a heightened emphasis on practical skill training and professional development. Only then can the nation's acute need for more good lawyers be adequately addressed, he maintains. Chapter 5 is titled *Successful Lawyer Skills and Behaviors*.

Chapters 6 and 7 speak to (i) the growing importance of and need for inclusive thinking in law practice, and (ii) the frustrating dual reality of, on the one hand, an extraordinary and expanding record of achievement by women lawyers and, on the other, persistent structural barriers to women's professional growth and access.

Consultant and author Dr. Arin N. Reeves, a pioneer in the field of "inclusive thinking" for lawyers and law organizations, posits and presents evidence that learning to think inclusively—that is, to make it a habit of always engaging diverse and divergent voices, perspectives and backgrounds in one's professional processes—represents not only adherence to professional ideals, but also the better path to professional effectiveness in an increasingly complex world. Dr. Reeves' contribution, *Inclusive Thinking: Essential Professional Value / Powerful Professional Advantage*, is Chapter 6.

Roberta (Bobbi) Liebenberg, chair of the ABA Gender Equity Task Force and past chair of the ABA Commission on Women in the Profession, wrote Chapter 7, *Women in the Law: Overcoming Obstacles, Achieving Fulfillment*. Ms. Liebenberg comprehensively and frankly addresses the seemingly intractable difficulties women still face in achieving equal status and power in the legal world, notwithstanding the impressive credentials, accomplishments and records of countless women lawyers and judges. Ms. Liebenberg offers high-value insights and guidance to women lawyers trying to make their way up law firm ladders. Among other things, she urges young women lawyers to make themselves invaluable through their competencies; to self-promote within their firms, as their male colleagues do; to develop professional networks and spread their base through articles and presentations; and to find mentors to teach them and sponsors to stand up for them when promotion and compensation decisions are made.

The next four chapters dig deeply into foundational duties—and qualities—of the professional lawyer. In Chapter 8, *Mastering the Craft of Lawyering*, ethics and lawyer discipline expert Mark A. Dubois explores the multiple dimensions of lawyer competence and the constant duty of every lawyer to be competent in all client representations, as well as the consequences of incompetence. A former chief disciplinary counsel for the state of Connecticut, Mr. Dubois defines what it is to be competent, and identifies proven paths to developing competence in legal practice.

In Chapter 9, authors Professor Daisy Hurst Floyd (also the author of Chapter 2) and Paul A. Haskins, ABA CPR senior counsel, examine *Diligence* as a professional attribute and an ethical duty. Though often overlooked or taken for granted, the duty of diligence has informed innumerable disciplinary cases against lawyers who have neglected client matters. The chapter also explores the relationship of diligence to other ethical duties. Chapter 10, *Honesty, Integrity and Loyalty*, again by former Connecticut disciplinary counsel Mark A. Dubois, untangles the web of interlocking and often inconsistent duties of the lawyer to client, court, adversaries, and the public. Mr. Dubois begins by noting that the public tends to take a dim view of attorney integrity, and sees most lawyers as dishonest. What new lawyers need to grasp, and get comfortable with, is that complex ethical duties will often compel them to act in ways—for instance, withholding knowledge of client guilt, or representing a murderer—that, while compelled by the rules and highest principles of the profession, may not pass the honesty or integrity test to the untrained eye of an average citizen. But that cannot be the lawyer's concern.

Chapter 11, *Navigating the Character and Fitness Process*, flows from the Chapter 10 discussion on honesty and integrity. Authored by Patricia A. Sexton, President of the Missouri Board of Law Examiners, this chapter carefully walks the bar admission candidate through the character and fitness review segment of the admissions process. Ms. Sexton gives assurances that most law students will sail through the process with little if anything to fear, as long as they conscientiously meet all process dates and disclose all requested information. For those who face a closer review by bar authorities, as consequence of past conduct or not taking the process seriously, Ms. Sexton offers expert guidance on getting through the process.

In Chapter 12, *Reputation*, Avarita L. Hanson presents a thoughtful, heartfelt and incisive essay on the real meaning of reputation, its centrality to lawyer professional identity and professional success, and ways to build and protect an excellent reputation in the legal profession. Ms.

Hanson is Executive Director of the Georgia Chief Justice's Commission on Professionalism.

A leading national expert on the lawyer mentoring process and programs, Lori L. Keating, and a practitioner and author committed to effective mentoring habits, Michael P. Maslanka, team up in Chapter 13 with a resource-rich examination of the criticality of lawyer mentoring to individual lawyer development and the future of the profession. Ms. Keating and Mr. Maslanka persuasively assert that all new lawyers must have mentors to succeed; describe the new national mentoring movement and the growth in states' formal mentoring programs; and urge veteran lawyers to become mentors, both because it is the right thing to do and because it can renew their own commitment to professional ideals. Ms. Keating, Secretary to the Ohio Supreme Court Commission on Professionalism, is Chair of the National Legal Mentoring Consortium. Mr. Maslanka is head of the Dallas office of Constangy Brooks & Smith. Chapter 13 is *Finding and Getting the Most out of a Mentor*.

In Chapter 14, *Handling Money*, writer Martha Middleton examines the ethical tripwire that the handling of client money places in front of a distressingly high number of lawyers, despite the legal ethics proscription of misappropriation of client and third-party property. Ms. Middleton reviews the controlling rules and reflects on the prevalence of abuse of the rule, usually with dire disciplinary consequences for the lawyer. Ms. Middleton also notes the strong nexus between lawyer substance abuse and lawyer disciplinary actions stemming from misuse of client funds.

eProfessionalism, Chapter 15, by Stephanie L. Kimbro, is *ea* fresh, penetrating, and important look at lawyers' growing use of social media, with a clear cautionary message on the ethical, professional, and practical need to keep one's personal and professional personas separate on public sites. Ms. Kimbro, a lawyer-consultant and expert in the field, stresses the importance of mastering privacy settings on social media applications and of avoiding undesirable consequences of inadequate management and understanding of one's web presence. She identifies best and problematic practices and offers "netiquette" guidance. The *eProfessionalism* chapter also covers online marketing tools for lawyers.

In Chapter 16, *Pro Bono and Public Service*, Professor Anthony C. Musto combines an illuminating recitation of every lawyer's pro bono and public service duty with a passionate appeal to new lawyers to discover their best selves while serving society and the profession through a real commitment to public service. With an emphasis on every lawyer's special responsibility to perform true pro bono—donating legal services to people of limited means—Professor Musto notes that pro bono work offers an invaluable opportunity to develop and expand legal skills as well as a chance to build key professional connections. A former prosecutor, he also makes the case that à career in government legal service can be a special and uniquely satisfying form of public service. Chapter 16 describes other categories of volunteer public service opportunities open to lawyers.

Health and Wellness, Chapter 17, by Frederic S. Ury and Deborah M. Garskof, urges young lawyers to recognize at the outset of their careers the close connection between career success and attention to personal health and wellness. Observing and documenting that the law is often a high-stress occupation and that stress unquestionably correlates with health problems, Mr. Ury and Ms. Garskof persuasively call upon lawyers to take ownership of their health by paying close heed to it throughout their careers. Regular exercise, good nutrition, the capacity to relax, and work-life balance are habits often associated with the successful and contented lawyer. The chapter pays special attention to the corrosive impact of substance abuse and untreated mental health issues on many careers, and offers resources. Mr. Ury is a Founding Partner of Ury & Moskow LLC, in Fairfield, Connecticut. Ms. Garskof is a member of the firm.

Chapter 18, *Mindfulness and Professionalism*, by Jan L. Jacobowitz, is a progressive and enlightening exposition of the adoption of mindfulness techniques by lawyers to moderate and avoid the kind of emotional reactions that precipitate uncivil and ill-advised conduct. Ms. Jacobowitz explains how the use of controlled breathing and other techniques can enable the lawyer's better judgment to prevail in challenging situations, such as insulting or overly confrontational behavior by opposing counsel. The author chronicles the growing adoption and advocacy of mindfulness practices within the bar and more widely in the private and public sectors. Ms. Jacobowitz has extensive experience with application of mindfulness techniques to the practice of law, and is a leading advocate of their use. Ms. Jacobowitz is a Lecturer in Law and the Director of the Professional Responsibility and Ethics Program at the University of Miami School of Law.

Chapter 19, *The Importance of Personal Organization*, by Kelly Lynn Anders, shows that being organized is more than a virtue—it can make legal practice in an increasingly complex world manageable, and in some cases even can prevent the lawyer from facing attorney discipline. Lawyers without a firm handle on the whereabouts of pleadings, client property, ever-expanding electronic data and other files are more prone to engage in negligence—for instance, a missed court filing date or misplaced client property. Ms. Anders, author of the book *The Organized Lawyer,* offers astute tips on getting one's office functionally organized, and keeping it that way.

The other anchor of this book, *Globalization and Professionalism*, Chapter 20, is the work of Professor Robert E. Lutz, a leading national and international expert in the area of the effects of globalization and technology on the legal profession. Surveying an array of problematic issues now confronting international law practice as a function of both cross-cultural fault lines and, in some parts of the world, pervasive corruption, Professor Lutz articulates an urgent need for development and adoption of comprehensive lawyer professionalism standards for international practice. For new and aspiring attorneys, Professor Lutz notes that boundless opportunities lie ahead for lawyers in the international arena, along with a responsibility to seize the mantle of lawyer professionalism and stand firm against corruption and socially irresponsible business practices in their future dealings with foreign clients, adversaries, and co-counsel.

A final note: All chapter authors were asked by the editor to forego the use of footnotes in their chapters, consistent with the plan and purpose of this book. Some but not all authors—depending on subject matter treatment—added at their option citations in a Sources/Reading list at the end of the chapter.

Paul A. Haskins, Editor
Senior Counsel, Center for Professional Responsibility
American Bar Association

ACKNOWLEDGMENTS

The twenty authors who contributed to this volume believed enough in its message, and the urgency of that message, to find space in their already full schedules to deliver chapters on a very tight timetable. They worked well and fast, and less than a year after the first author was formally enlisted for this project, an important new lawyer professionalism book is on the street, a testament to the authors' knowledge, skill, and level of personal commitment. In agreeing to meet this challenge, the authors of *Essential Qualities of the Professional Lawyer* were incentivized by nothing more than a chance to guide and support those now entering their profession.

Frederic S. Ury, Chair of the ABA Standing Committee on Professionalism since August 2012, has been a force behind the committee's accelerated drive to make this book happen and to deliver it to legal educators and the new and aspiring lawyers who can benefit from it most. Mr. Ury and the Standing Committee saw—and acted decisively to address—a palpable need for a practice-focused professionalism book to help law students and new lawyers absorb those core professional values that can enable them stay internally grounded in these uncertain times for lawyers, while taking on the skills to succeed.

The germ of a good book idea came from Mr. Ury's predecessor as committee chair, Dennis Honabach, who had urged development of a new kind of professionalism book built around a varied set of themes tied together by their relevance to practical aspects of lawyer professional development.

The members of the 2012–13 ABA Standing Committee on Professionalism fully bought into this book, by word and by deed. Notably, more than half of the committee roster—five of nine members—authored or co-authored chapters on topics drawing from their subject matter expertise. In addition to Fred Ury, the chair, Kelly Anders, Tony Musto, Jayne Reardon, and Patricia Sexton all conscientiously delivered chapters. All members of the committee passionately backed the book and encouraged its development while contributing ideas for promotion and distribution and next-step development of a teaching manual.

Avarita Hanson, Chair of the ABA Consortium on Professionalism Initiatives, an ABA affinity group of the Standing Committee, also delivered a chapter, as did Lori Keating, a Consortium member. Jan Jacobowitz, a new liaison to the Committee from the Association of Professional Responsibility Lawyers, produced a chapter as well.

Michael P. Downey, a partner with Armstrong Teasdale in St. Louis, Mo., provided peer review of Stephanie Kimbro's chapter on eProfessionalism.

Prof. Robert Lutz, author of Chapter 20 on globalization, expressed appreciation for comments on early chapter drafts by Michael Trayner and Hon. Gary Hastings.

Art Garwin, now Director of the ABA Center for Professional Responsibility, informed and facilitated the book's development, offering leads on author prospects, supporting and taking part in editing, dispensing sound judgment and drawing on his extensive experience throughout the project management process, and generally supporting the project's progress. Mr. Garwin and ABA Ethics Counsel Dennis Rendleman also supplied critical insights, ideas, and suggestions as the outline of the book took shape.

Kimley Grant, paralegal for the Center for Professional Responsibility, kept the project on track, pulling together the loose threads of the work in progress, coordinating with the authors and the editor, providing quality control, and helping to meet the ambitious target date for delivery of a completed manuscript to ABA Publishing. Natalia Vera, CPR senior paralegal, brought well-honed blue-booking skills to the enterprise.

ABA Deputy Regulation Counsel Theresa Gronkiewicz and CPR Associate Counsel Helen Gunnarsson provided critical readings of certain chapter drafts. Ellyn Rosen, Regulation Counsel of the ABA, also suggested chapter authors, as did Ethics Counsel Rendleman.

Standing Committee Chair Fred Ury was an important source of author and topic suggestions. The richness of the range of chapter offerings, as reflected in topics such as *Globalization and Professionalism, Health and Wellness,* and *Mindfulness and Professionalism,* can largely be credited to Mr. Ury's expansive vision of the things new lawyers should know as they brace themselves for a life in the law.

Jeanne Gray, the late Director of the ABA Center for Professional Responsibility (CPR) and ABA Associate Executive Director, strongly supported this project.

Ms. Gray and and Mr. Garwin created space in the schedule of CPR Senior Counsel and book editor Paul Haskins to take on and complete the job of planning, organizing, coordinating, and editing the book on a fast-track schedule—from concept to publication within one ABA year.

The book is dedicated to the memory of Jeanne Gray.

Angela Burke, CPR Director of Marketing and Planning, worked to secure the book's budget and spearheaded the marketing effort within CPR.

The highly professional work of ABA Publishing and Rick Paszkiet, the ABA Entity Book Content Publishing Director who ran the project on the publishing side, speaks for itself.

The Standing Committee on Professionalism and the editor are indebted to all.

—The Editor

THE AUTHORS

Kelly Lynn Anders is the author of *The Organized Lawyer* (Carolina Academic Press 2009) and *Advocacy to Zealousness: Learning Lawyering Skills from Classic Films* (Carolina Academic Press, 2012). She has published numerous articles on professionalism, diversity, film history, art law, and social media. Ms. Anders' work has appeared in the *ABA Journal*, *The National Law Journal*, *State Legislatures*, and *Journal of Public Policy & Marketing*, among others, and she has provided commentary to local and national media. She has chaired the Kansas Bar Association's Diversity Committee and co-chaired the American Bar Association's Committee on Visual Arts and Dramatic Works, Section of Intellectual Property Law. Ms. Anders currently serves on the editorial boards of *Court Review* and *The Nebraska Lawyer*. She was appointed to the ABA's Standing Committee on Professionalism in 2012. Her website is www.theorganizedlawyer. com (last visited April 11, 2013).

Mark A. Dubois is an attorney with Geraghty & Bonnano, LLC in New London, Connecticut. Mr. Dubois limits his practice to legal ethics and legal malpractice. From 2003 to 2011, he served as Connecticut's first Chief Disciplinary Counsel, responsible for the prosecution of cases involving attorney ethics violations, the unauthorized practice of law and attorneys convicted of crimes. Mr. Dubois is a graduate of the University of Connecticut School of Law, where he is an adjunct faculty member. He has also served on the faculty of Quinnipiac University Law School, where he was a Distinguished Practitioner in Residence. He lectures frequently in Connecticut and nationally on legal ethics matters. Mr. Dubois has served as an expert witness in legal ethics matters in state and federal courts. He is President-Elect of the Connecticut Bar Association and a member of several state and national bar groups, and he has been board certified in civil trial advocacy for more than 20 years.

Daisy Hurst Floyd is a University Professor of Law and Ethical Formation at Mercer University School of Law in Macon, Georgia, where she served as Dean from 2004 until 2010. She is the author of numerous law review articles and a frequent speaker at academic and law conferences. Her teaching and research interests include legal ethics, legal education, civil procedure, evidence, and interviewing and counseling. Professor Floyd was named a Carnegie Scholar by The Carnegie Foundation for the Advancement of Teaching and participated in the Foundation's study of legal education and its *Life of the Mind for Practice Seminar*, exploring the relationship between liberal education and professional education. She holds a BA and MA from Emory University and a JD from the University of Georgia School of Law. Professor Floyd is a Fellow of the American Bar Foundation, the Lawyers Foundation of Georgia and the Texas Bar Foundation. She is a member of the ABA President's Council on Diversity in the Profession.

Deborah M. Garskof is a member of the Ury & Moskow, LLC law firm in Fairfield, Connecticut, where she focuses her practice in the areas of appellate practice, commercial law, employment law, and real estate. Ms. Garskof previously was a trial attorney with the Federal Labor Relations Authority, where she practiced in the areas of labor and employment law and investigated and prosecuted unfair labor practices under the Federal Service Labor-Management Relations Statute.

Ms. Garskof has lectured on the topics of mechanic's lien law and employment law. She is co-author of "Asset Assignment from the FDIC, Debt Collection Strategies," *Connecticut Lawyer* (August, 1999), and co-author of "Parents Legal Primer: Teens, Trouble, Consequence, and Liability," *Connecticut Lawyer*, Vol. 14 No. 3 (November, 2003). She earned her JD from Suffolk University Law School, *cum laude,* in 1994 and her BA degree from the University of Connecticut Honors College, *summa cum laude*, in 1991, and was inducted into Phi Beta Kappa. Ms. Garskof is a member of the Massachusetts, Connecticut, and New York Bars.

Neil W. Hamilton is Professor of Law and Director of the Holloran Center for Ethical Leadership in the Professions at the University of St. Thomas School of Law (MN). He served as Interim Dean in 2012 and Associate Dean for Academic Affairs twice at St. Thomas. He served from 1980 until 2001 as Trustees Professor of Regulatory Policy at William Mitchell College of Law. He has taught both the required course in Professional Responsibility and an ethics seminar for thirty years. He is the author of three books, more than seventy longer law journal articles, and more than 100 shorter articles as a bi-monthly columnist on professionalism and ethics for the *Minnesota Lawyer* from 1999 to 2012. In 2002, the *Minnesota Lawyer* selected him as one of the recipients of its Lawyer of the Year awards, and in 2003 he received the Hennepin County (Minneapolis) Professionalism Award. In 2004, the Minnesota State Bar Association presented him its highest award, the Professional Excellence Award, given to recognize and encourage professionalism among lawyers. He received the University of St. Thomas Presidential Award for Excellence as a Teacher and Scholar in 2009. In 2012, *Minnesota Lawyer* honored him again for outstanding service to the profession and placed him in its Circle of Merit for those who have been honored more than once.

Paul A. Haskins is Senior Counsel in the American Bar Association Center for Professional Responsibility and Lead Counsel for the Standing Committee on Professionalism. He joined the ABA in 2005 as Staff Counsel in the Division for Legal Services, where he was staff originator of the ABA Military Pro Bono Project. Previously, Mr. Haskins practiced civil litigation in Chicago and was a newspaper reporter and columnist in Washington, D.C., and North Carolina. He holds a BA from the University of Michigan in Ann Arbor, and a JD from Northwestern University School of Law in Chicago.

Avarita L. Hanson is the Executive Director of the Georgia Chief Justice's Commission on Professionalism in Atlanta, Georgia, and has more than thirty years of experience in the law. She is the 2011–13 Chair of the ABA Consortium on Professionalism Initiatives. Ms. Hanson served as president of the Gate City Bar Association and Georgia Association of Black Women Attorneys. She is a member of the American Bar Association, State Bar of Georgia (Commission on Continuing Legal Competency, Bench and Bar Committee, and Professionalism Committee), State Bar of Texas, Atlanta Bar Association, Georgia Association for Women Lawyers, National Bar Association, Lawyers Club of Atlanta, and Legal Ministry of Cascade United Methodist Church. Ms. Hanson is the author of *Professionalism and the Judiciary: Lessons Learned as Georgia Approaches 20 Years of Institutionalizing Professionalism*, Chief Justice of Ontario's Advisory Committee on Professionalism Tenth Colloquium on the Legal Profession, http://www.lsuc.on.ca/media/tenth_colloquium_hanson.pdf (March, 2008). She regularly pens articles for the Professionalism Page of the *Georgia Bar Journal*.

William D. Henderson is a Professor of Law at the Indiana University Maurer School of Law, where he teaches courses on the legal profession, project management, business law, and law firm economics. His research, which focuses on the empirical analysis of the legal profession and legal education, has been published in leading law journals and leading publications for practicing lawyers, including *The American Lawyer*, the *ABA Journal*, and the *National Law Journal*. Bill's observations on the legal market and legal education are frequently quoted in the mainstream media, including *The New York Times*, *Wall Street Journal*, *The Los Angeles Times*, *The Atlantic Monthly*, *The Economist*, and National Public Radio. As a result of his analysis of the structural changes occurring in the legal profession, Professor Henderson was recently included on *The National Law Journal's* list of The 100 Most Influential Lawyers in America. In 2012, he was named among the Top 5 Most Influential People in Legal Education by *The National Jurist* magazine. In 2009, Professor Henderson was named a "Legal Rebel" by the *ABA Journal* in recognition of his influence on legal education and the changing economics and structure of the legal profession. Professor Henderson speaks to law firms, law schools, and legal organizations across the country, sharing insights on the future of legal services and the results of his empirical research.

Jan L. Jacobowitz is a Lecturer in Law and the Director of the Professional Responsibility and Ethics Program (PREP) at the University of

Miami School of Law. Under Ms. Jacobowitz's direction, PREP received a 2012 E. Smythe Gambrell Professionalism Award, for outstanding professionalism programming, from the Standing Committee on Professionalism of the American Bar Association. Ms. Jacobowitz has presented dozens of PREP Ethics CLE Seminars. She has been a featured speaker or panelist on various legal ethics topics, including social media, advertising, and mindful ethics. Ms. Jacobowitz co-developed and teaches "Mindful Ethics: Professional Responsibility for Lawyers in the Digital Age," and co-authored the book, *Mindfulness & Professional Responsibility—Incorporating Mindfulness* into the Law School Curriculum. She is on the board of the Association of Professional Responsibility Lawyers (APRL) and currently serves as APRL's special liaison to the ABA Standing Committee on Professionalism. Ms. Jacobowitz began her career as a Legal Aid attorney; prosecuted Nazi war criminals at the U.S. Department of Justice; was a litigator with private firms in Washington, D.C., and Miami; and served as in-house counsel for a large corporation. In addition to her current faculty position, Ms. Jacobowitz frequently consults on legal ethics matters.

Peter R. Jarvis leads Hinshaw & Culbertson LLP's national Lawyers' Professional Responsibility/Risk Management Practice Group and is licensed in California, New York, Oregon, Washington, and Alaska. He received his BA from Harvard (1972) and his MA (Economics) and JD from Yale (1976). His practice emphasizes advising lawyers and law firms on a broad range of legal ethics and risk management questions. He is a former member of two state bar ethics committees, a co-author (with Geoffrey C. Hazard, Jr. and W. William Hodes), of the national treatise, *The Law of Lawyering* and a co-author (with Anthony E. Davis) of *Risk Management: Survival Tools for Law Firms.* He is a member of the American Law Institute and has received the Oregon State Bar President's Membership Service Award, the Harrison Tweed Special Merit Award from ALI-ABA, and the Burton Award for distinguished legal writing. Mr. Jarvis is based in Hinshaw & Culbertson's Portland, Oregon, office.

Lori L. Keating is Secretary to the Supreme Court of Ohio Commission on Professionalism. As Commission Secretary, she oversees several statewide professionalism initiatives, including the Lawyer to Lawyer Mentoring Program. Ms. Keating is a faculty member of the Ohio Judicial

College, and a member of the Consortium on Professionalism Initiatives of the American Bar Association and of the Ohio State Bar Association. Ms. Keating is the Chair of the National Legal Mentoring Consortium. Previously Lori served as a trial court magistrate and as an appellate court staff attorney. She graduated *magna cum laude* from the University of Notre Dame in 1995, with a BA in the Great Books of the Western World and a minor in Gender Studies. Lori is a member of Phi Beta Kappa. She received her JD from Washington and Lee University in 1998.

Stephanie L. Kimbro is a lawyer with Burton Law, LLC, a virtual law firm based in Ohio, North Carolina, and Washington, D.C., and she provides consultations to law firms and legal technology startups. She is a member of the Standing Committee on the Delivery of Legal Services of the American Bar Association and Chair of the ABA Law Practice Management Section's Ethics and Professional Responsibility Committee. Ms. Kimbro teaches legal technology and ethics topics as an adjunct professor for Wake Forest University School of Law, Michigan State University School of Law, and the University of Dayton School of Law. She is the author of Virtual Law Practice: How to Deliver Legal Services Online (ABA 2010), Limited Scope Legal Services: Unbundling and the Self-Help Client (ABA 2012), and the forthcoming Consumer Law Revolution: Lawyers Guide to Online Marketing Tools (ABA 2013).

Katie M. Lachter practices in the New York office of Hinshaw & Culbertson LLP, where she is a member of the firm's national Lawyers Professional Responsibility/Risk Management Practice Group. Ms. Lachter's practice focuses on representation of lawyers and law firms in ethics and disciplinary matters. She is the Secretary of the New York City Bar Association's Committee on Professional Ethics and a co-author (with Peter R. Jarvis) of "Civility: The Ultimate Legal Weapon?" She is a 2012 recipient of the Burton Award for distinguished legal writing, for her article with Mr. Jarvis noted above, and is a 2009 recipient of the Legal Aid Society's Pro Bono Publico award.

Ms. Lachter co-authored two recent articles on lateral attorney movement: Anthony E. Davis and Katie M. Lachter, "Do's and Don'ts of Lateral Attorney Movement: Managing the Risks," *New York Law Journal* (March 5, 2012); and Anthony E. Davis and Katie M. Lachter, "Lateral Attorney

Movement: Pre-Departure and Recruitment," *New York Law Journal* (May 7, 2012). Ms. Lachter is a 2003 *cum laude* graduate of Harvard Law School and a 2000 *summa cum laude* graduate of Dartmouth College.

Roberta D. Liebenberg is a partner at Fine, Kaplan and Black, R.P.C. in Philadelphia and concentrates her practice in class actions, antitrust and complex commercial litigation, and white collar criminal defense. She is Chair of the ABA Gender Equity Task Force and former Chair of the ABA Commission on Women in the Profession. She has written and spoken extensively about issues of importance to women lawyers. The National Law Journal named her one of the "50 Most Influential Women Lawyers in America," and she has received awards from many organizations, including the National Association of Women Judges, Chambers Women in Law, and the Philadelphia and Pennsylvania Bar Associations. Pennsylvania's governor named Ms. Liebenberg a "Distinguished Daughter of Pennsylvania." She is Co-Chair of the Pennsylvania Interbranch Commission for Gender, Racial and Ethnic Fairness. She is a Leader in Residence at the Center for Women in Law, University of Texas Law School.

Robert E. Lutz is a Professor of Law at Southwestern University School of Law, in Los Angeles, where he teaches international law, international commercial law, and international dispute resolution. Professor Lutz is past chair of the American Bar Association (ABA) Section of International Law and the ABA Task Force on International Trade in Legal Services, and is Co-Chair of the Indo-U.S. Trade Policy Forum's Working Group on Legal Services. Professor Lutz recently served as the ABA representative to the Union Internationale des Avocats (UIA) and is a Lifetime Member of the American Law Institute, a member of Pacific Council on International Policy (affiliate of the Council on Foreign Relations), and a Lifetime Fellow of the American Bar Foundation. Mr. Lutz arbitrates public international and private international commercial disputes, actively serves on North American Free Trade Agreement bi-national arbitration panels, and he is a listed panelist for the World Trade Organization. Most recently, Professor Lutz participated in the three-year ABA Commission on Ethics 20/20, which analyzed the impacts of globalization and technology on the legal profession. Professor Lutz is the author or editor of several books as well as many book chapters and articles on public international law, international business law, and environmental law. He has served as editor-in-chief of several periodicals, including *The International Lawyer*.

Michael P. Maslanka is the Office Head of the Dallas office of Constangy Brooks & Smith, a national labor and employment firm. Mr. Maslanka litigates and tries cases across Texas. He blogs at Work Matters, twice named by the ABA Journal as the No.1 labor and employment law blog. Blog: Work Matters, http://www.texaslawyer.typepad.com/work_matters (last visited April 11, 2013). He is the author of "Maslanka's Pocket Guide to Employment Law" (American Lawyer Media 2013), and of the Maslanka Field Guide series on employment law, www.texaslawyerbooks.com. Mr. Maslanka has written a monthly newsletter on Texas employment law since January 1990. He is a National Institute for Trial Advocacy instructor on deposition techniques.

Martha Middleton is a legal researcher and writer who has reported for both the *American Bar Association Journal* and *The National Law Journal*. She is a graduate of DePaul University College of Law in Chicago.

Anthony C. Musto is Director of Community Outreach and Pro Bono Services and Visiting Assistant Professor of Law at St. Thomas University School of Law, Miami Gardens, Florida, where he teaches criminal law, criminal procedure, evidence, and appellate practice. Professor Musto is a member of the American Bar Association Standing Committee on Professionalism, a former member of the Florida Supreme Court Commission on Professionalism, and a recipient of The Florida Bar Claude Pepper Award, presented for "exemplifying the highest ideals of dedication, professionalism, and ethics" as a government lawyer. Professor Musto is the Chair-elect of The Florida Bar Public Interest Law Section. He has chaired three other Bar sections, the Bar's Council of Sections, and two Florida court rules committees. He is board certified by The Florida Bar in appellate practice and has handled well over 1,000 appellate proceedings, including more than 80 on the merits in the Florida Supreme Court.

Jayne R. Reardon is the Executive Director of the Illinois Supreme Court Commission on Professionalism, where she is responsible for programs and initiatives to increase the professionalism, civility, and inclusiveness of the legal system. Ms. Reardon and her team have developed and launched a statewide Lawyer-to-Lawyer Mentoring Program, which has been replicated in other jurisdictions. She is a member of the American Bar Association's Standing Committee on Professionalism, the American Bar Association Consortium on Professionalism Initiatives, and the National Legal Mentoring Consortium Steering Committee, and is a board member of the Phi Alpha Delta Legal Fraternity, Chicago Alumni Chapter. Ms. Reardon has authored many articles on professionalism topics, including "Civil Disagreement," Illinois Supreme Court Commission on Professionalism Pro Say Blog, http://blog.ilsccp.org/civil-disagreement/ (January 2013), and she maintains a blog and various social media channels on the Commission's website. Ms. Reardon is a graduate of the University of Michigan Law School and the University of Notre Dame.

Arin N. Reeves, PhD, JD, is an expert in the fields of diversity and inclusion and the President of the boutique consulting firm Nextions, based in Chicago. Born in India and raised in India, Libya, and Tanzania, Dr. Reeves studied business at DePaul University's College of Commerce, received her JD from the University of Southern California and her PhD in Sociology from Northwestern University. Dr. Reeves' work on women of color in the legal profession has been featured on National Public Radio, she is a Fellow of Leadership Greater Chicago, and she was recognized as a Rising Star by the Anti-Defamation League. In addition to numerous articles in both online and traditional media, Dr. Reeves is the author of the Chicago Lawyer column "Diversity in Practice" as well as the ABA bestseller *The Next IQ: The Next Level of Intelligence for 21st Century Leaders* (ABA 2010).

Patricia A. Sexton is a Shareholder in Polsinelli Shughart, P.C.'s Kansas City, Missouri, office, where she specializes in product liability and commercial litigation. In 2007, Ms. Sexton was appointed by the Missouri Supreme Court to serve as one of six lawyers on the Missouri Board of Law Examiners. She is the current President of the Board, and serves as Chair of the Character and Fitness Subcommittee of the American Bar Association's Standing Committee on Professionalism. Sexton is a former President of the Kansas City Metropolitan Bar Foundation, and is listed in the Best Lawyers in America. Ms. Sexton's other articles related to character and fitness include: "When Character and Fitness Disclosures Collide: The Dilemma of Inconsistent Law School and Bar Admission

Applications," *The Professional Lawyer*, Vol. 21, Issue 2 (June 2012), and "The Shifting Cultural Tides of Plagiarism: What Does It Mean For The Profession," *The Professional Lawyer*, Vol. 21, Issue 4 (Forthcoming).

Frederic S. Ury is a founding partner of Ury & Moskow, LLC in Fairfield, Connecticut. He is a Board Certified Civil Trial Lawyer and an AV rated attorney listed in Martindale Hubbell's Bar Register of Preeminent Lawyers. He concentrates his practice in the areas of civil and criminal litigation. Mr. Ury served as President of the Connecticut Bar Association from 2004 to 2005. He is a past member of the Board of Directors of the Connecticut Bar Foundation and is a member of the James W. Cooper Fellows. Mr. Ury is a founding member of Charity Treks, Inc., a non-profit organization dedicated to raising funds for AIDS and cancer research.

Mr. Ury served three years on the Executive Council of National Conference of Bar Presidents and was President of the NCBP from 2011 to 2012. Mr. Ury was a member of the American Bar Association's House of Delegates from 2004 to 2009 and served on the ABA Commission on Ethics 20/20 from 2010 to 2013. He is the Chair of the ABA Standing Committee on Professionalism, and he lectures nationally on the future of the legal profession.

Chapter 1

THE QUALITIES OF THE PROFESSIONAL LAWYER

NEIL W. HAMILTON

I. Introduction

Why would you, as a law student or early-career lawyer, want to internalize the qualities of the professional lawyer? Let me start with the bold proposition that the authors of the other chapters will reinforce: if, over a career, you build a strong internalized foundation of the qualities of the professional lawyer, you will continue over a career to become an increasingly effective and successful lawyer.

Section I below analyzes empirical data identifying the qualities that legal employers and clients want in a new lawyer. Section II analyzes the empirical evidence on what qualities of the professional lawyer inform the profession's understanding of professionalism, professional formation, and an ethical professional identity. That evidence reveals a powerful service ethic anchoring professional formation: an internalized moral core characterized by a deep responsibility for others, particularly clients. Section III explores how the qualities of the professional lawyer form the foundation upon which a law student and early-career lawyer builds over a career to develop all the values, virtues, capacities, and skills of an effective lawyer. Section IV reflects professional formation's central role in fulfilling the legal profession's "social contract" with the larger society. That section also considers the "moral insight" attained by lawyers at later stages of professional formation. Section V concludes with a discussion of some key lessons to remember going forward in your law studies and career as a lawyer.

II. What Are the Qualities That Legal Employers and Clients Want in a New Lawyer?

It would be good to start with a clear definition of "qualities." These constitute the distinguishing character or nature of an individual. In the context of this chapter, the focus is the distinguishing character or nature relating to the individual's role as a professional lawyer.

Empirical research makes it clear that legal employers evaluate qualities beyond a new lawyer's technical legal skills (e.g., knowledge of the law, legal analysis, and effective written and oral communication). They also evaluate a new lawyer's capacities for: integrity, honesty and trustworthiness; an internalized commitment to self-development toward excellence; self-awareness; the capacity to take feedback and reflect on weaknesses and mistakes; effective teamwork; strong client relationships; and good judgment. Law-firm consultants Susan Manch and Terri Mottershead explain that "a competency-based approach [known as a competency model] to talent development involves identifying the characteristics of a firm's most successful lawyers and using these characteristics to anchor the firm's talent management strategy."

Empirical studies also make it clear that corporate clients want and evaluate not just the quality of a lawyer's technical legal skills but also her good judgment; high commitment and responsiveness to the client; full understanding of the client's business and needs; and teamwork. Individual clients also want from their lawyers not just technical legal skills but honesty; integrity; diligence; good relationship skills; good judgment and creative problem solving; listening skills; ability to see things through the eyes of others; counseling proficiency; teamwork; and reflective self-development.

Table 1 below provides a synthesis of four empirical studies on the values, virtues, capacities, and skills that legal employers and clients want.

Table 1: Synthesis of Four Empirical Studies on the Values, Virtues, Capacities, and Skills That Legal Employers and Clients Want

Values and Virtues	Critical Thinking and Judgment	Service Orientation with Clients	Working with Others	Communications
- Commitment to self-development toward excellence in all competencies - Proactive initiative in exercising all competencies - Integrity, honesty, trustworthiness - Self-awareness, capacity to recognize strengths and weaknesses, and reflection - Resilience and perseverance	- Core understanding of the law - Legal analysis and reasoning - Good judgment and pragmatic problem solving - Strategic thinking Creativity and innovation	- Responsiveness to Client - Client rapport and strong relationships - Client commitment - Demonstrated value to client - Networking and business development	- Effective teamwork - Effective planning and organization of work on projects, including timeliness - Community/pro bono/bar/firm involvement	- Listening - Persuasive speaking and writing - Negotiation

It bears repeating that Table 1, which is a synthesized competency model, shows that legal employers and clients evaluate a new lawyer's effectiveness not just by looking at the quality of the lawyer's technical legal skills, but also by looking at the values and virtues relating to both the new lawyer's moral core and to the new lawyer's ability to build successful relationships with clients and work with colleagues in teams. For example, both law firm competency models and individual clients evaluate a new lawyer's (1) integrity, honesty, and trustworthiness, and (2) ability to take feedback and reflect to foster self-development. Law firm competency models evaluate whether a new lawyer has self-awareness and an internalized commitment to grow toward excellence in all the other competencies of being an effective lawyer. Law firm competency models and both individual and corporate clients also evaluate a new lawyer's (1) good judgment, (2) client relationship skills, and (3) teamwork skills.

A simple inspection of Table 1 also reveals the foundational importance of the values and virtues, in the left column, to a lawyer's career-long growth in terms of many of the other important capacities and skills of an effective lawyer. For example, an internalized commitment to career-long self-development toward excellence at all competencies and the capacity to recognize strengths and weaknesses and reflect about improvement are foundational for continued career-long growth in all of the competencies in Table 1. Integrity, honesty, and trustworthiness contribute substantially to successful long-term relationships with clients, and among teams.

Table 2 presents this visually, where the values and virtues that legal employers and clients want in a lawyer are the foundation on which an effective lawyer builds.

Table 2: The Foundation of Values and Virtues that Lead to Career-Long Development of the Other Capacities and Skills of an Effective Lawyer

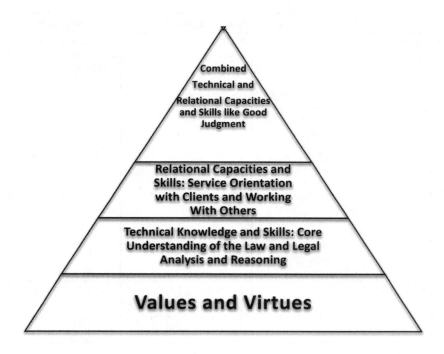

A last important point with respect to the values, virtues, capacities, and skills that legal employers expect is that the more sophisticated law firm associate evaluation systems (competency models) define developmental stages for each of the competencies expected. The employers recognize that a law student or early-career lawyer grows toward later stages in each of these competencies. For example, Table 3 describes the stages of development for good judgment for three larger law firms in Minnesota.

Table 3: Developmental Stages of Good Judgment From Three Larger Minnesota Firms

	Good Judgment	Good Judgment	Good Judgment
Junior Associate	- Demonstrates astute discernment and fitting behavior in interactions with others, even when under stress - Uses diplomacy and tact routinely - Knows when to ask for guidance and direction on work assignments - Demonstrates professionalism in personal appearance and attire - Accepts constructive feedback with maturity	Recognizes potential risks involved in client situations	Uses common sense and creativity in applying the law
Mid-Level Associate	In addition: - Able to grasp complex facts and aspects of law as well as practical aspects of matters - Understands the business issues concerning the matter and client priorities - Anticipates clients' needs - Shows good judgment in personal client intake decisions	- Identifies and evaluates risks involved in alternative courses of action. - Recommends appropriate course of action based upon evaluation of the relevant facts, issues, and risks	Uses both common sense and creativity in applying the law. Identifies and articulates alternative courses of action and strategies for consideration by the supervising lawyer, and identifies risks involved in such courses of action

	Good Judgment	Good Judgment	Good Judgment
Senior Associate	In addition: - Is a role model for, and can mentor newer associates - Can recommend alternatives to shareholders and clients in addressing clients' concerns (legal and business)	Evaluates the relevant facts, issues and risks, distinguishes among various options, and prepares and executes effective strategies to achieve the clients' objectives	- Uses common sense and creativity in applying the law. - Identifies and evaluates facts, issues and risks involved in alternative courses of action, recommends sound course of action to supervising attorney, and effectively articulates bases for recommendation

III. An Internalized Moral Core and Other Elements of Professional Formation

With a clear understanding of the values, virtues, capacities, and skills that legal employers and clients expect in their evaluation of new lawyers, the next step is to explore which of these capacities and skills are included in the profession's understanding of the qualities of the professional lawyer.

The research discussed and synthesized in this section converges on several essential elements of professional formation, with none more foundational to one's emergence as a true "professional" lawyer than an internalized moral core. As is also discussed below, the research points to the following additional elements of professional formation: an emphasis on professional feedback, a standard of lawyering excellence, integrity and honesty, public service, and sound judgment.

An exploration of the profession's notion of the qualities of the professional lawyer faces an initial challenge of creating definitional clarity about the most common terms that are used as synonyms in the scholarship in this area, including the qualities of the professional lawyer, professionalism, professional formation, and ethical professional identity. For example, the authors of the five Carnegie Foundation for the Advancement of Teaching studies of education in the professions used synonymously the terms professional formation, formation of a professional identity, professionalism, professionalism and ethics, and ethical comportment. In *Educating Physicians* (2010), the last in the series of studies, the Carnegie authors adopted "professional formation" rather than "professionalism" as the best term to use going forward because it emphasizes the developmental and multi-faceted nature of the construct. Professional formation indicates "an ongoing self-reflective process involving habits of thinking, feeling and acting and a lifelong commitment to continued progress toward technical excellence and the aspirational goals of the profession. For these reasons, I prefer "professional formation" but believe an even more specific statement—"professional formation toward a moral core of responsibility for others"—best captures both the developmental nature of the challenge for each law student and the "other-directedness" inherent in all of these synonyms. For purposes of brevity, in this chapter I proceed relying on the phrase "professional formation."

Relevant research and findings are summarized in the text box below.

Summary of Studies and Findings

Following the general principle of triangulation (that is, we can best understand the values, virtues, capacities, and skills of professional formation by using a variety of qualitative and quantitative research methods, and then looking for general areas of convergence where different methods corroborate the findings), I conducted six earlier studies analyzing different perspectives on the capacities and skills that define professional formation. I first looked at how the organized profession nationally has defined professionalism in its reports and in the ABA Model Rules of Professional Conduct. Then I analyzed how all legal scholars writing since 1980 have defined the elements of professionalism. In a third article, I analyzed how the five Carnegie studies of higher education for the professions (based on over fifty site visits) defined the elements of professionalism. Finally, Dr. Verna Monson and I conducted three qualitative empirical research studies focused on how entering law students, early-career lawyers, and peer-honored exemplary lawyers understood professionalism.

The most important findings of these studies are that a student's or new lawyer's understanding of professional formation depends upon the student's or new lawyer's stage of development, and that a student or new lawyer can eventually grow over a career toward the internalization of a later-stage understanding of professional formation (similar to the understanding of peer-honored exemplary lawyers). To be effective in fostering professional formation, senior lawyers must take into account the developmental stage of each student or new lawyer and engage each student or new lawyer at his or her developmental stage.

These studies also clarify the key elements of a later-stage understanding of professional formation. The studies of the understandings of professionalism from the organized legal profession, the legal scholars who have written on professionalism, and the five Carnegie studies on higher education for the professions, combined with the exemplary lawyers study, all agree that, as noted, professional formation encompasses an internalized moral core characterized by a deep responsibility for others, particularly the client, as well as some restraint on self-interest in carrying out this responsibility. Nearly all of the studies also agree that professional formation includes these elements: (1) ongoing solicitation of feedback and self-reflection; (2) an internalized standard of excellence at lawyering skills; (3) integrity and honesty; (4) adherence to the ethical codes; (5) public service (especially for the disadvantaged); and (6) independent professional judgment and honest counsel.

IV. The Qualities of a Professional Lawyer Are the Foundation on Which an Effective Lawyer Builds.

It is fair for law students or new lawyers to wonder whether the "real-word" pressures of law practice might pull them away from the values of a true professional motivated by a sense of service and commitment to values such as integrity, honesty, and trustworthiness. It is important to note that the latest research affirms that those professional values are largely in sync with the criteria used by legal employers and by clients to evaluate new lawyers.

Table 4 juxtaposes the values, virtues, capacities, and skills of a later-stage understanding of professional formation with those that legal employers and clients expect in evaluating the effectiveness of a new lawyer. As the table reflects, the overlap is substantial.

Table 4: Comparison of the Values, Virtues, Capacities, and Skills Defining Professional Formation with Those that Legal Employers and Clients Expect in Assessing the Effectiveness of a New Lawyer

Professional Formation Values, Virtues, Capacities and Skills	Values, Virtues, Capacities and Skills Legal Employers and Clients Evaluate (Beyond Technical Legal Skills)
Internalized Moral Core Characterized by Deep Responsibility for Others, Particularly the Client	
Integrity/Honesty	Integrity/Honesty/Trustworthiness
Internalized Standard of Excellence at Lawyering Skills and Career-long Growth Toward Later-stages of Professional Formation	Internalized Commitment to Grow toward Excellence in All Competencies
Ongoing Solicitation of Feedback and Self-Reflection	Ability to Take Feedback and Reflect to Foster Self-Development
Independent Professional Judgment and Counsel to the Client	Good Judgment/Creativity and Innovation, and Strategic Thinking
Adherence to Ethical Codes	
Public Service	Community/Pro Bono/Firm Involvement
	Client Relationship Skills Including Responsiveness and Commitment to the Client, Strong Client Rapport, Value for the Client, Empathy and Listening Skills
	- Effective Teamwork and Project Skills - Persuasive Speaking and Writing and Negotiation

Professional formation entails career-long growth toward an internalized moral core characterized by deep responsibilities for others, particularly the client. In my experience, a lawyer who has internalized deep responsibilities for others will, in fulfilling those responsibilities, work with integrity, honesty, and trustworthiness, and an internalized commitment to grow toward excellence at all the other competencies of an effective lawyer. In a sense, the values and virtues depicted in Table 2 in turn have an even more fundamental foundation—the internalization of deep responsibilities for others, particularly the client. This is essentially a fiduciary disposition, using "fiduciary" in the general meaning of founded on trustworthiness.

In addition, an internalized moral core is implicit in many of the values and virtues that legal employers and clients want in an effective lawyer. For example, the virtues of integrity, honesty, and trustworthiness, as well as the lawyer's internalized commitment to grow toward excellence, in all the capacities and skills of effective lawyering, by their very presence imply that a lawyer has an internalized moral core. A new lawyer who seeks ongoing solicitation of feedback and engages in self-reflection will foster growth of her moral core of responsibility for others over a career. Moreover, an internalized commitment to grow toward excellence in all the competencies of an effective lawyer will lead to ongoing improvement in a new lawyer's technical skills.

Finally, and most importantly, a new lawyer who has internalized a moral core characterized by deep responsibility for others (particularly the client) and also has integrity, honesty, and trustworthiness will be more effective in achieving successful long-term client relationships, effective teamwork, and persuasive speaking, writing, and negotiation.

V. Broader Benefits of Lawyer Professional Formation
A. *Fulfilling the Social Contract; Enhancing Lawyer Well-Being*
In addition to the importance of career-long professional formation for each student's and new lawyer's enlightened self-interest, there are three other reasons for each student and lawyer to internalize a later-stage understanding of professional formation. First, the professional formation of each law student and lawyer supports the legal profession's unwritten social contract whereby the public grants the profession substantial autonomy to regulate itself through peer review. In return, the organized profession and each lawyer commit both (1) to set and enforce standards of how individual lawyers perform their work so it serves the client and the public good, and (2) to foster the core values and ideals of the profession. The social contract is premised on the public's trust that the organized profession and each lawyer are serious about professional formation. For example, a lawyer will merit trust if the lawyer has internalized a moral

core characterized by: (1) deep responsibilities for others, particularly the client; (2) integrity, honesty, and trustworthiness; and (3) a standard of excellence at all lawyering skills.

The elements of professional formation capture the required and aspirational duties of the social contract for each lawyer. Failures of professional formation undermine the public trust in the profession and the social contract. In addition, the public's trust that the profession will monitor and foster the competence and trustworthiness of individual lawyers is a type of professional capital that accrues to each member of the profession. The higher the public's trust in the social contract, the more likely it is that members of the public will bring problems to lawyers.

Second, empirical research points toward the higher probability of (1) increased physical health and longevity from reaching out to others and giving back to a person's friends and community, and (2) increased levels of happiness and well-being from service to others and some suppression of self-serving impulses.

B. Attaining the 'Moral Insight'

Third, beyond the profession's and each student's and new lawyer's enlightened self-interest as a reason to foster formation of an ethical professional identity, the major faith traditions and moral philosophy call each person toward lifelong growth in understanding and living "the moral insight."

Business ethicist Ken Goodpaster, looking to nineteenth century philosopher Josiah Royce, observes that ethics is grounded in "the moral insight" or what philosophers today call "the moral point of view." Goodpaster notes, "The moral insight is the realization of one's neighbor, in the full sense of the word realization. . . . We see the reality of our neighbor, that is, we determine to treat him as we do ourselves." One's "neighbor" in many faith traditions includes especially the poor and disadvantaged. Goodpaster argues that the field of ethics is about understanding the full implications of the moral insight. The moral insight leads to growth of shared ethical norms and each individual's ethical principles—what philosophy calls normative ethics.

The medical profession has also defined professionalism and gives us another window through which to understand the concept. For example, the American Board of Medical Specialties (ABMS) professionalism working group recently gave a one-sentence definition of professionalism: "Medical professionalism is the assertion that doctors are worthy of public and patient trust."

The ABMS continues: "Medical professionalism is a belief system in which group members publicly declare ('profess') to each other and the public the shared values and competency standards that they promise collectively to upheld in their work. These declarations constitute a set of promises, and one-half of an ongoing dialogue with society, about what the public and individual patients can and should expect from medical professionals. At the heart of these ongoing declarations has long been a three-part promise about the science, art and service orientation of medical practice. Medical professionals promise to acquire, maintain and advance[:] (1) the scientific and technical skills necessary for competent medical practice, (2) the interpersonal skills necessary to work with patients to elicit goals and values that can help direct the use of the professional's medical knowledge and skills (sometimes referred to as the 'art' of medicine), and (3) a value system which upholds that medical professionals will use their medical knowledge and skills always in the service of patients and the public's health. Medical professionalism, therefore, pledges medical practitioners, as members of the profession, to a dynamic process of personal development (life-long learning and professional formation) and to participation in a social enterprise that continually seeks to express that expertise and caring in its work."

You can see in the ABMS definition that the foundation of professionalism includes life-long learning and professional formation toward an internalized value system that uses the professional's skills in service to the patient and the public's health. A physician (and by analogy a lawyer) who has internalized these deep responsibilities for others—the patient and the public's health (or the client and justice system)—is worthy of both patient and public trust. My experience is that any physician or lawyer who has internalized a deep responsibility for others is also highly attentive to developing excellent technical and interpersonal skills to fulfill these internalized responsibilities.

VI. Key Lessons to Apply Going Forward
A. Distinguishing Yourself in a Very Competitive Market
Chapter 5 author Bill Henderson emphasizes that "[s]tudents need the skills to differentiate themselves" in a very competitive market. A student who uses the three years of law school and then a career to internalize and demonstrate later-stage understandings of professional formation will be distinguishing herself as an effective lawyer for legal employers and potential clients. These are the competencies that law firms have identified as characteristics of the firms' most successful lawyers.

B. Professional Formation Has Developmental Stages.
Each peer-honored exemplary lawyer whom Dr. Monson and I interviewed talked about how he or she grew over a career, often through learning from setbacks (sometimes caused by their own mistakes), toward a fully internalized moral core of responsibility for others. Our empirical studies of entering law students, graduating law students, early-career lawyers, and senior peer-honored exemplary lawyers show clear developmental stages on moral reasoning and ethical professional identity. Each of us can grow toward being a virtuoso by practicing our art, seeking excellent mentoring and coaching, and reflecting on both our setbacks and the input our mentors and coaches give us. Use the three years of law school to start building your foundation of the attributes of a professional lawyer.

C. The Habit of Actively Seeking and Reflecting on Feedback
The most effective strategy to foster self-development in professional formation is to internalize the habit of actively seeking feedback and reflecting on it. Affirmatively seek out exemplary law professors, lawyers, and judges to be coaches and mentors who will give you honest and constructive feedback. You want coaches and mentors who will ask stage-appropriate questions that challenge your current assumptions, beliefs and performance, and support you to reflect and try again. Create your own "personal board of directors" for this purpose.

D. Risk of Excessive Focus on Technical Professionalism

Since legal education emphasizes principally a core understanding of the law, legal analysis, and to some degree, effective research and written and oral communication, a student is at risk of embracing too narrow an understanding of professional formation focused only on excellence at the technical skills such as knowledge of legal doctrine and legal analysis. Let's call this a technical professionalism without a strong foundation in deep responsibilities for others, especially the client, nor in the other values and virtues of professional formation.

In a globalized economy, lawyers who focus just on a technical professionalism are increasingly like a commoditized service that can be secured from suppliers world-wide at lower prices. In contrast, a lawyer who internalizes a moral core of professional formation over a career will benefit from excellent trustworthiness, relationship skills, teamwork skills, and persuasive communication that flow from a deep understanding of others.

E. Community and Pro Bono Service Are Important.

Community service and pro bono legal work are important and are rooted in each lawyer's internalization of deep responsibilities for others, as well as the profession's social contract with society. Both are part of professional formation as well as the values, virtues, capacities, and skills that legal employers and clients want.

F. The Importance of Dialogue with Other Law Students and Lawyers About the Traits and Qualities of the Professional Lawyer

The American Board of Medical Specialties professionalism working group emphasizes the importance of an on-going dialogue within the profession and with society about what the public and individual patients can expect from medical professionals. The same is true for law students and lawyers. This book is an important part of the ongoing dialogue.

VII. Conclusion

Many of the chapters of this book analyze values, virtues, capacities, and skills that are rooted in the law student's or lawyer's moral core of responsibility for others and for self. For example, the chapters on authenticity, respect for others (inclusion), diligence, honesty and integrity, excellence at the craft of lawyering, fiduciary duties, and public service implicitly assume a moral core that informs the law student's or lawyer's exercise of those values and virtues.

There is no perfect consensus on the values, virtues, capacities, and skills listed in Table 4 for professional formation—or, for that matter, that the chapter themes of this book capture all qualities and traits of the professional lawyer. Ongoing dialogue and debate among us and personal reflection about the core elements of professional formation, however, are how we help each other grow.

Sources/Reading

THE ART AND SCIENCE OF STRATEGIC TALENT MANAGEMENT IN LAW FIRMS (Terri Mottershead ed., 2010).

Kenneth E. Goodpaster, CONSCIENCE AND CORPORATE CULTURE (2007).

Neil W. Hamilton et al., *Encouraging Each Student's Personal Responsibility for Core Competencies Including Professionalism*, 21 PROF. LAWYER, no. 3, 2012, *available at* http://www.americanbar.org/content/dam/aba/administrative/professional_responsibility/tpl_21_3_20121105.authcheckdam.pdf.

Neil Hamilton & Verna Monson, *Legal Education's Ethical Challenge: Empirical Research on How Most Effectively to Foster Each Student's Professional Formation (Professionalism)*, 9 U. ST. THOMAS L.J. 325 (2011).

Neil Hamilton & Verna Monson, *The Positive Empirical Relationship of Professionalism to Effectiveness in the Practice of Law*, 24 GEO. J. LEGAL ETHICS 137 (2011).

Neil Hamilton et al., *Empirical Evidence that Legal Education Can Foster Student Professionalism/Professional Formation*, 10 U. Sт. Tнoмаs L.J (forthcoming 2013), *available at* http://papers.ssrn.com/sol3/papers.cfm?abstract_id=2205447.

NEIL W. HAMILTON is Professor of Law and Director of the Holloran Center for Ethical Leadership in the Professions, University of St. Thomas School of Law (MN). Professor Hamilton has authored a series of empirical studies on the essential qualities of the professional lawyer, including *Empirical Evidence That Legal Education Can Foster Student Professionalism/Professional Formation to Become an Effective Lawyer*, accessible at http://ssrn.com/abstract=2205447.

Chapter 2

THE AUTHENTIC LAWYER: MERGING THE PERSONAL AND THE PROFESSIONAL

DAISY HURST FLOYD

I. Introduction

Law school is a transformational experience. Students take on a new professional identity as they transform from non-lawyers to lawyers. They learn about the law, acquire the distinctive skills and habits of being a lawyer, and develop an understanding of the many ethical obligations that guide a professional's actions. They develop new ways of thinking, talking, writing, and interacting with others. This transformation is the result of an educational process that is successful for many reasons, including that it is so challenging.

But legal education carries a risk: that students will experience a damaging loss of self because they replace the identities they brought to law school with a brand-new professional identity. The goal instead should be to integrate a new-found professional identity with personal values and skills, so that one can live authentically as a lawyer.

This chapter will discuss the importance of remaining authentic as both a law student and lawyer, identify some of the challenges to doing so, and offer practical strategies for overcoming those challenges.

II. What Is an Authentic Lawyer, and Why Does It Matter?

Being an authentic lawyer means living consistently with one's deepest values and core beliefs. Authenticity refers to the ability to hold on to personal values and goals while integrating them with a newly-acquired identity as a lawyer. A person's actions, including the decisions she makes, the ways that she spends her time and treats others, and where her priorities lie, can either be consistent with her true self or at odds with it. In other words, one chooses to live either authentically or inauthentically.

Why should one strive to be an authentic lawyer? Studies of lawyers and law students demonstrate links between authenticity and being a good lawyer as well as a fulfilled person. There is ample empirical research to show that those who live authentically are better at what they do and are also happier. Living authentically has consequences for the individual and for others: if one lives authentically, she will be a better lawyer and a better spouse, friend, parent, and community member. When she does not live authentically, there are negative consequences for her and for those in her life. Inauthentic lawyers are more likely to act unethically, experience anxiety and stress, and damage both personal and professional relationships.

III. The Authentic Law Student

The very thing that makes law school a powerful formative experience can also pose challenges to living authentically. Students arrive at law school as adults informed by prior life experiences, including family and other relationships; physical, mental and emotional experiences; and completion of high school and college. They have developed beliefs about a number of things, including a set of moral and ethical values that guide their conduct. The fact that they have been successful through the competitive process of law school admissions means that they have made good choices, worked hard, and lived honorably. There is every reason to think that they are fully-formed ethical beings and that the values developed to that point will be all they need to guide them in living out their new lives as law students and lawyers.

Yet, importantly, many people who had just such a beginning lose their moral compass in law school or afterward. Some get into explicit ethical difficulties, running afoul of honor codes or lawyer disciplinary rules. Others, while avoiding ethical sanctions, find themselves unsatisfied with their professional lives and, as a result, fail to offer the best of themselves to their clients, friends, and families. There are disheartening statistics about the rates of clinical depression and substance abuse among law students and lawyers, and rates of attrition from law practice indicate that many people do not find what they were hoping for in their professional lives.

During the last couple of decades, lawyers and legal educators have closely examined why so many lawyers' lives do not turn out as they had hoped. Research has shown us that law school and the practice of law have an unintended consequence of separating people from themselves, which is to say that many law students and lawyers lack authenticity. This inauthenticity in turn has two results: An inauthentic person is likely to be unhappy and unfulfilled, and an inauthentic person is more likely to act unethically.

IV. Staying True to Intrinsic Motivations

Some of the pertinent research has focused on the role that intrinsic and extrinsic motivations play. Intrinsic values are fulfilled when a person chooses an action that she genuinely enjoys or that furthers a fundamental purpose. Examples of intrinsic motivations include spending time with a loved one or reading a good book. Another is volunteering to clean a public park because of a commitment to taking care of the environment. Picking up trash may not be enjoyable but it advances a purpose that is important to the person doing it. In contrast, extrinsic values drive a person to choose an action because of external rewards, such as money, grades, or honors; the avoidance of guilt or fear; or a desire to please or impress others. If a student picks up trash in a public park only because she needs the money and is being paid to pick up trash, she is motivated extrinsically, unlike her classmate who fulfills a personal commitment to the environment by the same action.

The research informs us that when intrinsic values are primary, people experience satisfaction and well-being. When extrinsic values are primary, people experience angst and distress. To be sure, most people are motivated by both extrinsic and intrinsic values. Often, they are motivated by some combination of both. The law student who is committed to environmental causes may choose to earn money by picking up trash in a park rather than earning the same amount of money by doing something else; she combines her need to earn money with fulfilling a purpose that is important to her. A similar combination of purposes guides most people in their professional work. Most work because they need to earn money, which fulfills an extrinsic value. But those who can combine their need for money with doing something that fulfills a fundamental purpose will be both happier and better at what they do.

Keep in mind that there is nothing inherently wrong with extrinsic values or motivations. They can often produce positive results. A desire to receive an award for volunteer service may cause someone to spend time in activities that benefit others. A desire for a good grade can lead a law student to improve skills and knowledge that will be of service to clients in the future practice of law. The difficulty arises when extrinsic values become sole or primary motivators for conduct. When that happens, one is less likely to be satisfied than when her primary motivations are intrinsic. If a person is solely motivated by receiving an award or grade, receiving those things is less likely to be fulfilling than if doing those things also fulfills some intrinsic values.

There is another consequence as well. A person who is motivated primarily by external rewards is less likely to do a good job at whatever she is doing. It also becomes easier to justify acting in ways that violate a personal value system for the sake of obtaining those awards. The extreme example is a student who cheats to obtain a good grade because she is so motivated by the grade that she believes that she should use any means to achieve it or a lawyer who overbills a client because he is being considered for partner and reacts to perceived pressure from the law firm to produce billable hours. He may justify the conduct to himself by focusing on all of the reasons that the extrinsic reward of partnership will be good for him and his family. Being primarily focused on extrinsic awards, however, can also tempt people to act in ways that do not necessarily violate written rules or codes of conduct but that still may be at odds with deeply-held belief systems. For example, a student who is motivated solely by good grades may neglect a good friend or family member in a time of crisis, or deny help to a weaker fellow student, or study only to the test rather than really trying to learn the material so that it can be used effectively later. While these actions may not violate the honor code, they are at odds with a personal belief system that values relationships, helping others, and becoming the best lawyer one can be. So, the student—whether or not she obtains the desired grade—may begin to feel at odds with herself. That student is not likely to be happy or fulfilled by the law school experience.

The psychological research has particular relevance for law students. Studies reveal that many law students experience a shift in their motivations during the first year of law school. Law professor Larry Krieger and psychologist Kennon Sheldon have found that most entering law students are primarily motivated by intrinsic values. During the first year of law school, however, there is a shift: law students become primarily motivated by extrinsic values. Moreover, this shift is not transient. It cannot be explained by a temporary adjustment to a new environment. The same studies demonstrate that upper-level students do not experience a shift back toward intrinsic values during the second or third year of law school. The questions are why, and what can be done about this?

V. The Challenge of Law School

American legal education is rightly valued for its strength in teaching students critical intellectual and verbal skills in a rigorous learning environment. Other countries have looked to American legal education as a model for their own professional reforms. Indeed, the learning methods developed and practiced by American law faculty are often cited as examples of effective teaching. As students become lawyers, they acquire valuable skills and knowledge that will benefit them and others for a lifetime. It is important, however, to be self-aware about what is happening during the transition to being a lawyer, including the potential risks inherent in the process. Law students report that they find both positive and negative aspects of legal education.

As a positive, law students report becoming more disciplined and developing greater confidence. They also acquire an improved ability to articulate arguments and to depersonalize disagreement. They become proficient at "thinking like a lawyer," the skill that is promised to them when they begin law school. They report a great deal of justifiable pride in successfully meeting a challenging educational program. These positive consequences will serve them well in both their personal and professional lives.

Students also report some negative consequences of their time in law school. Law school can make them feel as if they are losing a sense of self. Many report that it is difficult to hold on to the sense of purpose that guided them to law school. In other words, the process of legal education makes it difficult for them to be authentic. What is it about law school that presents this challenge?

A. *The Downside of Learning to Think like a Lawyer*

Learning to think like a lawyer is one of the positive consequences of a legal education, but it has a downside. The educational theory behind much of law school is that students must set aside old ways of thinking and being in order to see clearly the new ways they are being taught. They must move from novice to expert, and doing so is easier when beginning with a clean slate. For example, students in first-year courses are taught the basic skills of legal analysis. They learn the substantive law through reading and synthesizing appellate opinions, and they learn to sort relevant from irrelevant facts. In developing these vital skills, they are taught that many things that we use in our everyday lives to give meaning to stories and relationships are irrelevant facts. This includes such things as parties' names and the emotional consequences of what has happened to them. It also includes students' personal feelings of justice or compassion. Indeed, every lawyer has a story of hearing a professor tell a first-year student that he must set aside his personal feelings to make a sound legal argument.

This mechanistic sorting is necessary for the novice law student to learn the essentials of legal reasoning. It teaches students early in their legal educations to compartmentalize their personal feelings and values, and it unintentionally sends a broader message that the personal and professional must always be kept separate. As part of this same process, skills other than those necessary for the cognitive task of legal analysis are devalued. Students may perceive that relationship skills such as listening, compassion, and empathy are not important for being a lawyer. Likewise, they may perceive that their personal value systems, including considerations of fairness and justice, must be replaced with a cold, rational analysis, which further separates them from the things that matter most to them. They perceive that taking on a new identity as a lawyer means letting go of those values. In other words, it is easy for law students to perceive an institutional message that being a lawyer requires inauthenticity.

Not only does this learned compartmentalization result in inauthenticity, but it also inaccurately describes the skills needed in the practice of law. Being a good lawyer requires integrating the new skill of objective, reasoned analysis with personal skills of empathy and compassion as well as a personal sense of justice. Yet, because of its emphasis on teaching a new skill, law school does a better job of teaching students to compartmentalize than it does of teaching them how to re-integrate their personal values with their newly-acquired professional skills and values.

B. The Competitive Environment of Law School

Another challenge of law school arises from its highly competitive environment. Just as with the important skill of legal reasoning, competition has its place in both legal education and the practice of law. Students are being prepared for an adversarial and competitive profession, and learning to deal with the rigors of law school is good preparation for being a lawyer. However, there is a downside to the competitive aspects of legal education. The law school environment includes artificially constructed bases of competition that can cause students to lose sight of a larger perspective, including what matters most to them. Unhealthy aspects of the

25

law school environment stem from an emphasis on grades, supported by grading curves, class rank, and the rewards that flow from grades, such as law journal membership, high-paying summer jobs, and prestigious first jobs upon graduation. This emphasis is exacerbated by the fact that, in most law school classes, grades are determined by performance on tests that measure only legal reasoning skills, further devaluing non-cognitive abilities. In this environment, winning at law school becomes about these external rewards. If, instead, winning at law school is perceived in terms of what brings most students to law school in the first place—the goals of graduating, passing the bar, and undertaking a satisfying career—it becomes clear that almost every student can win.

For all its benefits in preparing people for a highly competitive professional world, the competitive environment of law school has concerning consequences. It devalues collaboration, leading some students to feel isolated from their peers. This sense of isolation affects interactions both inside and outside of the classroom. Additionally, the competitive environment seems to value toughness and perfection. Students report that they feel that they must put on a mask, presenting themselves to others as free of fear or anxiety. They perceive that good law students and lawyers are perfect and that mistakes must be hidden rather than dealt with forthrightly. These effects of a competitive academic environment not only affect the conduct of law students, they also may be carried over into a lawyer's life after graduation from law school.

VI. The Gap Between Law School and the Legal Profession

Another aspect of law school that causes difficulties is its disconnection from law practice and the profession. American legal education has primarily taken place in universities since the late 1800's. Like other university-based graduate education, law schools have adopted many of the values and characteristics of academia, increasing the gap between legal education and the profession. This means that performance in law school is based primarily upon the kinds of things that universities value most highly, therefore placing a high priority on cognitive skills such as research, writing, and test performance. This is one of the reasons that the law school curriculum is more focused on teaching the content of the law than it is on teaching the skills and values of law practice. At most law schools, students can get through their entire legal education without interacting with a practicing lawyer or meeting a client who needs a lawyer's services. While legal education has made recent progress in these areas, adding more clinic and externship experiences, those opportunities are usually not available to all students and are very rarely available to first-year students. Therefore, the early messages that students receive about being a lawyer are more reflective of what it takes to study law than reflective of all that is involved in being a good lawyer. Any lawyer will tell you that law school and law practice are very different from each other.

This academic emphasis has two consequences: it separates students from the larger goal of being a lawyer and the reasons they want to become lawyers, and it leads students to conclude that, if they are not enjoying law school, they will not enjoy being lawyers. Both of these consequences fuel the temptation to focus on external motivations—rather than internal motivations—for managing the day-to-day tasks of being a law student. Therefore, the relative disconnection from practice contributes to the separation of the personal and professional selves.

VII. Meeting the Challenge: The Cultivation of Habits

Given these challenges, what can one do to maintain authenticity as a law student and then as a lawyer? Understanding the challenges is important but is not enough. There are habits that students can develop that will help them remain authentic as law students and later as lawyers. While it is true that law students arrive at law school as developed adults with a set of moral and ethical values, it is not true that they have completed the process of ethical formation. Nor will they have completed it when they graduate from law school. Human beings continue their ethical development throughout a lifetime, affected by a wide range of choices and experiences. Law school graduates encounter situations as lawyers that will present ethical dilemmas and tensions unlike those they have previously encountered. The practice of law is a complex and demanding profession; among its other challenges, it requires lawyers to make judgments under conditions of inherent uncertainty and to do so on behalf of not just themselves but also of their clients. Some of those challenges will require them to act quickly, with perhaps only a few seconds to think before making a decision with long-lasting consequences. They will not have time to decide what matters and what their primary motivations should be when a difficult situation arises. Therefore, they should use their time as students to prepare for these situations by developing the right habits of thinking, doing, and being. These habits will help them to remember who they are and to understand who they are becoming. They will guide conduct in a complex and demanding future.

What kinds of specific habits are helpful? Two categories of habits can help one to be authentic: habits of connection and habits of reflection.

A. *Habits of Connection*

It is easy to let the pressures of law school interfere with relationships. One of the negative consequences of law school reported by students is an eroding of relationship skills. Yet relationships are vital to sustaining one's well-being, and having good relationships is an intrinsic value for most people. Relationship skills are also invaluable for lawyers. If one does not know how to form and sustain human relationships, it will be more difficult to be an effective lawyer. Law can be practiced only in relationship to others. Law practice is a collaborative endeavor, requiring skills of listening, empathy, and cooperation. Just as with habits of reflection, habits of connection will not only make one happier, but also a better lawyer.

Habits of connection can help students to focus on both sustaining existing relationships and fostering new ones. One way to begin building habits of connection is by listing important relationships—friends, family, professional colleagues, etc. Next, think about where those relationships fit within priorities of time and attention. Become mindful of the ways in which new lawyering skills may interfere with those relationships. For example, the fact that law students learn to depersonalize disagreement and to enjoy critical analysis of ideas—and likely enjoy the art of argument—may be distressing to family and friends who are not law students or lawyers. Be conscious of using those new skills appropriately, of understanding that forceful advocacy that is appropriate in a courtroom may not be similarly appropriate in a friendship or marriage. Part of integrating new professional skills with a personal life may mean understanding when those skills should be modified or even set aside for the moment.

Relationships will also be enhanced by effective time management of the new professional demands that law students experience. Attorney Nancy Miller-Herron has described the "tyranny of the urgent," and has noted that for most of us, "the challenge is not finding important work to do and pressing needs to address. . . . [T]he challenge is to move past the *urgent* to be about the *important*." As with extrinsic rewards, there is nothing inherently bad about urgent matters. In fact, most of the urgent matters in our lives are about good things. Yet the urgency of paper deadlines, moot court briefs, work schedules, student leadership responsibilities, or job applications can cause us to ignore other important things that do not seem urgent. Often, those things are the people in our lives. While in law school, students should develop effective time management skills that will allow them to spend time with family and friends while also meeting other obligations.

Second, students should take the opportunity in law school to form new relationships, both personal and professional. Fellow students will be professional colleagues in the future, and many of the relationships formed with them will last a lifetime. There is another benefit. Developing relationships with fellow students can reduce a sense of isolation as well as help students cope with the demands of law school and, later, with the demands of practice. Students are often surprised to learn that other students are experiencing law school the same way that they are. By forming relationships, students can help each other with the challenge of integrating a new professional identity with their personal values and skills. They will learn firsthand that they are not alone in finding law school challenging. Some law students believe that their struggles with law school are a sign that they are not doing what they should be doing or that they will not be good lawyers. Forming relationships with other law students will help students see that these reactions are a normal response to a challenging and demanding environment whose purpose is to provide them with new ways of thinking, speaking, and acting.

Third, students should look beyond their classmates for new professional relationships. They should seek out opportunities to meet lawyers and to ask them about their lives. Forming connections with lawyers will help to overcome the gap between law school and practice. It will expand students' imaginations about the many ways to practice law. Some students do this through paid employment while a student, but there are many other ways. Most law schools provide elective externship courses and volunteer opportunities that will expose students to a variety of lawyers in diverse practice settings. Another idea is to attend CLE programs or bar association events—most will allow students to attend for reduced or no cost. Students should identify alumni of their law schools (or colleges) who practice in the subject area or region in which they are interested. Students can ask family and friends if they know of such lawyers and then contact these lawyers to ask for advice about the best way to reach their goals. Most lawyers enjoy mentoring new colleagues and will be glad to correspond with students or perhaps even meet with them.

Students should not forget about faculty members as they seek to expand their professional relationships. Faculty come from a variety of educational and practice backgrounds, and talking with them about their perspectives on legal education or their career decisions can assist students' own decision-making.

B. Habits of Reflection

In the midst of the sometimes overwhelming pressure of law school, it is helpful to cultivate habits of reflection. Students should set aside time to reflect upon what matters to them and why they are in law school, and let those reflections guide the choices they make. Reflection will help reconnect them to the things that matter most. When a student feels the pressure of an impending paper deadline or disappointment over an unsatisfying grade, a time of reflection will help her to gain some perspective. By focusing on her long-term goal of becoming a lawyer, she will realize that she is well on her way to achieving that goal.

For example, a student could complete this sentence: "I decided to go to law school because..." The exercise asks one to spend three to five minutes thinking about the reasons she chose law school among the variety of experiences and educational pathways that could lead to a career. Is it because of a lawyer she has known whom she admires? Is it because she enjoys the intellectual aspects of thinking about the law, or because she has good oral or writing skills? Or, does she feel that understanding the substantive and procedural aspects of our legal system is a way to effect needed change in the world or to help individuals with problems resolve those problems and move on with their lives?

All of these are good reasons, as are dozens of others, that people invest time and energies into this demanding endeavor. Yet in the face of the intensive day-to-day challenges of becoming a lawyer, it is easy to lose sight of those long-range goals. Even though individual reasons vary and many law students are unclear about their professional goals, most of them have chosen to come to law school because they want their work to have meaning. They want what they do for a living to help others as well as to provide a good living for themselves and their families. This means that, like the environmentalist law student who picks up trash as a way of both helping the environment and earning needed money, everyone has the option of combining both internal and external rewards in their lives as lawyers. It is up to you to choose a way to live that integrates both, and reflection will help you do that.

Reflection helps students make the right choices in law school and later, so that they can be true to their intrinsic values as well as extrinsic goals and can live their lives consistently with their deepest beliefs. These choices include such things as the courses they take, their extracurricular activities, and their job searches. When students are choosing which courses to take, they should think about what their goals are and which courses will help meet them. For example, traditional law school courses measure primarily cognitive skills through a fairly limited range of assessments. A student who is frustrated that she has other skills that are not being allowed to shine in those settings should look for elective courses or extracurricular activities that will focus on those skills.

There are many ways to develop habits of reflection: exercises that can be found in books or on websites, keeping a journal, meditating or praying, listening to classical music, or simply taking a walk. The options are endless, and what works for one person will be different than what works for another. What is important is not so much how one engages in regular reflection but rather that one makes a habit of reflection.

VIII. Conclusion

Students have chosen to invest time, hard work, and financial resources into becoming lawyers. They are likely feeling pressure to become a certain kind of lawyer and are thinking about that decision in terms of practice specialties such as prosecution or defense, civil or criminal, real estate, transactional, or in-house counsel. This chapter has challenged law students and new lawyers to think about that decision a bit differently: to choose to become an authentic lawyer, regardless of the practice area or setting. As a law student or lawyer, each person has the potential to lead a fulfilled life of service to others in which they are both happy and good at what they do. They can choose that future, but doing so requires that they be aware of both the positive and the potentially negative consequences of becoming and being a lawyer. It also requires that they find intentional ways of meeting those challenges. The effort will be worth it. Long-time Dallas attorney John McShane describes it best when he reflects on a lifetime as a lawyer: "I want lawyers to know that it is not only possible to have a joyful, meaningful law practice, but that there isn't another activity around that offers more opportunity for both personal growth and making a difference in other people's lives."

Sources/Reading

Derrick Bell, Ethical Ambition: Living a Life of Meaning and Worth (2002).

Steven Keeva, *Passionate Practitioner*, 86 A.B.A.J. 56 (2000).

Steven Keeva, Transforming Practices: Finding Joy and Satisfaction in the Legal Life (2011).

Lawrence S. Krieger & Kennon Sheldon, *Does Legal Education Have Undermining Effects on Law Students? Evaluating Changes in Values, Motivation and Well-Being*, 22 Behav. Sci. & L. 261 (2004).

Lawrence S. Krieger, *Institutional Denial About the Dark Side of Law School, and Fresh Empirical Guidance for Constructively Breaking the Silence*, 52 J. LEGAL EDUC. 112 (2002).

Nancy C. Miller-Herron, *On Maintaining Spiritual Sanity in a Secular Vocation*, 27 TEX. TECH L. REV. 1221 (1996).

DAISY HURST FLOYD is University Professor of Law and Ethical Formation at Mercer University School of Law, in Macon, GA, where she served as Dean from 2004 until 2010. She was named a Carnegie Scholar by the Carnegie Foundation for the Advancement of Teaching, in support of her work on American legal education.

Chapter 3

CIVILITY AS THE CORE OF PROFESSIONALISM

JAYNE R. REARDON

Civil behavior is a core element of attorney professionalism. As the guardians of the Rule of Law that defines the American social and political fabric, lawyers should embody civility in all they do. Not only do lawyers serve as representatives of their clients, they serve as officers of the legal system and public citizens having special responsibility for the quality of justice. To fulfill these overarching and overlapping roles, lawyers must make civility their professional standard and ideal.

I. What Exactly Is "Civility"?

Let's do what all good lawyers do—agree first on the definitions. The concept of civility is broad. The French and Latin etymologies of the word suggest, roughly, "relating to citizens." In its earliest use, the term referred to being a good citizen, that is, exhibiting good behavior for the good of a community. The early Greeks thought that civility was both a private virtue and a public necessity, which functioned to hold the state together. Some writers equate civility with respect. So, civility is a behavioral code of decency or respect that is the hallmark of living as citizens in the same state.

It may also be useful at the outset to dispense with some widely held misconceptions about civility, likening it to: (1) agreement, (2) the absence of criticism, (3) liking a person, and (4) good manners. These are all myths.

Civility *is not* the *same as agreement.* Just as disagreement does not equate to incivility, the presence of civility does not mean the absence of disagreement. In fact, underlying the codes of civility is the assumption that people will disagree. The democratic process thrives on dialogue and dialogue *requires* disagreement. Civil dialogue over differences is democracy's true engine. Individuals must disagree in order to debate, debate in order to decide, and decide in order to move. Professor Stephen Carter of Yale Law School has stated, in one of his many writings on civility, "[a] nation where everybody agrees is not a nation of civility but a nation without diversity, waiting to die."

Civility *is not the* same *as liking someone.* It is a myth that civility is more possible in small communities where everyone knows each other. The duty to be civil toward others does not depend on liking the other person. It doesn't even necessarily require knowing the other person. Civility compels us to show respect even for strangers who may be sharing our space, whether in the public square, in the office, in the courtroom, or in cyberspace.

Civility *is not the absence of criticism.* Respect for the other person or party may in fact call for criticism. For example, a professor who fails to point out an error in a student's research paper is not being civil—he isn't doing his job. And a law firm partner who fails to point out an error in a young lawyer's brief isn't being civil—she isn't doing her job.

Civility *should not be equated with politeness or manners* alone. Although impoliteness is almost always uncivil, good manners alone are not a mark of civility. Politely refusing to serve someone at a lunch counter on the basis of skin color, or cordially informing a law graduate that the firm does not hire women, is not civil behavior.

Civility is a code of decency that characterizes a civilized society. But how is that code reflected in the practice of law?

II. Civil Conduct as a Condition of Lawyer Licensing

A civility imperative permeates bar admission standards. The legal profession is largely self-governing, with ultimate authority over the profession resting with the courts in nearly all states. Courts typically set the standards for who becomes admitted to practice in a state and prescribe the ethical obligations that lawyers are bound, by their oath, to fulfill.

Candidates for bar admission in every state must satisfy the board of bar admissions that they are of good moral character and general fitness to practice law. The state licensing authority's committee on character and fitness will recommend admission only where the applicant's record demonstrates that he or she meets basic eligibility requirements for the practice of law and justifies the trust of clients, adversaries, courts, and others with respect to the professional duties owed to them. Those eligibility requirements typically require applicants to demonstrate exemplary conduct that reflects well on the profession. Representative language in the Illinois bar application, for example, requires every applicant to "conduct oneself with respect for and in accordance with the law and Rules of Professional Conduct, the ability to conduct oneself diligently and reliably in fulfilling all obligations to clients, attorneys, courts, creditors, and others and to conduct oneself in a manner that engenders respect for the law and the profession."

Capacity to act in a manner that engenders respect for the law and the profession—in other words, civility—is a requirement for receiving a law license and, in some jurisdictions, for retaining the privilege of practicing law. It follows that aspiring and practicing lawyers should be disabused of the notion that effective representation ever requires or justifies incivility.

III. Beyond Client Representation: Lawyer as Public Citizen

Notions of a lawyer's core civility duty also are rooted in ethical principles informing and defining the practice of law. Those principles, having evolved over the centuries to lend moral structure and a higher purpose to a life in the law today, speak plainly to a lawyer's dual duties as officer of the legal system and public citizen, beyond the role client advocate. At the very top of the lawyer's code of ethics—in the Preamble to the Model Rules of Professional Conduct—we read of those larger civic duties binding every practicing lawyer.

Civility concepts suffuse the hortatory language of the Preamble. For example, the Preamble makes clear that even in client dealings, counsel is expected to show respect for the legal system in his or her role as advisor, negotiator or evaluator (Preamble Cmt. 5). The Preamble also states that "as a public citizen having special responsibility for the quality of justice," a lawyer should seek improvement of the law, access to justice and the administration of justice, cultivate knowledge of the law beyond its use for clients and further the public's understanding of and confidence in the rule of law and the justice system (Preamble Cmt. 6).

IV. Tension Between Zealous Advocacy and Civility

Living the role of lawyer means carefully balancing duties to client, the legal system, and the lawyer's own interest. Lawyers should resolve conflicts inherent in those duties through the exercise of discretion and judgment "while maintaining a professional, courteous, *and civil attitude* toward all persons involved in the legal system" (Preamble Cmt. 9, emphasis added).

Even for the most ethically conscientious lawyers, there is seemingly ubiquitous tension between the duty of zealous advocacy and the duty to conduct oneself civilly at all times. Model Rule 1.2 compels zealous advocacy, and Comment 1 to the Rule speaks to the depth of that duty, noting that a lawyer

> should pursue a matter on behalf of a client despite opposition, obstruction or personal inconvenience to a lawyer, and take whatever lawful and ethical measures are required to vindicate a client's cause or endeavor. A lawyer must also act with commitment and dedication to the interests of the client and with zeal in advocacy upon the client's behalf. (Rule 1.2 Cmt. 1)

The distorted image in popular culture of lawyer as a zealot, both partisan and combative, would seem to preclude civil behavior as the preferred approach to legal practice. Not so. That same comment goes on to explain:

A lawyer is not bound, however, to press for every advantage that might be realized for a client. . . . The lawyer's duty to act with reasonable diligence does not require the use of offensive tactics or preclude the treating of all persons involved in the legal process with courtesy and respect. (Rule 1.3 Cmt. 1)

Thus, there are firm limits to the lawyer's duty to act with zeal in advocacy, but the precise location of those limits is not always easy to discern. Therein lies the tension. Appropriate zeal, however, never extends to offensive tactics or treating people with discourtesy or disrespect.

The individual lawyer is the guardian of the tone of interactions that will serve both the client and the legal system well. Clients may not understand these limits. Many clients in fact are under the misconception that because they hired the lawyer, they have the power to dictate that lawyer's conduct. It falls to the lawyer, then, to manage and correct that expectation, whenever needed, and to let the client know the lawyer is more than a "hired gun." In practice, that often means refusing a client's demand to act uncivilly or to engage in sharp or unethical practices with other parties in a case or matter.

The rules themselves make it clear, of course, that the lawyer is not just a hired gun. Model Rule 1.16(b)(4) of the ABA Model Rules of Professional Conduct provides that a lawyer may withdraw if the client insists upon taking action that the lawyer considers repugnant or with which the lawyer has fundamental disagreement, and Rule 3.1 provides that a lawyer cannot abuse legal procedure by *frivolously* bringing or defending a proceeding, or asserting or defending an issue. Egregious forms of uncivil behavior in a court proceeding also may constitute conduct prejudicial to the administration of justice, within the meaning of Rule 8.4(d).

V. The Problem of Declining Civility in the Legal Profession

Civility, then, is a central pillar deeply anchored in the ethical and public-service bedrock of the American legal profession. Like the work of vandals in ancient temples, however, substantial evidence points to a steady rise in *incivility* within the American bar. It is problematic to pin down the incidence of incivility and unprofessional conduct because incivility, without some associated violation of the ethical rules, historically has not been prosecuted by the regulatory authorities. Thus there is no good systemic data on incivility's prevalence. There have been countless writings, however, about widespread and growing dissatisfaction among judges and established lawyers who bemoan what they see as the gradual degradation of the practice of law, from a vocation graced by congenial professional relationships to one stigmatized by abrasive dog-eat-dog confrontations.

Discussion of the problem tends to dwell on two areas: (1) examples of lawyers behaving horribly, from which most of us easily distinguish ourselves; and (2) possible causes and justifications of that behavior—rather than possible solutions. Traditional media and social media carry countless accounts of lawyers screaming, using expletives, or otherwise being uncivil. Lawyers who reflect on the trend generally pin the cause on any of a combination of factors, including the influence of outrageous media portrayals; inexperienced lawyers who increasingly start their own law practices without adequate mentoring; and the impact of modern technology that isolates lawyers and others behind their computers, providing anonymous platforms for digital expression.

The scattered data that is available tends to confirm that uncivil lawyer conduct is pervasive. A 2007 survey done by the Illinois Supreme Court Commission on Professionalism, for example, took a close look at specific behaviors of attorneys across the state and concluded that the vast majority of practicing lawyers experience unprofessional behavior by fellow members of the bar. Over the prior year, 71 percent had reported experiencing rudeness—described as sarcasm, condescending comments, swearing, or inappropriate interruption. An even higher percentage of respondents reported being the victim of a complex of more specific behaviors loosely described as "strategic incivility," reflecting a perception that opposing counsel strategically employed uncivil behaviors in an attempt to gain the upper hand, typically in litigation. The complained-of conduct included, for example, deliberate misrepresentation of facts, not agreeing to reasonable requests for accommodation, indiscriminate or frivolous use of pleadings, and inflammatory writing in briefs or motions.

"There is a general view that zealous representation means doing whatever it takes (legally) to win or promote a client's position."

—Respondent to Illinois Supreme Commission on Professionalism Survey

Whatever the causes, the first step toward a real remedy to the incivility pandemic is recognition of the deeply destructive impact of uncivil conduct on individual lawyers who engage in it, on those subjected to it, on the bar as a whole, and ultimately on the American system of justice. It begins with recognition that civility is, and must be, the cornerstone of legal practice.

VI. Benefits of Civility

Aside from the most obvious reasons that lawyers should act civilly—that is, that the profession requires it of them and it's just the right thing to do—a number of tangible benefits accrue from civil conduct in terms of reputational gain and career damage avoidance, as well as strategic advantage in a lawyer's engagement (*See* the accompanying Chapter 4, by Peter R. Jarvis and Katie M. Lachter, *The Practical Case for Civility*, page 49.).

Lawyers who behave with civility also report higher personal and professional rewards. Conversely, lawyer job dissatisfaction is often correlated with unprofessional behavior by opposing counsel. In the 2007 Survey on Professionalism of the Illinois Supreme Court Commission, 95 percent of the respondents reported that the consequences of incivility made the practice of law less satisfying.

Other research shows that lawyers are more than twice as likely as the general population to suffer from mental illness and substance abuse. Law can be a high-pressure occupation, and it appears that needless stress is added by uncivil behavior directed to counsel. "Needless" is used as a descriptor here because the consequences of incivility, as acknowledged by over 92 percent of the survey respondents, often add nothing to the pursuit of justice or to service of client interests. Consequences include making it more difficult to resolve our clients' matters, increasing the cost to our clients, and undermining public confidence in the justice system.

They are the exact *opposite* of the goals we should strive to accomplish as lawyers.

Moreover, judges are not fond of being asked to decide disputes between opposing counsel extraneous to deciding the merits of the respective clients' case. Judges will tell you that mediating bickering between counsel is the least tasteful part of their job. Even if a judge avoids wading into a dispute between counsel, the fact that a lawyer was disrespectful or used bad behavior cannot help but register on the judge's consciousness. Then, if there is a close call on a motion or other issue, and the judge has a choice between ruling in favor of the client whose lawyer was civil and professional or in favor of the client whose lawyer has been a troublemaker, the Judges-Are-Human rule may well control. Similarly, juries also report being negatively affected by rude behavior exhibited by trial attorneys. In sum, lawyer conduct can and does affect the results lawyers deliver to their clients, and ultimately the success of their practices.

It naturally follows that a lawyer's reputation for professional conduct is part and parcel of her reputation for excellence in practice. Before the advent of the Internet, evaluations of attorneys were conducted and disseminated largely by and for lawyers and published yearly in books with entries listing an attorney's achievements by name, geographic region, and specialty. Now, any person who has contact with an attorney may rate and comment on the attorney's performance and professionalism on websites devoted to rating and ranking attorneys or through general social media channels. It is well worth noting that in the realm of the Internet, one uncivil outburst may haunt an attorney for years; and reputations may be built and destroyed quickly. (*See* 12, Reputation, by Avarita L. Hanson, page 151). Even a cursory search of some of these websites shows that clients regularly comment (especially if they are displeased) about an attorney's communication style and respect for her clients and the system of justice.

Not surprisingly, research shows that clients evaluate a lawyer who exhibits civility and professionalism as a more effective lawyer. If clients evaluate their lawyers as being effective, they stay with them; if they see their lawyers as ineffective, they will go elsewhere for legal services, particularly in a climate in which the supply of lawyers exceeds the demand for legal services.

Moreover, recent law firm industry research shows that the vast majority of clients would consider switching law firms if another law firm could deliver better services or results and, similarly, that superior service, in which relationship abilities are central, increases client retention rates by about one third. The research also found that effective client service and positive relationships, in turn, increase profit to the lawyers by about the same rate.

VII. Bad Behavior / Bad Consequences

Historically, incivility *per se* has by and large not been prosecuted by attorney regulatory authorities, but the tide seems to be turning. Since 2010, several attorneys have been suspended by their states' high courts for uncivil conduct implicating a lawyer's duty to uphold the administration of justice and other ethics rules.

The Supreme Court of South Carolina has disciplined several attorneys for incivility, citing not only ethics rules but that state's Lawyer's Oath, taken upon admission to the bar. The oath contains a pledge of civility. In *In the Matter of William Gary White III*, the lawyer had sent a letter to his client, a church, which had received a notice from the town manager regarding compliance with zoning laws. The town manager was copied on the lawyer's letter. The letter questioned whether the town manager had a soul, said the town manager had no brain, and characterized the leadership of the town as pagans and insane and pigheaded.

The court found that respondent White had sent the letter as a calculated tactic to intimidate and insult his opponents, violating his obligation to behave in a civilized and professional manner. In imposing a ninety day suspension, the court noted that "the legal profession is one of advocacy; however, Respondent's role as an advocate would have been better served by zealously arguing his client's position, not making personal attacks . . . and Respondent's conduct in this matter reflects poorly on himself as a member of the legal profession and reflects negatively upon the profession as a whole."

In Illinois, respondent Melvin Hoffman was prosecuted by disciplinary authorities for oral and written statements made to judges and an attorney. His offensive statements included calling a judge a "narcissistic, maniacal, mental case," who "should not be on the bench." In an administrative proceeding before the Illinois Department of Children and Family Services, Hoffman's comments included saying that "this is a kangaroo court"; that the judge was "an advocate and adversary to my position in everything that's done here"; that he would be "embarrassed to have to take such jobs [as Administrative Law Judge]"; and that the proceeding was "no more a fair hearing than they had in Russia when they were operating under the Soviet system." Hoffman also was charged with saying to another attorney in a courtroom that the attorney was "unethical" and "you must be from a Jewish firm." The Illinois Supreme Court upheld the findings that the lawyer violated various ethical rules, including Illinois Rule 8.4(a) (modeled after the corresponding ABA Model Rule), prohibiting conduct prejudicial to the administration of justice, and suspended Hoffman for six months and until further order of court.

Outside of the courtroom, much of the uncivil arrow-slinging between counsel historically has occurred during discovery disputes in litigation. However, the growing influence of technology in litigation, with its potential for marshaling exponentially more information and data at trial than ever, and the commensurate need to control and limit that information to what is relevant and manageable, suggests courts will grow even less tolerant of lawyers trying to manipulate the pre-trial fact discovery process or engaging in endless, contentious discovery disputes. Moreover, while never wise or virtuous, it is no longer profitable to play "hide the ball" in litigation as clients are demanding better results at reduced costs.

VIII. Movement Toward Systemic Solutions to Incivility

There have been programmatic efforts, largely led by judges, to address and curb spreading incivility in the legal profession. In 1996, the Conference of Chief Justices adopted a resolution calling for the courts of the highest jurisdiction in each state to take a leadership role in evaluating the contemporary needs of the legal community with respect to lawyer professionalism. In response, the supreme courts of fourteen states have established commissions on professionalism to promote principles of professionalism and civility throughout their states.

Many more states have, either through their supreme courts or bar associations, formed committees that have studied professionalism issues and formulated principles articulating the aspirational or ideal behavior the lawyers should strive to exhibit. These professionalism codes nearly all state at the outset that they do not form the basis of discipline but are provided as guidance—attorneys and judges should strive to embody professionalism above the floor of acceptable conduct that is memorialized in the attorney rules of ethics. They also typically echo a theme found in the Preamble to the Model Rules of Professional Conduct: that lawyers have an obligation to improve the administration of justice.

In 2004, a relatively aggressive stance was taken by the Supreme Court of South Carolina. The South Carolina high court amended the oath attorneys take upon admission to the bar to include a pledge of civility and courtesy to judges and court personnel and the language "to opposing parties and their counsel, I pledge fairness, integrity, and civility, not only in court, but also in all written and oral communications." It also amended the disciplinary rules to provide that a violation of the civility oath could be grounds for discipline. In 2011, the Supreme Court of Florida added a similar pledge to that state's oath of admission to the bar.

Some jurisdictions, in states including New Jersey, Illinois, Georgia, Florida, Arizona, and North Carolina, have taken the voluntary aspirational codes further and have adopted an intermediary or peer review system to mediate complaints against lawyers or judges who do not abide by the aspirational code. Because compliance with the mechanism, like the aspirational code, is voluntary, the success of these mechanisms has been inconsistent. It can be challenging to implement an enforcement mechanism in a way that inspires voluntary compliance with an aspirational code without straying into the area of attorney discipline.

Without question, the most effective ways of addressing incivility entail bringing lawyers together for training and mentoring. The American Inns of Court, modeled after the apprenticeship training programs of barristers in England, brings seasoned and newer attorneys together into small groups to study, present, and discuss some of the pressing issues facing the profession. Through specialized bar associations and other organizations, educational efforts bringing together both prosecutors and defenders are lauded as successful vehicles for airing diverse perspectives in a way that promotes civility.

IX. Conclusion: A Time to Recommit to Civility

The needed rebirth of civility, at a critical juncture in the evolution of the legal profession, should be seen by lawyers not as pain, but as gain. As the research conclusively bears out, (1) civil lawyers are more effective and achieve better outcomes; (2) civil lawyers build better reputations; (3) civility breeds job satisfaction; and (4) incivility may invite attorney discipline. The rapid changes that technology and globalization are bringing to the practice of law make civil behavior more important than ever. Those two monumental change agents introduce conditions clearly conducive to conduct unbecoming a legal professional, that is, more stress, the dehumanizing effect of electronic interfaces, inexorable pressure to compete or perish, the demands of information overload, and incessant pressure to behave more "like a business" and less like a legal professional in the traditional sense. In the face of all that, one might ask, why bother trying? The answer—again besides the obvious: that the profession requires us to be civil, and it is simply the right thing to do—ultimately speaks to the challenge to preserve a great profession, and that level of professionalism among lawyers that the larger American society requires in order to survive as a civil society bound to the Rule of Law.

Sources/Reading

Stephen L. Carter, Civility: Manners, Morals, and the Etiquette of Democracy (1998).

Neil Hamilton & Verna Monson, The Positive Empirical Relationship of Professionalism to Effectiveness in the Practice of Law, 24 Geo. J. Legal Ethics 137, 140 (2011).

Leo J. Shapiro & Assoc. L.L.C., *Survey on Professionalism: A Study of Illinois Lawyers December 2007* (2007), *available at* http://www.ilsccp.org/pdfs/surveyonprofessionalism_final.pdf.

JAYNE R. REARDON is the Executive Director of the Illinois Supreme Court Commission on Professionalism and a member of the ABA Standing Committee on Professionalism. Ms. Reardon has written many articles on professionalism topics, including Civil Disagreement http://blog.ilsccp.org/civil-disagreement/ (January 2013).

Chapter 4

THE PRACTICAL CASE FOR CIVILITY

PETER R. JARVIS AND KATIE M. LACHTER

I. Introduction

Some lawyers believe that their duties to clients require an absolutely no-holds-barred approach meant to make life as unpleasant as possible for the clients' legal adversaries. Truth be told, some clients want this kind of lawyer. Whether described as Rambo lawyers, pit bulls, avenging angels, or an opponent's worst nightmare, these lawyers seem to believe that anything less will fail to maximize client objectives.

In this chapter, we do not assert that such an approach, whether within or outside of ethical bounds, can never, in fact, serve a client's interest. The argument is simpler: regardless of how often this may be true, client interests are far more often better served when lawyers behave civilly.

The focus here is not manners or social etiquette as ends in and of themselves, or virtue as its own reward. Nor is it the general moral or philosophical benefits of harmony over disharmony. What we mean to say is that very often the best way forward for even the most egotistical, self-interested, and self-absorbed lawyers and their egotistical, self-interested, and self-absorbed clients is through, rather than around, civility. Stated another way, this chapter makes the practical case for civility on its objective merits.

In this chapter, we will first define what we mean by "civility," then turn to what we see as the principal benefits of civility in a lawyer-client context, and finally examine specific uses of civility in potentially difficult circumstances.

II. Defining Civility

For our purposes, "civility" includes but is not limited to treating others with courtesy and respect. It also extends to the avoidance of unnecessary rhetorical excesses, gratuitous insults, quarrels for the sake of quarrels, creating additional work for an adversary just because it is possible to do so, and intimidation for the sake of intimidation. Civility requires self-restraint and, at times, a willingness to make an extra effort to address or even calm the concerns of others who may be behaving uncivilly. On many occasions, the cause of civility compels a search for common interests with an adversary rather than an emphasis on the usually more evident areas of disagreement. And civility often requires clear, active reflection on one's own contributions to difficult situations, rather than just those of others, and the capacity to find humor rather than outrage when a problem arises.

Importantly, to act civilly is not to abandon key client objectives or to give in to bullies. Civility is focused not so much on the "what," or objectives, of lawyering as on the "how." One can be civil or uncivil in any line of practice. As the Supreme Court noted many years ago, civility allows the striking of hard blows, but not the striking of foul ones. *Berger v. United States*, 295 U.S. 78, 88 (1935).

III. The Benefits of Civility

Civility has at least six practical benefits.

First, most lawyers—and, we submit, most human beings—do not do their best work when they are angry or irate. Even if one leaves aside the personal health benefits of limiting or avoiding prolonged and extreme emotional states, a lawyer consumed with ostensibly righteous zeal may consequently fail to see one or more better ways to pursue client or lawyer objectives. Most of us have experienced personal situations outside of the practice of law in which our anger toward a friend, relative, or situation has caused us to say things we later regret and has at least temporarily blinded us to better problem-solving. It is so in the practice of law as well.

Second, most lawyers—again like most human beings—don't do their best *listening* when they are angry or irate. Thus, the opportunity for successful resolution of a matter may be lost if counsel for the parties are not listening to each other or if, in a fit of pique, they intentionally or unintentionally fail to suggest potential resolutions.

Third, while uncivil behavior sometimes is the squeaky wheel that gets the grease, what goes around generally does come around. Experience teaches us that if it has any effects at all, uncivil behavior is likely to backfire and invite an equal or greater measure of uncivil behavior in return. For every cowardly lawyer who will turn tail and run at the first sign of trouble, there are far more who will dig in their heels and push back as hard or harder. It is very easy to sin in haste by dashing off an offensive email, only to repent in the fullness of time when the other side replies in kind or ups the ante. Moreover, although a client's appetite for litigation or for protracted business negotiations may decrease over time, the resolution of such matters on favorable and acceptable terms may be far more difficult to achieve with an opponent who feels disrespect.

A fourth and no less significant benefit concerns respect for client resources. Clients are the entities and individuals whom we expect to pay our bills and who, in turn, expect us to serve their interests rather than the other way around. Being in "confrontation mode" all the time is not just wearing upon the confronters and the confronted; it also takes a lot of time and costs a lot of money. Consider, for example, the time that can be spent in an email or letter-writing campaign or on a series of sanctions motions detailing every conceivable misstep an opponent may have made. Many lawyers charge for their time in six-minute increments, and the increments add up. In depositions, clients not only pay the attorney for asking or listening to questions and answers but also for counsel quarrels and for each page or electronic recording of the transcript. A fifteen-minute argument between counsel costs as much as fifteen minutes of probing testimony and likely does nothing to advance client objectives. Few clients will care even a fraction as much about wounded legal egos as their lawyers do, and clients can and will refuse to pay legal bills that reflect unnecessary diatribes and wasted time and effort. Bickering over items that, in the grand scheme of things, should have been resolved between lawyers may even lead clients to choose new counsel altogether.

A fifth benefit of civility has to do with the effects that uncivil behavior may have on third parties—including judges. On the whole, judges do not appreciate having to spend time refereeing what they see as personality spats or minor issues that counsel could have worked out for themselves. Adding to a judge's workload is a good way to alienate a judge, and sufficiently uncivil behavior can even lead to sanctions. But behaving badly before a judge poses an even greater danger. Imagine two cases raising the same legal issue before two different judges at the same time. In one case, counsel for both parties have engaged in extreme rhetorical excesses, misstatements of the opposing party's position, etc. In the other case, one side has engaged in such behavior, but every word from the other side, while firm, is also calm and rational. Other things equal, the lawyer who appears to have kept his or her head is more likely to emerge the winner. As one judge stated, "You spent two pages telling me you don't like this guy? Get to what you want me to do." Newhouse, *Lawyers Learn How Not To Behave*, Brooklyn Daily Bulletin (Mar. 10, 2011).

In short, conducting oneself civilly is, entirely as a matter of lawyer and client self-interest, an excellent way to build a positive record that will improve the odds of winning over judges, juries, and others who may subsequently review the lawyer's conduct (including disciplinarians and plaintiff-side legal malpractice lawyers). One also cannot assume that ostensibly private but hostile and intemperate communications will remain private. A string of civil emails, letters, or moving papers can go a long way toward getting the judge and others on a lawyer's side. Tone, as well as content, matters. "Facts – not adjectives – will get you where you want to go." Ponsor, *Effective Oral Argument*, I Fed. Civil Litig. In the First Circuit § 4.3.1, FCLI MA-CLE 4–1 (2011).

The first five benefits of civility all speak to situations in which lawyers must deal with adversaries. A sixth and final benefit concerns the relationships between attorneys and clients. A surprisingly large number of bar complaints and legal malpractice claims can be traced to lawyers' failing to exhibit the common courtesy of returning client phone calls or responding to emails or letters on a timely basis. Some lawyers may attribute their non-responsiveness to benign forgetfulness, disorganization, or preoccupation with other matters. But to clients, such inattention is often seen as rude, insulting, unethical, and uncivil in the extreme. Ignoring one's clients is asking for trouble.

Formal complaints against lawyers also often arise from intemperate responses to clients. Even where a sharp response to an out-of-line client seems justified at the time, be assured there is no better way to turn a salvageable relationship or a friendly parting of the ways into a donnybrook. In one case, an entire law firm was publicly censured in part for "rude and uncivil conduct to a client." *In re Law Firm of Wilens and Baker*, 9 A.D.3d 213, 214, 777 N.Y.S.2d 116 (1st Dep't 2004). And at the risk of repetition, bar disciplinarians and plaintiffs' legal malpractice lawyers may attach great significance not only to what the lawyer said but also how the lawyer said it.

IV. Civility as a Strategy

Experience suggests that most lawyers recognize the practical benefits of civility and do act civilly most of the time. Yet all of us could benefit from thinking harder, and more strategically, about how and when specific civil conduct can advance the clients' interests, and our own. This section presents three not-so-hypothetical situations where a civil approach best serves the interest of client and lawyer. As the reader will note, these examples relate directly back to the benefits of civil conduct discussed above.

A. Lawyer receives what Lawyer perceives as an intemperate letter or email from Opposing Counsel that threatens motions for sanctions and other harms if Opposing Counsel's demands are not fully met by a date that Lawyer perceives to be unreasonable.

We start our analysis with the reminder that civility principles do not require Lawyer to sacrifice substantive client rights or objectives when efforts in support of the client may be unpleasant. If, in fact, Lawyer is not willing to serve client objectives because of a distaste either for the objectives of the representation or for the situations in which the lawyer may be placed, Lawyer should consider resignation (or, where appropriate, rejecting the matter in the first place). But suppose that none of these problems exists. In that case, a lawyer acting with civility in mind should ask herself at least the following questions before responding, because her answers to these questions may affect the tone and substance of any response:

1. Is it completely clear what Opposing Counsel is saying and why Opposing Counsel is saying it? For example, is it at least possible that Opposing Counsel may be operating on the basis of different factual or legal assumptions than Lawyer as a result of prior misunderstandings or miscommunications between the two? Alternatively, is Opposing Counsel's communication really as threatening as it first seemed or can it also be interpreted in a less threatening manner? And has Opposing Counsel been told why the proposed deadline or timeline is unworkable?

2. Is it at least possible that a face-to-face meeting with Opposing Counsel, rather than a written or telephonic shouting match, will enable the lawyers to understand each other and find common ground?

3. Is there someone else in Opposing Counsel's or Lawyer's firm whom Lawyer might consult in an attempt to lower rhetorical levels and move things forward?

4. To the extent that a written response must be sent, is it in the client's best interest (i) to respond with the same or even more strident tone and approach, or (ii) to at least appear to be rational, thoughtful and considerate?

As noted, a judge or others who may view both the rational and the irrational lawyer at a later time are more likely to be favorably inclined toward the rational. Moreover, alternative 4(ii) above is more likely to induce more civil behavior going forward by Opposing Counsel, who presumably also knows how judges tend to respond to strident lawyers. Upon reading Lawyer's civilized response and sensing a trap, Opposing

Counsel may well decide that it is best not to continue stridently but instead to try to work through problems on a constructive and less acrimonious basis. This result goes just as much into the "win" column as a successful judicial decision on the issue. Moreover, the expense to the client is likely to be far less.

B. Lawyer receives an intemperate and overbroad demand from Opposing Counsel for discovery to which Lawyer believes Opposing Counsel is probably not entitled. Lawyer is inclined to want to force Opposing Counsel to file a motion to compel in part in order to "educate the judge" about what lousy human beings Opposing Counsel and his client truly are. Lawyer takes an extremely aggressive position in response.

Like the prior example, this one implicates the benefits of better communication between counsel as a means to avoid costly and needless misunderstandings. And it introduces additional permutations to the civility analysis. Before deciding to act, Lawyer might ask the following:

1. To what extent, if any, are the issues raised in Opposing Counsel's communication truly material and worth fighting over?
2. By her willingness to take an extremely aggressive stance, is Lawyer testing the boundaries of civility herself, while creating a risk that her client will be cast in a negative light and needlessly inviting additional client expense related to the anticipated motion that would follow her contemplated aggressive stance?
3. To what extent is there a possibility of win-win alternatives that would leave all parties and counsel just as well off or better off and at lower cost?
4. Even if Lawyer is absolutely morally convinced that the judge should see things her way, isn't there also a risk that the judge may not do so?
5. Alternatively, how sure is Lawyer that the parties (or counsel) will not encounter future situations in which their roles may be reversed?

C. Lawyer begins case with Opposing Counsel on a cordial basis. Early in the proceedings, however, Client tells Lawyer that Client does not want Lawyer extending any courtesies or making life any easier for Opposing Counsel or Adverse Party on any issues—large or small, material or immaterial—than is absolutely necessary.

This example raises questions both about the lawyer-client relationship and about relationships between counsel. At a minimum, we believe a civil approach would suggest the following:

1. Particularly if Lawyer has not already done so, this would be a good time for Lawyer to explain to Client how cooperation can be a two-way street, how non-cooperation can make things more expensive and take them longer to resolve, and how it is difficult to predict at that time which side may need additional "slack" in the future. Even if Client is not persuaded, Lawyer can at least document this advice as protection against future assertions by Client that Lawyer unnecessarily ran up the bills.

2. Lawyer may consider whether it is in Client's interest for Lawyer to explain to Opposing Counsel at the time that Lawyer will be proceeding in this manner rather than leaving Opposing Counsel to conclude over time that Lawyer is just an incompetent jerk.

One of the authors of this chapter faced such a situation and chose to inform Opposing Counsel of the constraints under which that lawyer was operating. The result was that when the client finally decided to consider settlement negotiations, the relationship between counsel was positive and constructive, allowing a mutually favorable settlement to be reached in a fairly short time. Even if the case had not settled well or quickly, however, the author's client would have been no worse off as a result of the early communications with Opposing Counsel.

V. Conclusion

Although this article contains only three examples, many more can easily be imagined. Our hope is that this discussion of the practical benefits of civility will encourage lawyers facing currently or potentially uncivil situations to consider all options before heading down what may, with the benefit of 20/20 hindsight, prove to be an unnecessarily difficult path.

Before the age of comparative fault, there was a tort doctrine called "last clear chance" that sometimes placed responsibility on a party who was not initially at fault but who nonetheless had the last opportunity to avoid the harm that ultimately occurred. This chapter suggests a kind of "last clear chance" approach to lawyer-lawyer and lawyer-client relationships—not just because of whatever moral benefits civility may bring but also because of its often high potential for effectiveness. While fighting fire with fire is dramatic, fighting fire with a fire extinguisher may do more to save the lawyer's (and his client's) property. And avoiding fire altogether through the use of fire prevention techniques will most often, if not always, be better still.

PETER R. JARVIS leads Hinshaw & Culbertson LLP's national Lawyers' Professional Responsibility/Risk Management Practice Group and is licensed in California, New York, Oregon, Washington, and Alaska. He is a co-author (with Geoffrey C. Hazard, Jr. and W. William Hodes) of the national treatise, *The Law of Lawyering*.

KATIE M. LACHTER is a member of Hinshaw & Culbertson LLP's national Lawyers' Professional Responsibility/Risk Management Practice Group and Secretary of the New York City Bar Association's Committee on Professional Ethics.

Chapter 5

SUCCESSFUL LAWYER SKILLS AND BEHAVIORS

WILLIAM D. HENDERSON

I. Overview

It would be nice if science would deliver a definitive list of skills and behaviors that resulted in lawyer success. The law schools could teach it, employers would hire for it, and clients and society would be better off. Alas, this is unlikely to happen. The first stumbling block is our inability to agree on an adequate definition of success. Is the yardstick for success income or fame? Alternatively, is success the result of justice advanced through brilliant advocacy, or can it flow from justice delayed through mastery of procedure, thus pleasing the client who benefits from the delay? Or perhaps true success occurs outside the limelight and is derived from the admiration and respect of one's peers and clients, or some internal scorecard that connects lawyers to the rest of humanity. Suffice it to say, even if all stakeholders agreed on a single measure of success, these issues raise difficult problems of measurement.

Rather than select one definition of success and invite the usual lawyer skepticism, this chapter works backward and identifies examples that suggest that success—however it might be defined—requires something more than high cognitive ability as measured by standardized test scores or academic achievement. As simple and obvious as this statement might sound, it is fundamentally at odds with how lawyers are hired out of law school. Whether it is white shoe law firms hiring associates, federal judges hiring clerks, federal agencies or elite public interest organizations hiring staffers, or the legal academy hiring professors, law school pedigree and grades—common proxies for intelligence—reign supreme. Ironically, as important as intelligence is for hiring, it is all too often the absence of various non-cognitive factors that cause lawyers to be fired (e.g., inability to relate to clients or colleagues, lack of drive or passion) or hit a permanent plateau (e.g., inability to effectively supervise or delegate legal work, lack of a professional network).

The core message of this chapter, supported by ample social science and empirical evidence, is that highly effective lawyers draw upon a diverse array of skills and abilities that are seldom taught, measured, or discussed during law school. One of the major implications of this analysis is that the heavy emphasis placed on academic credentials by elite legal employers, such as large law firms, is misplaced. As discussed below, these practices are largely the relics of a bygone area that persist long after their original business purpose has evaporated. For new and aspiring attorneys who may lack the cognitive markers to make the cut for these seemingly elite institutions, the encouraging word is that the markers themselves have precious little ability to predict future performance as a lawyer.

This chapter also has clear implications for legal education. Since the advent of the *U.S. News & World Report* rankings, law school admissions offices have adopted a near-exclusive focus on LSAT scores and undergraduate GPA, ignoring a wide range of relevant information that signals other significant life accomplishments. This systemic mis-weighing of ability, or future ability, creates a counterproductive expectations gap that negatively affects law students' belief in what they can accomplish in their legal careers. This "capping" of expectations also undercuts the perceived value of innovation in legal education, as the overemphasis on elite credentials arguably holds its greatest sway among the legal professoriate (Sullivan et al., 2007). The flipside of the overemphasis on academic markers is an underestimation of the true power of excellent teaching, training, intensive practice, feedback, and coaching to create truly outstanding advocates, counselors, and problem solvers. This is an opportunity for all stakeholders—students, employers, and law schools—to make a giant leap forward for the benefit of the legal profession and society as a whole.

II. Intelligence Versus Other Factors In Determining Lawyer Effectiveness

George E.P. Box, a renowned statistician, once wrote that "all models are wrong but some are useful" (Box 1979, p. 2). Figure 1 summarizes a simple model of lawyer performance. It may be wrong, but it has the virtue of being clear.

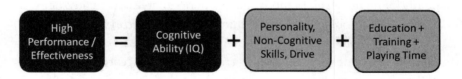

Figure 1

According to the model in Figure 1, high performance as a lawyer depends upon a confluence of three factors: intelligence/cognitive ability; motivation, drive, personality, and various non-cognitive abilities (e.g., "people skills"); and the quality of education and playing time a lawyer received to practice and develop her craft.

Regarding the first factor, practicing law requires an accumulation of legal knowledge and the ability to formulate appropriate legal solutions. This requires some reasonable quantum of cognitive ability. For reasons of lawyer competence, state bar examinations set the minimum cut-off. Scores on the LSAT, which measures verbal reasoning ability (Henderson, 2004), are consistently and meaningfully correlated with scores on the bar exam, even after controlling for law school grades (see, e.g., Wightman, 1998, pp. 37–54). Thus, higher levels of cognitive ability clearly help law school graduates acquire sufficient legal knowledge to pass the bar exam, though an important caveat is warranted. When LSAT and law school grades are placed in the same statistical model, law school grades are a much stronger predictor of bar passage than LSAT scores. This strongly suggests that effort or drive, apart from cognitive ability, is a key prerequisite for acquiring the knowledge necessary to pass the bar (Wightman, 1998)— presumably, the more drive and effort, the better. (Short citations in this chapter refer to longer citations in the Sources/Reading list at the end of the chapter).

The basic empirical facts on cognitive ability and bar passage need to be acknowledged. Yet, these same facts also raise a far more fundamental question: If a law student has the requisite minimum threshold of intelligence needed to enter the profession, what is the relative tradeoff (to an employer or client) of the three factors presented in Figure 1? Stated more concretely, would it be wise for an employer to trade five or ten LSAT points for higher levels of motivation, a more suitable personality, or excellent legal skills obtained through intensive practice with a great mentor?

These tradeoffs, though often ignored or undervalued by legal employers at the time of entry-level hiring, are very real. According to the late Arthur Jensen, an eminent educational psychologist who devoted his career to the study of intelligence, differences in IQ are useful and valid for predicting the ability to progress from one educational level to the next. According to Jensen, an IQ of 115 (one standard deviation above average) is the approximate cutoff for the ability to complete "an accredited four-year college with grades that would qualify for admission to a professional school or graduate school" (Jensen 1980, p. 113). This amounts to roughly one in six adults. Jensen observed that beyond this threshold, "IQ differences in this upper part of the scale . . . are generally of lesser importance for success in the popular sense than are certain traits of personality and character" (*Id.*).

A vivid example of this observation is Richard Feynman, who won the 1965 Nobel Prize in Physics. In the 1980s, Feynman told the story of his trip home from the Nobel ceremonies in Stockholm. Feynman decided to stop by his high school in Far Rockaway, Queens and look up his grades and IQ score. "My grades were not as good as I remembered," Feynman reminisced, "and my IQ was 124 or 126, considered just above average." His wife Gweneth reported his delight, "He said to win a Nobel prize was no big deal, but to win it with an IQ of 124, now that was something" (Faber, 1985).

If, beyond a certain threshold of intelligence, personality and character are critical determinants of professional accomplishment and success, another distinguishing factor might be creativity. Yet, there is no useful academic proxy for creative ability. Similar to Jensen's observations, academic researchers have found that "the association between intelligence [as measured by cognitive ability tests] and creativity is very weak for both child and adult samples." In fact, the correlation tends to become negligible for populations that are above-average in intelligence (Simonton, 2008, pp. 681–82). Another academic study documented the experience of Louis Terman, an early believer in the power of IQ to predict great accomplishment later in life. Terman assembled a group of 1,500 young children based on high IQ scores and conducted a longitudinal study that tracked their future professional success. Although many in the sample achieved professional prominence, none won a Nobel Prize. Yet, William Shockley and Luis Alvarez were two youngsters who applied for admission to the Terman's elite program but were excluded because they were below the IQ cutoff. Both went on to win the Nobel Prize (Winner, 1996; Hulbert, 2005).

III. Labor Markets and Law Schools

It is worth noting that the reputations of the nation's leading law schools were established long before the first LSAT was administered. In the early part of 20th century, a small number of university-based law schools (primarily those in the Ivy League, but a handful of others schools) began to differentiate themselves based on the case method, scholarly faculty, and admission criteria that required undergraduate study. Relative to other law schools, these innovations produced a better-trained law graduate. Thus, during the early 20th century, these schools became the preferred recruiting grounds for the small number of legal employers with large corporate clients.

The firm history of Cravath Swaine & Moore, a leading New York City corporate firm (Swaine 1948), provides a vivid example of this practice. As of 1948, the firm had employed a total of 454 law school graduates. Of this total, 67.7% attended Harvard (128), Columbia (124), or Yale (54), with the remainder allocated to "other law schools of high repute, such as Pennsylvania, Cornell, Virginia, Michigan and Chicago" (Swaine 2 n.2, 1948). These law school graduates became the core input of the "Cravath system," which was a sophisticated training methodology designed to produce, over a period of years, first-rate partner-level lawyers.

The primary business purpose for privileging the national law schools was not the high aptitude scores required for admissions—the LSAT was not administered for the first time until 1948. Rather, these schools only admitted students with an undergraduate education, and "Cravath believed that disciplined minds are more likely to be found among college graduates than among men lacking in formal education" (Swaine, 1948). In a talk given at Harvard Law School in 1920, Cravath told students that a successful "lawyer of affairs" (i.e., a corporate lawyer) required "the fundamental qualities of good health, ordinary honesty, a sound education and normal intelligence. . . . Brilliant intellectual powers are not essential."

The allegiance to top students at national law schools was not limited to the east coast corporate bar. In the 1920s in Cleveland, the law firm of Jones Day demanded law review credentials of Harvard Law School graduates as a condition of being hired (Scheler, 2000). Thirty years later in nearby Detroit, sociologist Jack Ladinsky surveyed lawyers in the city's metropolitan area and found that 73 percent of all lawyers working in a law firm—i.e., a partnership of two or more lawyers—attended one of five law schools: Harvard, Yale, Columbia, Michigan, or Chicago (Ladinsky, 1963). Regional law school graduates, in contrast, overwhelmingly worked as solo practitioners.

When the LSAT was finally introduced in 1948, the vast majority of national law schools were among the early adopters (Johnson, Olsen & Winterbottom 1955). One of the most striking features of the early years was relatively large proportion of students in the traditional applicant profile who had very low scores. The original LSAT was scaled on a 200 to 800 point scale, with a mean of 500 and standard deviation of 100. For the 1948 academic year, 45% of the incoming class at the University of Pennsylvania Law School (116 out 265) scored below 475 nationally (a total of 18 law schools participated), a proportion that decreased in future years as the test's strong predictive validity changed admissions practices. Similarly, among incoming law students at UC Berkeley who enrolled between 1950 and 1953, 35 percent scored below the 50th percentile. For Harvard Law School, two-thirds of students admitted between 1949 and 1954 scored below 600. During the sample period, 7.2 percent of all entering students flunked out of Harvard Law, with a disproportionately large number toward the lower end of the LSAT scale. Thus, Harvard Law, like many other schools, moved toward the implementation of LSAT cutoffs (*Id.* at 94).

By the late 1950s, the influence of the ABA and the Association of American Law Schools effectively universalized the educational features of the national law schools (Stevens 1983). The rise of the great public law schools and federal loan programs also improved access to legal education by making it available to students who formerly could not afford to take three years out of the labor force. By mid-century, these changes in U.S. legal education enabled a large swath of first-generation college graduates to attend law school, thus expanding the talent pipeline. With the advent of accreditation standards, the quality of pre-law preparation and law school instruction was improved and made more uniform.

Although these were significant, broad-based innovations in legal education, they had markedly little effect on the hiring patterns of the large and growing corporate bar. By this time, elite educational credentials had become an engrained part of the firms' identity and culture (Henderson, 2009). Further, corporate law firms were about to enter a period of astonishing growth and economic prosperity (Galanter & Palay, 1993; Galanter & Henderson, 2008; Henderson, 2011). With the supply of elite graduates far in excess of demand, why tinker with the model? Thus, for the next several decades, long after the condition for the original business logic had evaporated, the nation's leading law firms continued to ply their traditional credentials-based recruitment model. Albeit, this model was gradually modified to include top academic students at regional law schools as the supply of national law school graduates gradually became inadequate to keep up large law firm growth (Heinz et al., 2006). This credentials-based labor market cast a very long shadow on the incentive structure of the entire legal education hierarchy.

IV. The Impact of the *U.S. News & World Report* Rankings

If a labor market continues to provide a large reward to a discrete number of law schools for innovations that occurred several decades earlier, despite widespread adoption of those practices at virtually all other law schools, new and more timely innovations in legal education will grind to a halt. This is, unfortunately, an accurate description of the current state of U.S. legal education. (At the time of this writing, the bleak employment numbers and declining volume of law school applicants were starting to bring this sector back to the life (Henderson, 2013), but the scale of promising new initiatives is tiny relative to the magnitude of the underlying problems.)

The stagnant incentive structure of legal education has been further compounded by the advent of the annual *U.S. News & World Report* law school rankings. Since the magazine began ranking all law schools in the mid-1990s, law schools have devoted enormous time and resources toward increasing their relative standing (Sauder, Espeland & Nelson, 2009). Competition is thus largely defined by the various input factors that comprise the magazine's composite score. These input factors include reputation scores among academics and practicing lawyers (40%), educational resources, such as faculty-student ratio, student scholarship funds, and size of library (15%), employment and bar passage rates (20%), and student quality based on undergraduate GPA, LSAT scores, and admissions selectivity (25%).

Among the input factors, the 25% allocated to student quality is subject to immense strategizing because, in theory, these input statistics can be directly influenced through a school's admissions policies. The strategy is straightforward: aggressively market the school to prospective students and allocate limited scholarship dollars to optimize median undergraduate GPAs and LSAT scores (Henderson & Morriss, 2006). As the logic has spread through the law school hierarchy, it has produced a self-fulfilling prophecy. According to a 1998 report prepared by the Association of American Law Schools, "90% of the overall differences in ranks among schools can be explained solely by the median LSAT score of their entering classes" (Klein & Hamilton, 1998). Indeed, over the last two decades, institutional pressures for higher rankings have fundamentally altered admissions practices. In order to preserve or increase rankings, admission resources and merit scholarship dollars are deployed toward the goal of achieving the highest possible median LSAT and UGPA scores. This pattern can be observed in Figure 2, which compared the median LSAT of the top 50 ranked law schools in 1994 with the top 50 ranked in 2012.

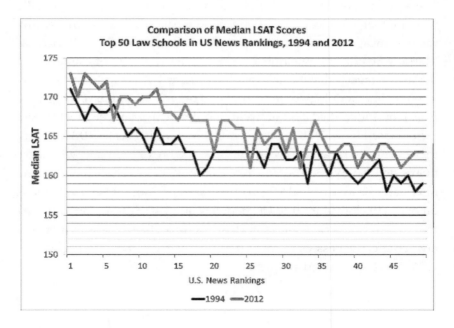

Figure 2

Over the nearly two decade period covered in Figure 2, the median LSAT scores increased an average of 3.1 points. Remarkably, this increase was spread relatively evenly across all top 50 law schools despite the fact that the applicant volume was smaller in 2012 by over 10,000 prospective students (89,600 in the fall of 1993 versus 78,800 in the fall of 2011). Comparable increases can be observed with undergraduate GPAs (Henderson, 2010).

The consequence of placing such heavy weight on numerical credentials is that there is precious little room to consider other relevant factors, such as the rigor of an undergraduate major, work experience, letters of recommendation, personal accomplishment, or diversity. In essence, law school admissions have largely become a sterile, mechanical process based on two numbers, LSAT and undergraduate GPA.

V. Empirical Evidence of Successful Lawyer Behavior

The emphasis on LSAT and undergraduate grades has fundamentally reshaped legal education. Yet, are these measures of academic ability the best measures of lawyering potential? A recent study by Professors Marjorie Schulz and Sheldon Zedeck at the University of California at Berkeley suggests that the answer is no (Schulz & Zedeck, 2008). Drawing upon the methodology of industrial and organizational psychology, the researchers identified a set of twenty-six distinctive lawyer effectiveness factors (see Figure 3). Behaviorally anchored rating scales (BARS) were then created to measure lawyer effectiveness on a 1 to 5 scale, with increments defined by specific, concrete examples of lawyer behaviors. The next step was to use the BARS to obtain peer and supervisor evaluations on over 1100 law alumni of UC Berkeley and UC Hastings and approximately 200 UC Berkeley law students. In turn, these measurements of lawyer effectiveness were correlated with participants' undergraduate GPA, LSAT scores, and 1L grades.

Figure 3. Schultz & Zedeck 26 Lawyer Effectiveness Factors

Intellectual & Cognitive	Conflict Resolution
Analysis and Reasoning	Negotiation Skills
Creativity & Innovation	Able to See the World Through the Eyes of
Problem Solving	Others
Practical Judgment	
	Client/Business Relations:
Research & Information Gathering	**Entrepreneurship**
Researching the Law	Networking and Business Development
Fact Finding	Providing Advice & Counsel & Building
Questioning & Interviewing	Relationships with Clients
Communications	**Working with Others**
Influencing and Advocating	Developing Relationships within the Legal
Writing	Profession
Speaking	Evaluation, Development, and Mentoring
Listening	
	Character
Planning and Organization	Passion and Engagement
Strategic Planning	Diligence
Organizing/Managing One's Own Work	Integrity/Honesty
Organizing/Managing Others (Staff/	Stress Management
Colleagues)	Community Involvement and Service
	Self-Development

Consistent with the thesis of this chapter, the results of the Shultz-Zedeck study suggest that academic factors are profoundly under-inclusive of future lawyering potential. Among the law school graduates in the sample, factors such as Analysis & Reasoning, Researching the Law, Writing, and Problem Solving showed modest, positive correlations with grades and LSAT scores (between 0.10 and 0.15, $p > .05$). Yet, some correlations with effectiveness factors were negative. For example, LSAT scores and first year grades were negatively correlated at statistically significant levels with Networking (-.122) and Community Service (-.96). In the student sample, undergraduate GPA was positively correlated with no effectiveness factors but negatively associated with Practical Judgment (-.169), Seeing the World through the Eyes of Others (-.170), Developing Relationships (-.195), Integrity (-.189) and Community Service (-.152). Similarly, LSAT scores were positively correlated with Analysis and Reasoning (.254), Creativity (.190), Problem Solving (.243), Influence and Advocacy (.148), and Writing (.259), but negatively associated with Networking (-.195).

A second part of the Shultz-Zedeck study correlated the BARS scores with established, off-the-shelf personality assessments. For example, on the Hogan Personality Inventory (HPI), the Adjustment construct measures emotional stability and steadiness under pressure. In the alumni sample, the HPI Adjustment scores were positively correlated at statistically significant levels with 22 of the 26 effectiveness factors (ranging from .072 to .220) and negatively correlated with none. Similarly, the HPI Prudence scale measures self-control and conscientiousness. Scores on Prudence were correlated with 18 effectiveness factors (ranging from .071 to .189) and negatively correlated with none. Another factor included in the study was the HPI Ambition scale, which measures achievement and leadership orientation. Scores on Ambition were positively correlated with 14 effectiveness factors (ranging from .076 to .239) and negatively correlated with none.

The poor correlation between lawyer performance and academic predictors and law school prestige can also be observed in the outcomes of the leading student trial court tournaments. If high LSAT and undergraduate grades are meaningful predictors of lawyer ability, we would expect to see top-ranked law schools dominating these competitions. But, in fact, we observe no such relationship.

For example, one of the most prestigious and longest running is the Texas Young Lawyers Association's National Trial Competition (NTC), which is an invitation-only event based on the results of fourteen regional competitions. Since the NTC's founding in 1975, the school with the most wins (5) has been Stetson University College of Law. Stetson is currently rated #109 in *U.S. News & World Report* rankings. Two schools have won four times: Northwestern (#12) and Baylor (#54). And three schools have won three times each: Temple (#56), Chicago-Kent (#68) and Loyola University-Los Angeles (#68). Harvard won once (in 1976), but so did unranked California-Western (in 1987). Similar results emerge from other high-profile skills competitions. Since the founding of the National Institute for Trial Advocacy's (NITA) Tournament of Champions in 1989,

Stetson and Temple have won five and four times respectively. The American Association for Justice (AAJ), which is comprised of practicing trial lawyers, runs the Student Trial Advocacy Competition. Since 2004, the top winners have been Baylor, Stetson, and Samford University, which as of 2013 were all ranked in the second and third tiers of *U.S. News & World Report*.

In the national trial advocacy competitions, the efficacy and quality of student courtroom legal work are blind-graded by panels of accomplished trial lawyers. The results raise two interconnected questions. First, the large number of non-elite schools in the winner's circle suggests that marginally higher academic credentials are not particularly useful for predicting trial performance—arguably the quintessential lawyer skill set. Second, the prevalence of a handful of repeat winners across the broad spectrum of the legal education (Stetson, Temple, Northwestern, Baylor, Chicago-Kent, Samford) suggests that the quality of coaching is a key explanatory factor. This is entirely consistent with the model set forth in Figure 1 above—not only does intelligence matter, but so do things like (motivation, drive, and the quality of experience, training, and practice time available to the student or junior lawyer.)

Ironically, the excessive weight given to pedigree can also be observed in the hiring and promotion patterns of large law firms. For example, each year the *National Law Journal* compiles data on the number of associates hired and partners promoted based on law school attended for the 250 largest law firms. In 2011, 53.7% of entry-level associates hired attended a law school ranked in the top 14 by *U.S. News and World Report* (the top 14 cut-off is significant because no school inside the top 14 has ever fallen out—these are the perceived national law schools). Yet, only 29.4% of the lawyers promoted to partner attended these same elite schools. This is an enormous skew that favors the long-term promotion prospects of the regional law school graduates. Stated more concretely, for every 5.4 graduates from elite law schools, one elite graduate is promoted to partner. For all other law schools, that corresponding statistic is 1.95. Further, even when the analysis is limited to the top 50 based on profitability, there remains a large, persistent disparity that favors regional law graduates. Among the 50 most profitable firms, there are 4.9 top 14 associates hired for every top 14 lawyer promoted to partner, compared to regional law schools, where the ratio of associates hired to partners promoted is only 1.9 (Henderson, 2012).

What explains this large disparity? A simple explanation is that the national law schools are overfished. Specifically, many aspiring government lawyers, public interest advocates, and non-profit executives are lured into large, elite law firms because they possess the requisite pedigree and the starting salaries are so high. Indeed, the *After the JD* study, a major longitudinal study of law graduates sponsored by the American Bar Foundation, found that lawyers from elite law schools were, as a group, the least satisfied with large firm practice and were the most likely to leave (Dinovitzer & Garth, 2009). Indeed, it is probably very hard to stick around for partnership when one's personality, motivations, and values are pulling in a different direction. When a law firm is making astronomical sums of money from a conservative business model, it can afford to ignore the data in order to retain hiring policies that have become integral to the firms' own self-image. But in an increasingly competitive legal marketplace, at least some employers are likely to revisit basic assumptions on recruitment that are nearly 100 years old.

VI. Conclusion

It is time for legal education and the legal profession to think seriously about the skills and behaviors that produce great lawyers. The reason is simple: The world needs more of them. The evidence assembled in this chapter suggests that the raw inputs are in plentiful supply—a large number of students throughout the law school hierarchy possess the requisite intelligence, personality, drive, and character. All that is missing is, one, a first-rate education taught by professors who truly believe in the students' potential, and two, a chance to develop as lawyers through intensive practice and first-rate mentorship. For most promising law graduates, astronomical salaries are neither expected nor required. Remarkably, a large portion of the profession is blind to this opportunity. Why?

In his 2011 book, *Thinking, Fast and Slow*, the Nobel Laureate Daniel Kahneman, discusses his lifelong research on cognitive biases. One of the most prevalent is what Kahneman refers to as the availability heuristic.

Rather than undertake the rigor of gathering relevant and reliable data to answer difficult questions, the human mind naturally gravitates to information that appears relevant and has the virtue of being readily available (Kahneman, 2011, pp. 129–36). In many respects, the availability heuristic explains the disproportionate weight many lawyers give to various markers of academic achievement, intelligence and law school prestige. Lawyers and law professors can easily construct a narrative around the utility and reliability of these measures, as constructing plausible arguments is the profession's stock-in-trade. Yet, the narrative is largely an illusion—an illusion that is stifling the profession's ability to adapt to changing times. It is time to collect and analyze the relevant data and use the findings to make more great lawyers.

Sources/Reading

George E.P. Box, *Robustness in the Strategy of Scientific Model Building, in* ROBUSTNESS IN STATISTICS: PROCEEDINGS OF A WORKSHOP (R.L. Launer & G.N. Wilkinson eds., 1979).

Nancy Faber, *An Irreverent Best-Seller by Nobel Laureate Richard Feynman Gives Nerds a Good Name*, PEOPLE MAG., July 22, 1985, at 92, *available at* http://www.people.com/people/archive/article/0,,20091337,00.html.

Marc Galanter & William D. Henderson, The Elastic Tournament: the Second Transformation of the Big Law Firm, 60 STAN. L. REV. 102 (2008).

Marc Galanter & Thomas Palay, The Tournament of Lawyers: The Transformation of the Big Law Firm (1991).

John P. Heinz et al., Urban Lawyers: The New Social Structure of the Bar (2005).

William D. Henderson, *A Blueprint for Change*, 40 PEPP. L. REV. 461 (2013).

William D. Henderson, *The Bursting of the Pedigree Bubble*, 21 NALP BULL., no. 7 (July 2009).

William D. Henderson, *Law Firm Strategies for Human Capital: Past, Present, Future, in* LAW FIRMS, LEGAL CULTURE, AND LEGAL PRACTICE 73–106 (Austin Sarat ed., 2010).

William D. Henderson, Three Generations of Lawyers: Generalists, Specialists, Project Managers, 70 Md. L. Rev. 373 (2011).

William D. Henderson, The LSAT, Law School Exams and Meritocracy: The Surprising and Undertheorized Role of Test-Taking Speed, 82 Tex. L. Rev. 975 (2004).

Ann Hurley, *The Prodigy Puzzle*, N.Y. Times Mag., Nov. 20, 2005.

Arthur R. Jensen, Bias in Mental Testing (1980).

Daniel Kahneman, Thinking, Fast and Slow (1st ed. 2011).

Stephen P. Klein & Laura Hamilton, *The Validity of the U.S. News and World Report Ranking of ABA Law Schools* (Feb. 18, 1998), http://www.aals.org/reports/validity.html.

Jack Ladinsky, Careers of Lawyers, Law Practice, and Legal Institutions, 28 Am. Soc. Rev. 47 (1963).

A. Pemberton Johnson et al., The Law School Admissions Test and Suggestions for its Use: A Handbook for Law School Deans and Admissions Officers (1955).

Michael Sauder & Wendy Nelson Espeland, *The Discipline of Rankings: Tight Coupling and Organizational Change*, 74 Am. Soc. Rev. 63 (2009).

Curt Schleier, *Consulting Innovator Marvin Bower: His Vision Made McKinsey & Co. A Pioneer*, Investor's Bus. Daily, Nov. 9, 2000, http://news.investors.com/management-leaders-in-success/110900–349324-consulting-innovator-marvin-bower-his-vision-made-mckinsey-and-co-a-pioneer.htm.

Majorie M. Schultz & Sheldon Zedeck, *Identification, Development, and Validation of Predictors for Successful Lawyering* (Sept. 2008), http://www.law.berkeley.edu/files/LSACREPORTfinal-12.pdf.

Dean Keith Simonton, *Creativity and Genius*, in Handbook of Personality: Theory and Practice (Oliver P. John, Richard W. Robins & Lawrence A. Pervin eds., 2008).

Robert Stevens, *Law School: Legal Education in America from the 1850s to the 1980s* (1983).

William M. Sullivan et al., *Educating Lawyers: Preparation for the Profession of Law,* Carnegie Foundation for the Advamcement of Teaching (2007).
2 Robert T. Swaine, *The Cravath Firm and its Predecessors,* 1819–1948 (1948).
Linda F. Wightman, *LSAC National Longitudinal Bar Passage Study* (1998).
Ellen Winner, Gifted Children: Myths and Realities (1996).

WILLIAM D. HENDERSON is Professor of Law at the Indiana University Maurer School of Law, where he teaches courses on the legal profession, project management, business law, and law firm economics. His research, which focuses on the empirical analysis of the legal profession and legal education, has been published in leading law journals and leading publications for practicing lawyers.

Chapter 6

INCLUSIVE THINKING

Essential Professional Value /
Powerful Professional Advantage

ARIN N. REEVES

I. Overview

The practice of law, at its core, is about people. Achieving excellence in the practice of law requires excellence in inclusive thinking—in understanding and navigating the many different ways in which people think, interact, negotiate, and connect with each other and the world around them. As the legal profession demands increasingly rapid access to intelligent insights, creative problem solving skills, a wide variety of communication strengths, and the ability to lead collaboratively, inclusive thinking has emerged as both an essential professional value and a potent professional advantage. Regardless of the specific area of law involved or the role of a legal advocate in a particular situation, the practice of law today calls for the understanding of complex issues from multiple perspectives. Thinking inclusively about differences is the intellectual gateway through which these multiple perspectives are most effectively accessed.

II. What Is Inclusive Thinking?

The research on inclusive thinking has evolved from a body of work on differences between people that began with anti-discrimination and affirmative action and now encompasses diversity and eventually inclusion. While anti-discrimination and affirmative action—legal constructs that focus on compliance with laws about how to treat differences—continue to play a vital role in creating fair and effective workplaces on national and organizational levels, the work on diversity and inclusion has evolved into a separate field of inquiry not directly concerned with legal mandates and compliance. Where the treatment of differences in a legal compliance context has stressed what employers can and cannot do, diversity and inclusion efforts have focused on what employers can aspire to do in order to thrive in today's global marketplace.

Organizations, regardless of geography or industry, today embrace diversity of perspectives because changes in demographics (increases in numbers, purchasing power, and influence of racial and ethnic minorities, women, gays and lesbians, and other previously underrepresented groups) have changed the ways in which businesses connect with consumers, talent, vendors, and the marketplace in general. Demographically diverse workforces and leadership teams, once a "nice to have" factor, have become a "must have" for success. As organizations increase the diversity of identities, experiences, and perspectives in their ranks, they soon realize that differences between people cannot be managed or leveraged without inclusive thinking. A focus on differences in the workplace requires an equal focus on people's skill sets in working effectively across those differences.

The focus on inclusion and inclusive thinking has emerged as a central tenet of those organizations and individuals looking to attract diverse perspectives from a variety of backgrounds, cultures, experiences, strengths, work styles, and the like, and to successfully leverage this diversity as a competitive advantage in the marketplace.

Diversity thus is the representation of diverse perspectives, and inclusive thinking is the skill involved in using those differences to create a collective intelligence that is greater than any one individual's intelligence.

Figure 1

In order to think inclusively, it is helpful first to understand why inclusive thinking is not necessarily the way in which we have traditionally been taught to think. The legal profession, historically, has touted the primacy of individual expertise and the adversarial "right vs. wrong" thinking as the cornerstones of legal practice. The American legal culture remains rooted to a significant degree in an adversarial-model justice system, where plaintiff and defendant stand in opposition to each other before a court of law. While that adversarial paradigm persists, today's effective legal advocate must adopt more flexible approaches to problems and people in sync with rapidly changing global, demographic, political, business, and legal environments. In today's world, individual expertise and adversarial thinking alone cannot ensure success in our legal culture; they must be combined with inclusive thinking in order to lead to a competitive advantage in the marketplace.

A Timeless Indian Fable

One day an elephant walked into a village where none of the villagers had seen an elephant before. The villagers were frightened by the beast and asked the most intelligent men in the village—six blind men who were renowned for both their intellect and their courage—to examine the elephant so that the villagers could figure out what the beast was and what they should do with it.

The six blind men were led to the elephant and encircled it to examine it. Each man reached out and touched the part of the elephant in front of him—one touched the side, one touched an ear, one touched a tusk, one touched a leg, one touched the trunk, and one touched the tail. Each man spent ample time absorbing the nuances of what he was touching, and each was satisfied that he now knew the full and true nature of the beast.

"I know for sure that this beast is like a wall," said the man who had touched the side, and he went on to discuss what that meant.

"Not at all like a wall," interrupted the man who had touched an ear. "I know for sure that this beast is like a large fan."

"Both of you are clearly wrong," said the man who had touched a leg. "This animal is much more like a solid tree."

"I think you all are quite confused. It may not even be an animal," said the man who had touched a tusk. "This creature is hard as stone and sharp as a spear."

"I think perhaps you are one that is confused," replied the man who had touched the trunk. "This beast is very much alive, and it is like a large snake."

"Not a snake, but maybe a rope," said the man who had touched the tail.

Then, the six men began to argue about the true nature of the beast.

As the six blind men argued about the true nature of the creature, the other villagers waited anxiously to find out which of the men was right. The longer they argued, the more strongly each of the men clung to what he knew to be true based on his experience.

As the men argued, a young boy standing nearby listened to their conversation earnestly. He finally interrupted the discussion to say, "From what I can see, it looks like all of you are right. The beast has a body like a wall, two ears like large fans, two tusks like spears, four legs like large trees, a trunk like a snake, and a tail like a rope."

The men were silent as they digested what the young boy had just said. They wondered if they could all truly be right, so they decided to walk around the elephant and see if they could feel the different things that they had heard described. After circling the elephant a few times, the men congratulated the young boy for having the vision to overcome their intelligence.

The fable above offers a metaphor that illustrates our tendency to value the need to be right over the need to think inclusively. As each of the men explored the issue in front of him, he defined the issue through his perspective. When confronted with perspectives other than his own, each man reacted by arguing his own perspective as right and dismissing the other perspectives as wrong. Although each man was absolutely right, from one isolated perspective, each man's understanding of the issue was significantly incomplete.

Recognizing that individual intelligence is enhanced when collective intelligence is embraced is the foundational core of inclusive thinking as a professional value. While the legal system continues to be an adversarial system, the lawyers who succeed within this evolving culture will be those able to shift away from rigid "right vs. wrong" or "win/lose" thinking to "full picture with multiple rights" thinking. In order to build and sustain this foundation of inclusive thinking, an individual must develop various diverse perspectives from which to create a more informed and intelligent opinion. Therefore, the ability to actively seek out diverse perspectives is essential to inclusive thinking, even if we are not taught to do so formally during our legal education.

Further, while inclusive thinking as a general professional value can enhance the way a lawyer learns, thinks, and practices law, the variety of diverse perspectives a lawyer can draw on, and the depth of one's inclusive thinking, can transform this professional value into a professional advantage.

III. How Does Inclusive Thinking Work?

Practicing law in the 21st century means practicing law with increasingly diverse clients who have increasingly diverse problems in increasingly diverse markets in front of increasingly diverse juries and judges. With the concept of diversity itself becoming more intricate as we understand all the ways in which we think, learn, and work differently, the ability to compete as a lawyer will depend, to a significant degree, on the ability to gather perspectives, especially perspectives that differ from and even contradict one's own perspectives, from as many different places as possible. Once the perspectives are gathered, the ability to understand and integrate these varying and often conflicting perspectives into well-informed insights is a significant competitive edge. Lawyers who maintain this edge can compete effectively in various arenas against varying challenges from peers whose success is fenced in by limited perspectives, narrow realms of expertise, and the inability to appeal to a broad base of clients and influencers.

An Illustration of the Positive Impact of Inclusive Thinking

A legal team comprised of lawyers from a corporation's legal department and lawyers from a law firm representing that corporation submitted a proposal to public officials to rezone several acres of residential land to allow for the development of a commercial retail campus of outlet stores. The land was located in an economically blighted area filled with empty lots, abandoned homes, and unused parking lots. The development of the retail campus would bring jobs to the surrounding area, infuse the economy with much-needed tax revenues, and usher in other support services for the overall community. The corporation was willing to compensate the landowners in the area at market value for the land, and it was willing to contribute to the cost of new infrastructure necessary to support the development and maintenance of the retail campus. The corporation's legal team also held a few town hall meetings with public officials and residents in the area to hear their concerns before it put together the bid.

The legal team was excited about its proposal. It was submitted to the appropriate public agencies with full expectation of approval with very few changes. But the bid was rejected in full within a week. Stunned, the legal team determined to meet with the responsible officials individually to figure out what happened. The team learned that although its proposal was technically sound, it had missed or misunderstood many of the social and cultural expectations of the residents in the area. As a result, the proposal lacked public support needed for approval. The officials explained to the bid team that three mistakes in particular had damaged the corporation's proposal:

1. There was a high distrust of strangers in this area, and the town hall meetings were hosted by the corporation's representatives instead of a neighborhood organization.

2. The area had a high concentration of regular church-goers, and several of the town hall meetings had been scheduled for Sunday morning (prime church attendance time) and Wednesday evenings (the most common day for churches in the area to hold Bible study). The scheduling offended many residents greatly!

3. Not a single person from the legal team attending the meetings resided in the state where the property was located.

> The corporation's legal department regrouped and resubmitted the proposal with the assistance of a different law firm after finally understanding and integrating the various perspectives it needed to be successful. Their second proposal was accepted, but the detour of not thinking inclusively cost the company millions of dollars, and cost the original law firm a very large client.

In the fable about the elephant, imagine what would have happened if one of those men had tried to understand the creature, and the other five had not been around to disagree with him. One man, based on his one perspective, would have assumed that he could describe the entire animal, and he would have been partially right but mostly wrong. Similarly, lawyers who assume that what they see is all of what there is to see risk being partially right and mostly wrong.

The legal team in the example above was not wrong in its analysis underlying the proposal (the same analysis had worked in other areas), but without the diversity of local perspectives that the team had missed, its analysis was more incomplete than correct. The team members were forced to think inclusively only after their initial way of thinking failed. The good news is that one doesn't have to fail in order to learn the lesson that inclusive thinking nets greater success than thinking in more limited ways.

Inclusive thinking works by infusing our thought process with information and insights that we cannot access on our own. It causes us to think critically about our own perspectives, while forcing us to consider that contradictory points of view may not only be compatible with each other, they may actually be the missing pieces we need in order to fully understand the issue.

IV. What Are the Challenges to Thinking Inclusively?

If inclusive thinking is a significantly better way to think, why don't more lawyers adopt it as their primary mode of thinking? The simple answer is that they would if they could, but their conscious choices to think inclusively and their unconscious patterns of thinking—patterns that they revert to without their conscious consent—do not align naturally without deliberate focus. Most thought patterns—even in the midst of being intellectually challenged—gravitate toward that which feels similar, easy, and predictable. This is especially true when there is STUFF© involved—**Stress, Time** constraints, **Uncertainty, Fear,** and/or **Fatigue.** Given the overabundance of all five of these factors in most legal workplaces, the tendency to gravitate toward the similar, easy, and predictable is even more prevalent.

The main barriers between the conscious choice of inclusive thinking and the unconscious patterns of the similar, easy, and predictable are implicit biases. Implicit biases are unconscious decisions made about people, events, or things that are based in stereotypes, cultural expectations, or other cognitive shortcuts that brains take to think faster. Implicit biases prevent rational choices predicated on real and verified information. These cognitive shortcuts actively hinder inclusive thinking, not because of any explicit decision to think a particular way, but because of a process that occurs almost entirely without the thinker's conscious recognition. Actively recognizing and interrupting these cognitive biases—decidedly easier said than done—is the key to becoming a more inclusive thinker.

Please read the five examples below, keeping in mind lessons to be learned in the context of inclusive thinking. What are some implicit biases playing out in the various scenarios?

1. A young lawyer is asked by his supervising attorney to gather a lot of information about a specific client very quickly. The lawyer asks other lawyers in the office for information and spends the majority of a day gathering the information and organizing it. He learns later that one of the legal secretaries who worked on this client's matter had already gathered and organized the information several weeks prior, but the associate had not bothered to ask anyone other than the lawyers on the matter for guidance and information.

2. A senior lawyer asks a junior lawyer to research a health care matter. The junior lawyer researches the legal issue but also talks with a couple of physician friends of hers unrelated to the case to see what they thought about the issue, protecting the actual identities of the parties and others involved in the matter. Her friends give her

names of hospital administrators and nurses who, though unrelated to the specific client matter being researched, had great insights on the issue. After talking with people who are directly affected by this issue, she revises her memo accordingly and is commended by the senior lawyer for addressing issues that he had not even considered.

3. A team of federal lawyers is dispatched to a predominantly minority area to interview people about a recent crime there. They get very little information in the interviews and are frustrated by their lack of progress in the case. One of the community organizers in the area gives them the advice that no one in the neighborhood will talk openly in front of "all white men." The team then realizes how it appeared from the outside, and it is recomposed with more minority lawyers. One of the newly added minority lawyers laughingly tells his colleagues that if they had talked to any minorities on a regular basis, they would have known not to walk into this investigation with an "all-white team."

4. A lawyer is about to try a case in an unfamiliar town, and he blocks out "case preparation" time for himself and his colleagues to meet some residents and try to learn what is important to the townspeople. In the course of these conversations, the lawyer and his colleagues learn that the town has a minor league baseball team that is dearly beloved in the area, that there had been a months-long drought that had devastated the economy in the area, and that the newly elected Governor of the state was not popular at all in this area (a political reality that tangentially impacted how the issue in the case was perceived). Those and other cultural facts went into the team's trial strategy to gain credibility with the jury.

5. A male partner in a law firm pulls together a group of male associates for a golf outing with a client. In the middle of the outing, one of the in-house lawyers for the client—a woman—asks the partner why he did not bring the female associate who actually did much of the work on the client's matters. The partner answers that he did not think that the associate would be interested in playing golf. The in-house lawyer casually mentions that she has golfed often with the female associate and that the associate is a very good golfer.

In common parlance, the concept of "biases" has developed negative connotations in our culture, and we are socialized to believe that being biased is a bad thing. Biases are a natural aspect of being human, and there is nothing intrinsically negative about biases, as long as we are aware of them and interrupt their ability to unduly influence our decisions. Acknowledging our biases, moreover, is a crucial step toward inclusive thinking because one cannot interrupt that which one does not acknowledge. Once acknowledged, biases become background noise instead of active challenges to our inclusive thinking processes.

Inclusive thinking can provide an important edge in expected and unexpected ways in the course of practicing law, but only when there is a conscious vigilance to think beyond comfort zones and well-tread patterns of similarity, ease, and predictability. Thinking inclusively may feel uncomfortable and even difficult at first, but the probability of success through inclusive thinking is far greater than the probability of success while staying in one's comfort zones.

V. Seven Steps to Thinking Inclusively

1. Examine your personal network. How much diversity of identity, experience, perspective, and personality do you have in your personal network? The more diverse your personal network, the more honed your inclusive thinking skills get. Do one thing every month to diversify your personal network beyond your comfort zones.

2. Examine your professional network. How much diversity of identity, experience, perspective and personality do you have in your professional network? As with your personal network, the diversity in your professional network enhances your ability to think inclusively. Do one thing every month to diversify your professional network beyond your comfort zones.

3. Infuse your problem solving style with inclusive thinking. When you have to solve a problem, try to identify all of the different perspectives that you need to consider in order to comprehensively understand the problem. Think of the fabled elephant and consider whether there could be facets of the issue that you haven't seen at all or perhaps hadn't imagined were possible. Identify at least five

people who can help you see completely different aspects of this issue and listen to each of their perspectives with an open mind and with the intention of integrating these differing perspectives into the way you think.

4. Create productive conflict in your thought process. Challenge your core beliefs and ask yourself why you believe what you believe. Make yourself defend your positions to yourself. Before making a final decision, hypothetically explore what the opposite of the decision—and corresponding consequences—would look like. The productive conflict in thinking can be a good substitute for an external point of contradiction.

5. Identify a time when you were unable to achieve something that you really wanted to achieve. Were there perspectives that were missing from your life that could have helped you identify the information, resources, and relationships you needed in order to improve your probabilities for success? If so, how could you have accessed these perspectives?

6. Pay attention to surprises. (If you are particularly ambitious, keep a surprise journal!) Every time you are surprised by something or someone, make a mental or written note of it. Surprise is the brain's way to remind you that there is a gap between what you thought would be reality and actual reality, so ask yourself what you thought the reality would be. The more you identify the sources of surprise, the better you get at recognizing and eventually interrupting your implicit biases.

7. Meet someone new once a week. That may sounds onerous, but it is not as bad as it sounds, and it is especially necessary if you don't already have diversity in your personal or professional networks, or both. Introduce yourself to someone and get to know the person's name. Get to know one or two additional details about that person and see what gets sparked. Every time you meet someone new, you add fuel to your inclusive thinking processes!

Sources/Reading

Malcolm Gladwell, Blink: The Power of Thinking Without Thinking (1st Back Bay trade pbk. ed. 2007).

Daniel Kahneman, Thinking, Fast and Slow (2011).

Arin N. Reeves, The Next IQ: the Next Level of Intelligence for 21st Century Leader (2012).

James Surowiecki, The Wisdom of Crowds: Why the Many Are Smarter Than the Few and How Collective Wisdom Shapes Business, Economies, Societies and Nations (2004).

Andres T. Tapia, The Inclusion Paradox: The Obama Era and the Transformation of Global Diversity (2009).

ARIN N. REEVES, PhD., J.D., is the President of Nextions, a boutique consulting firm based in Chicago and specializing in leadership and inclusion. She is the author of the Chicago Lawyer column "Diversity in Practice" as well as the ABA bestseller, *The Next IQ: The Next Level of Intelligence for 21st Century Leaders.*

Chapter 7

WOMEN IN THE LAW
Overcoming Obstacles,
Achieving Fulfillment

ROBERTA D. LIEBENBERG

I. Introduction

Women in the law have made great progress over the past several decades. Women now comprise one-third of the United States Supreme Court, for example, and more than 30 percent of the judges on the federal and state appellate courts. More and more women are being named general counsel of corporations, deans of law schools, and heads of law firm departments and practice groups. Every day, successful trailblazers are demonstrating it is indeed possible—and manageable—for female lawyers to achieve both professional and personal fulfillment.

Notwithstanding the notable successes of many individual women in practice, and despite the fact that women have been graduating from law schools at approximately the same rate as men for the past 20 years, female lawyers still confront unique and formidable challenges. Unfortunately, they remain grossly under-represented in positions of real power and influence in the profession. Moreover, attrition among all women lawyers remains disproportionately high, and female attorneys of color continue to face particularly daunting obstacles.

This chapter briefly examines how female attorneys are now faring and the persistent gender inequalities in the profession. It then explores some proven best practices and strategies a woman new to the legal profession can embrace to transcend systemic obstacles, further her career development, and attain the full measure of professional fulfillment that our profession can offer.

II. Persistent Gender Inequality

While the pace of change in modern society is often quite rapid, within the legal profession the progress of women is glacial. Notably, the percentage of female equity partners at the country's largest law firms has remained stagnant, stubbornly failing to cross the 16 percent threshold. As of 2012, women comprised only 20 percent of the members of the management committees of those law firms, and 70 percent of those firms had either no women or only one woman on their partnership compensation committee. Distressingly, almost half of the largest firms had no women among their "top 10" rainmakers and only 4 percent had women managing partners. In addition, compensation for female lawyers continued to lag behind that of their male counterparts, with the pay gap increasing with seniority.

The higher up one looks at every level of most law firms—and certainly the larger firms—the smaller the percentage of women one finds. Simply put, there is an inverse pyramid for women at law firms. As of 2012, they occupied 70 percent of law firm staff attorney positions; 45 percent of associate positions; 35 percent of "of counsel" positions; and 16 percent of equity partner positions.

The statistics for female attorneys of color are even more sobering. In 2012, they comprised less than 2 percent of law firm equity partners and only 11 percent of associates. Female attorneys of color occupy the lowest rung on the compensation ladder—earning less than white male and female attorneys and male attorneys of color. Minority women partners are rarely represented on important firm committees, such as the executive or compensation committee. Being both a woman and a person of color creates a "double bind" that makes it more difficult for female attorneys of color to succeed.

The gender inequality that persists in the legal profession contributes to the disproportionately high rate of attrition of women. Research indicates that this pervasive inequality may also be deterring some women from entering law school in the first place. In fact, there has been a steady decline in the percentage of women entering law school since 2000, and the percentage of women among all law firm associates declined each year from 2009–2012. Unless there is a profound commitment to changing the paradigm, the pipeline of women entering the profession will continue to shrink, while disaffected women lawyers will continue to vote with their feet by leaving their firms.

These statistics underscore the unique challenges that women continue to confront from the time they enter the profession—challenges that women lawyers nonetheless can and do overcome or work around each day through sound career strategies and a thoughtful commitment to professional growth.

III. Perfecting Legal Skills and Finding a Niche

Regardless of whether a woman lawyer practices in a large or small firm, or in a corporate or government setting, the single most important prerequisite to her success is the development and honing of her legal skills. While business development is increasingly important, even for young lawyers, it is imperative first to become an excellent lawyer. To be sure, business development becomes easier after one has gained a reputation, both within and outside the firm, as a talented lawyer who can be entrusted to handle matters effectively.

Law has become more and more specialized. Irrespective of practice setting, it is crucial for every lawyer to identify a specific practice area that she will find personally and professionally rewarding and in which she can excel. Unless a lawyer really enjoys her work, the many demands of practicing law will simply not be worth the tradeoff.

Finding the right niche is particularly important for women, who continue to face implicit biases in the workplace that impede their progress. Implicit biases are unconscious biases that affect everyone, both men and women, and influence what we notice about people, how we interpret their behavior, and what we remember about them. These implicit biases stem from everyone's natural desire to associate with those who look, act, and think like them and share similar characteristics and backgrounds. Research has shown that, as a result of these unconscious biases, women often must demonstrate greater levels of competence and proficiency, and are held to higher standards than their male colleagues. Implicit bias affects women lawyers' assignments, evaluations, promotions, and compensation. However, the woman lawyer who shines in her particular area of practice is far better positioned to succeed, notwithstanding these implicit biases.

In addition, it is important to continue to refine one's legal skills, and to develop a good reputation among more senior associates and partners. After all, they are the ones giving out assignments and conducting evaluations. Therefore, treat them as if they were clients who need to be favorably impressed. Keep them well-informed of the status of the work being performed, meet deadlines, and review work carefully before submission. It is important to bear in mind that first impressions are very important and, once formed, difficult to dispel. Once again, research shows that mistakes that women lawyers make are more likely to be remembered and ascribed greater significance than comparable mistakes by their male counterparts. Unlike men, women lawyers are often judged solely on their performance, rather than their potential. This double standard is obviously unfair, but nonetheless must be kept in mind.

IV. Developing a Strategic Plan and Seeking Out Mentors and Sponsors

Ascertaining an area of concentration that is the best fit, while essential to professional success and satisfaction, is just a starting point. As early in one's career as possible, a strategic plan should be created that contains both short-term and long-term goals. Ambition is a desirable trait, but research again confirms that many women are conditioned by society not to actively pursue their aspirations as aggressively as their male colleagues.

Strategic planning is all about identifying one's talents and the various options available for maximizing them. The strategic woman lawyer will objectively and frankly assess her existing skill set in order to identify the additional skills and knowledge needed to reach her identified goals. A beginning litigator, for example, should assess whether she has obtained sufficient deposition or trial experience. If not, what action steps need to be taken? Feedback should be sought from others to determine whether a self-assessment of strengths and weaknesses is realistic. A strategic plan should include timelines and mileposts.

The more well-defined one's goals are, the easier it will be to make the right career decisions. In a law firm setting, consider carefully and at regular intervals whether attaining partnership is the long-term goal. If not, it is important to evaluate whether transitioning from law firm practice to an in-house counsel or government position would be more satisfying professionally, and, if so, the appropriate time to make that move. For female lawyers in particular, career goals often evolve over time, especially when family obligations start to come into play.

Once there is a clear picture of career objectives, one shouldn't hesitate to share them with those who are in a position to help. No one succeeds on her own, and there should be no reluctance to identify and reach out to women and men, both inside and outside one's law firm or employer, who can provide the necessary guidance and assistance.

All workplaces are inherently political environments. To succeed, one must learn the "rules of the game" and find the right mentors and sponsors. While many women gravitate more naturally to other women as mentors, it can be particularly helpful to have one or more male mentors, since men continue to exercise a disproportionate amount of power in law firms. The key is finding mentors who can help in the development of legal skills, ensure exposure to a broad spectrum of work assignments, provide introductions to clients, and impart guidance and insights on firm politics and culture, thus helping avoid potential minefields that may impede career progress. Several mentors may be necessary to fill these different roles.

Importantly—and many lawyers fail to grasp this point until it is too late—women need to be pro-active in developing sponsors. Sponsors differ from mentors in that sponsors have the power and influence to advocate on one's behalf and champion one's career at critical junctures. Sponsors go beyond the mentor role of providing feedback, friendship, and advice. Sponsors occupy a seat at the table, and their clout is indispensable in helping to secure a role in the next big matter or the desired pay raise or promotion. Having the right sponsor can make all the difference in a career. Women tend to be over-mentored and under-sponsored, and that is particularly true for women attorneys of color.

In the search for potential mentors or sponsors, it is generally not a good idea to approach someone with the amorphous request, "Will you help me?" It is better to begin the relationship with a far more specific and targeted request (e.g., "Can you put me on this case to work with you?"; "Can you take me to the client pitch meeting?"; "Can you introduce me to the chair of that bar committee or get me invited to speak at that seminar?"). Because sponsors are influential people who are being asked to vouch for a younger lawyer, it is all the more important that any approach to them be carefully considered and focused, and that trust, confidence, and rapport be established before any specific requests are made to them.

V. The Self-Promotion Imperative

The stark reality for all lawyers, both women and men, is that it is simply not enough to sit in one's office, work hard, and produce outstanding work. It is also necessary that one's talents and accomplishments become widely known, both within and outside the firm. Enhancing one's profile and reputation within the firm is indispensable to obtaining more significant assignments from influential partners and referrals from important clients. It is also critical when compensation and promotion decisions are being made.

Studies have repeatedly shown that women are more reluctant than men to engage in self-promotion, believing that their work will speak for itself. Although self-promotion may not come naturally, it is imperative if one is to receive the recognition and credit necessary to advance and succeed. Female lawyers need to advocate just as vigorously on their own behalf as they do for their clients. Male colleagues will undoubtedly be touting their own accomplishments, and a female lawyer's failure to self-promote will leave her competitively disadvantaged.

Self-promotion must be done tactfully, however. Studies have shown that self-promotion can sometimes have negative consequences for women, as they may be viewed by some as being too pushy or assertive. Again, the research shows that there is a double standard in this regard, as men are criticized less frequently for self-promotion. Women need to be mindful of this implicit bias in the workplace and be savvy when they attempt to gain recognition for their work. For example, it may be helpful to enlist sponsors, mentors, and other colleagues to tout one's accomplishments at meetings where compensation, promotion, and partnership decisions are made.

A woman can become more visible and enhance her reputation and stature, both within and outside of her workplace, through bar association work, community involvement, publications, or speaking engagements. Once again, it is never too early to develop a strategic approach that maximizes one's skill set and is aligned with one's practice area. Involvement in local, state or national bar associations, or community organizations often pays great dividends. Many bar associations offer free or deeply discounted memberships for law students.

In terms of strategic planning, it makes sense to identify the particular organizations that are most closely related to one's interests and goals and to become active in those organizations. There is no benefit to be gained by joining a plethora of organizations to which one simply cannot commit sufficient time and energy. Active participation in organizations that closely fit one's practice and interest areas is a tried-and-true path to increased visibility and a higher public profile. Through active involvement, moreover, one learns who the key players are, a necessary step before entering an organization's leadership track.

VI. Strategies for Business Development

Becoming an active leader in bar and civic associations not only helps to increase one's visibility in a law firm, it often provides invaluable networking opportunities that will lay the groundwork for potential future referrals of business. In fact, research confirms that female lawyers who attain leadership roles in organizations have a greater likelihood of becoming rainmakers and have higher origination fees than their colleagues.

In addition, serving as a speaker or panelist at seminars or CLE programs, publishing articles, or even writing blog posts are relatively easy ways of enhancing one's professional stature, which enhances prospects for business development. Affirmatively seek out these opportunities in the subject area of your expertise. Whether giving a speech or writing an article, one must take the time necessary to do an outstanding job. Public speaking can be unnerving for many people. Training and practice go a long way toward building up confidence and the refinement of skills. As with any other activity, the more public speaking one does, the more polished one will become. A lawyer's articles and the written materials prepared in connection with speaking engagements should demonstrate mastery of the subject matter and impart valuable and useful information to the target audience. A lawyer should always let potential clients and law firm colleagues know about her speaking engagements and articles.

Business development can seem daunting, but it is really all about establishing and sustaining personal connections and relationships. Effective networking includes setting aside time every month to cultivate new contacts. It is also useful to maintain prior relationships with classmates from college and law school and friends in the community. Business referrals come from myriad and sometimes unexpected sources, but the key is developing as broad and deep a network of contacts and relationships as possible.

Once a relationship has been established, a lawyer should not be reluctant to make a pitch for business, consistent, of course, with the ethical rules governing client solicitation. Pitches are most successful when one is fully informed about the nature of the client's business and able to explain in a concrete and persuasive fashion how the lawyer or her firm's expertise can help the client achieve a desired solution. While women are often very good at building relationships, many are reluctant to ask for business. Absent a willingness to make a pitch, however, it is very unlikely that the business will magically land in one's lap. Keep in mind that a pitch need not be a "hard sell." It is often most effective when presented simply as an offer to provide much-needed assistance. To be sure, a lawyer will encounter some rejections along the way, but with increased experience, she will refine her technique and achieve greater success.

The good news for women at law firms is that the percentage of women general counsel and senior in-house counsel is increasing. They, along with their corporations, are striving to ensure that the law firm teams that represent them are diverse. In addition, the ever-increasing number of women-owned businesses provides great potential for female lawyers to cultivate new clients. Also, many law firms have implemented "Women's Initiatives" to help women lawyers network and develop business. If one's firm has such an initiative, take advantage of it. One who practices in a small firm or on her own may seek out other opportunities to interact with women in-house lawyers, such as meetings of bar associations, organizations of professional women, and community organizations.

Business development will not happen overnight, but persistence, commitment, and strategic planning will help achieve success in the long run. It is always important to be authentic and to develop one's own individual approach. Taking risks and venturing beyond one's comfort zone are also integral to professional growth and success, as is not being deterred by the occasional and inevitable setbacks.

VII. The Never-Ending Search for Work-Life Balance

A major contributing factor to the exodus of women from the profession continues to be the great difficulty that many women face in balancing their professional life with their personal family obligations. In truth, no one can achieve a real "balance." Instead, each woman needs to make an inherently individual decision concerning her own personal priorities and objectives. While some women may ultimately conclude that practicing law is unduly interfering with their commitment to their family, it is important to adopt a long-term perspective and to make prudent decisions. Unfortunately, research repeatedly confirms that women who leave the profession for several years encounter enormous obstacles if and when they try to re-enter. Moreover, those who successfully re-enter the profession after a hiatus of several years find themselves disadvantaged in terms of compensation and promotion opportunities.

Some female lawyers try to achieve work-life balance by utilizing their firm's alternative work arrangements. By now, almost all law firms of any size have adopted part-time and flex-time policies. Less than 6 percent of all lawyers avail themselves of these policies, however, and the economic downturn has reduced the number of attorneys who work on a part-time or flex-time basis. Not surprisingly, the overwhelming majority of attorneys who participate in these programs are women.

The implicit biases that affect all women in the workplace have a particularly significant impact on women who work part-time. The "maternal wall" bias is well documented. Women attorneys with children are perceived to be less committed. They tend to receive more negative performance evaluations and are assigned fewer challenging and important matters. Consequently, their careers often suffer, and they are far less likely to remain on a partnership track.

When starting one's career, it would be wise for the woman lawyer to exercise due diligence by looking for places of employment that are truly committed to the success of their alternative work policies. Find out how many women with children and other family responsibilities have achieved partnership and leadership roles in the firm. Ask about "on ramp" programs that facilitate the return of women to their firms after taking a leave of absence.

For women lawyers who choose to work part-time, maintaining accessibility and flexibility is key. Given the advances in technology, it is much easier to remain connected to the office even while working from home. Also militating in favor of part-time work is the fact that several large corporations are actively encouraging their law firms to promote the utilization of alternative work arrangements. Some are requiring law firms to provide billing credit to a designated part-time partner and are asking firms to submit statistics concerning the number of part-time lawyers, the types of cases to which they are assigned, and how part-time lawyers are faring in terms of compensation and promotion. The intended goal is to help remove the stigma that has long been attached to part-time attorneys. Part-time programs can and should be a "win-win" both for female participants and for their law firms, which have invested considerable time and money in the hiring, training, and development of their women attorneys.

VIII. Conclusion

While women have yet to achieve true equality in the profession, progress is being made and will surely continue given the now-widespread recognition of the importance and value of diversity. Meaningful change will require women lawyers to achieve a critical mass in positions of power and leadership in their law firms, corporate legal departments, and other practice settings. In short, it is essential that more than token numbers of women occupy seats at the table where policies are being set. Young women are the future of the legal profession and hopefully will become change agents to transform the long-desired goal of gender equality into a reality.

Even though the culture in many law firms continues to perpetuate gender inequality, women entering the practice of law can realize their professional dreams by thinking and acting strategically, perfecting their legal skills, and identifying the right mentors and sponsors. Young women lawyers entering the profession have much to look forward to, as the potential rewards of a legal career are limitless, and their successes will also redound to the benefit of future generations of women.

Sources/Reading

ABA Comm'n on Women in the Profession, *A Current Glance at Women in the Law February 2013* (2013), http://www.americanbar.org/content/dam/aba/marketing/women/current_glance_statistics_feb2013.authcheckdam.pdf.

Catalyst, *Sponsoring Women to Success* (Aug. 2011), http://www.catalyst.org/system/files/sponsoring_women_to_success.pdf.

Catalyst, *Women in Law in the U.S.* (Mar. 2013), http://www.catalyst.org/knowledge/women-law-us.

Vivia Chen, *At Big Firms, Equity Gender Gap Continues*, NAT'L L.J., July 26, 2012.

N.Y. City Bar Association, *2011 Diversity Benchmarking Study: A Report to Signatory Law Firms* (Oct. 2012), http://www.nycbar.org/images/stories/pdfs/diversity/2011_law_firm_diversity_benchmarking_report.pdf.

Karen Sloan, *Companies Push For Flexible Schedules to Boost Women Attorneys*, NAT'L L.J., Dec. 3, 2009, *available at* http://www.lawjobs.com/ newsandviews/LawArticle.jsp?id=1202436003132&rss=newswire &slreturn=20130311185646.

Law School Admission Council, *LSAC Volume Summary: Matriculants By Ethnic And Gender Group*, http://www.lsac.org/lsacresources/data/ vs-ethnic-gender-matrics.asp (last visited April 11, 2013).

Leigh Jones, *Women, Associate Numbers Drop For Third Straight Year*, NAT'L L.J., Dec. 12, 2012.

Major, Lindsey & Africa, L.L.C., *Partner Compensation Survey 2012* (2012), http://www.mlaglobal.com/partner-compensation-survey/2012/ FullReport.pdf.

Minority Corporate Counsel Association, *13th Annual General Counsel Survey: Measuring the Progress of the Nation's Legal Leaders*, DIVERSITY & THE BAR 18–36 (Sept./Oct. 2012).

National Association for Law Placement, *The Demographics of Equity – An Update* (Feb. 2013), http://www.nalp.org/ demographics_of_equity_update.

National Association for Law Placement, *Representation of Women Among Associates Continues to Fall, Even as Minority Associates Make Gains* (Dec. 2012), http://www.nalp.org/2012lawfirmdiversity.

National Association of Women Lawyers & NAWL Foundation, *Report of the Seventh Annual National Survey on Retention and Promotion of Women in Law Firms* (Oct. 2012), http://nawl.timberlakepublishing. com/files/NAWL%202012%20Survey%20Report%20final.pdf.

Project for Attorney Retention, *Diversity and Flexibility Connection Best Practices* (Oct. 29, 2009), http://worklifelaw.org/Publications/ DiverFlexConn_BestPractices.pdf.

Project for Attorney Retention & Minority Corporate Counsel Association, *New Millennium, Same Glass Ceiling? The Impact of Law Firm Compensation Systems on Women* (July 2010), http://worklifelaw. org/Publications/SameGlassCeiling.pdf.

ROBERTA D. LIEBENBERG is a Partner at Fine, Kaplan and Black, R.P.C. in Philadelphia and Chair of the ABA Gender Equity Task Force. She also served as Chair of the ABA Commission on Women in the Profession. Ms. Liebenberg has written many articles concerning gender equality, including "The Retention and Advancement of Women at Law Firms-Strategies for Success," U.S. News & World Report (Nov. 2012).

Sorry we could not buy
your item.
OrderNumber:3146949
Reason: Rou
Date: 2024-04-16

0006858 7359

000685873594

Chapter 8

MASTERING THE CRAFT OF LAWYERING

MARK A. DUBOIS

I. The Process of Lifelong Learning

Many law students believe that graduation marks the end of the "learning" and the beginning of the "doing" phase of their career. While the "doing" phase may indeed be starting, the "learning" phase never ends. Learning in this sense means becoming acquainted with the legal doctrine that may govern the client's problem. But it also means acquiring the skills necessary to effectively identify and frame the issue, counsel the client on alternative options, assist her in choosing a wise course, and present her case in an appropriate forum, all while balancing the sometimes competing duties and responsibilities that come with membership in a profession.

Law schools offer some practical training in this regard, through legal research and writing courses, in "lawyering" classes, in clinics, and in internships and externships. But these experiences can never replace the deep learning that occurs when a new lawyer ventures into actual practice. Law school education, even at its most robust, can only impart a superficial understanding of the substantive law in a particular subject area. Deep subject-matter knowledge, understanding the interplay of various areas of relevant law, appreciating the intersection of statutory, regulatory, and common law, mastering matters of procedure and protocol, and integrating the principles of professionalism are all best learned—really, only learned—in practice.

Successful lawyers understand that the process of learning does not end with law school. It continues with admission to the bar and throughout a lawyer's career. New lawyers who are hired into large firms or large governmental enterprises may be carefully socialized, mentored, and developed as professionals in a supportive environment. Others, such as those in solo or small firm practice, may need to locate resources that will duplicate these experiences. The common thread linking all of them is the proposition that, to be successful, they will learn more about their profession every day of their careers.

II. The Duty of Competence

It is no accident that the first rule of professional responsibility is dedicated to competence. First, last, and always, it is the lawyer's responsibility to know the law. No representation can be successful unless the lawyer possesses a solid knowledge of the legal principles relevant to the client's problem. Knowledge is not static, however. What may have been relevant to one client or one case may be irrelevant to a new one.

A. *Knowing One's Limits*

Fulfilling the ethical duty of competence requires an ability to honestly evaluate the limits of one's knowledge. Overconfidence in one's abilities often goes hand-in-hand with a failure to appreciate the complexity of a particular matter. New and experienced lawyers alike can find themselves in trouble when they undertake representation outside of their field of knowledge and fail to acquire the skills to do so successfully.

New lawyers often find themselves in a bit of a box when assessing their own competency to handle a matter. They may lack the experience to readily recognize that they are well out of their depth on a particular matter, and therefore should decline the matter, enlist competent counsel, or commit to quickly attaining competence in the subject.

The mere fact that a client's problem may involve law or a practice area that is unfamiliar does not mean that a lawyer has to reject it or refer the client to a more experienced practitioner. As long as a lawyer understands the limits of her knowledge and is willing to do what is necessary to acquire and maintain competence, she may take on a problem in an area new to her. Similarly, once a lawyer has a good grounding in the basic law of a particular area, he may ethically take on more complex matters in the same area. While it can be a difficult choice to make, ethical lawyering sometimes requires a lawyer to admit to himself that his client would be better served with a different lawyer. The lawyer may simply refer the matter to another practitioner.

New lawyers may join firms or organizations where they will focus or concentrate on a limited area of the law. A lawyer joining a district attorney or public defender office will soon find her attention limited to criminal law and procedure. Similarly, a new lawyer in a large firm may be assigned to a particular practice area, such as trusts and estates or litigation. In both of those practice settings, new lawyers will soon begin to concentrate their learning in a narrow area and will soon possess basic competence in the subject matter.

Others may join smaller or more general practices or open their own offices. Some may try to limit or focus their practice in a particular area, while others may take a broader approach and allow the marketplace to dictate the nature of their practices. For these "generalist" lawyers, a real challenge can be understanding the limits of their knowledge and abilities and being able to evaluate whether it is realistic for them to expect to "learn while they earn" in a particular case.

When faced with a new type of matter, sometimes a new lawyer will partner with a more experienced lawyer or firm. The senior lawyer may be happy for the business, and the new lawyer will be grateful for the chance to work collaboratively with an experienced practitioner. Such arrangements can lead to very successful relationships, where solo or small firm lawyers refer large or complex matters to a bigger firm, which may reciprocate by referring other matters, as when a conflict prevents the firm from representing multiple parties in a particular litigation.

In sum, understanding one's limits as a new lawyer, or as a lawyer new to a particular field, can present a significant challenge.

B. Researching the Law

Inherent in the concept of competence is an appreciation that the law is fluid and ever-changing. The legal principles that drove yesterday's case may no longer be relevant today. The importance of redundant and fresh research, even with regard to what may appear to be a simple or routine matter, cannot be overstated.

Donald Rumsfeld, while talking about perceived failures of intelligence in the Iraq war, famously noted that in any area of inquiry, there are "known knowns," "known unknowns," and "unknown unknowns." Most new lawyers will have a sense of both the known knowns (relevant facts and law, basic procedures) and the known unknowns (further facts that need to be discovered, the current state of the law, recent cases) related to a particular matter.

For new and experienced lawyers alike, the biggest danger is the unknown unknowns: principles, procedures, and protocols that will have an effect on the outcome of the client's matter but that the lawyer is not aware of. Mastering the skill of identifying the areas where more knowledge is needed is a life's work.

The unknown unknowns related to a particular matter may be found in statutes, regulations, or case law. They may not be easily discoverable. They may be counterintuitive. They may lurk in cases that have been overruled by recent statutory enactments or by fresh legal precedent. Unknown unknowns may arise out of pending appellate cases that have the potential to alter the present state of the law. They may be hidden in federal law that renders state statutes or case law unavailing because of the supervening nature of federal authority. Only when a practitioner has discovered and mastered all of the unknown unknowns as well as the full body of "known" information can he give competent and appropriate advice and counsel to his client.

The uninitiated are prone to overestimating their ability to successfully navigate practice in complex areas, especially when they assume case law is the correct starting point for all research. Bodies of law found in different sources, such as the Code of Federal Regulations, statutes and regulations, legislative histories, and agency procedures and protocols represent important sources of relevant law often missed in case law database searches. Policy manuals maintained by an agency can be a useful tool, but they may be hard to find and not easily understood or navigated by novices in the subject matter. Such resources can be very hard to research using computer tools.

Unlocking the relevant law requires strong research skills. Many lawyers, having been trained in the "case book" method, will first go to case law, believing that appellate cases are the best source of relevant law. Case law often will yield an answer, but one that may be insufficient. It may not provide a full explanation of all of the legal principles relevant to a particular matter. Precedent may be stale. There may be a split of authority, not readily evident in case research, on a particular issue between courts of equal authority. Thus, secondary resources such as casebooks, treatises, restatements, and law review articles may be a better place to begin when learning a new area. They organize the often confusing and sometimes contradictory mass of information that an unfocused search may produce.

Most legal research today is computer assisted. While the field has traditionally been dominated by Westlaw and Lexis, there are many new entrants, some offering free or very low cost access to large libraries of information.

III. Learning to Listen

The need for thorough preparation is not limited to legal issues. It extends to mastering skills such as deep listening, empathy, skilled counseling, and effective advocacy. Listening, in its highest form, is a function of humility. Cases belong to clients, not to lawyers. A good lawyer will understand that it is the client's goals, values, needs, and wishes that will guide a successful representation. Helping the client to articulate her needs and wishes and using them as the basis of the representation will ensure that the client feels invested in the process.

A good listener will be able to develop an empathic relationship with his client, built on respect and trust. Such a partnership will be more successful than one characterized by the lawyer telling the client what is best and calling the tune irrespective of the client's wishes. Even if the result is not what the client had hoped, the client can better understand the process and may be less inclined to blame the lawyer for a bad outcome or occurrence if they have been partners from the inception of the process.

Good listening skills also will allow a skilled lawyer to respond quickly and effectively to a judge's signals about which avenues might be favored and which will be non-starters. Similarly, skilled listeners make for excellent cross-examiners. They can respond to nuances in a witness's voice or body language and shape their questioning accordingly. It is poor practice for a lawyer to prepare a script for an argument or a presentation and to be so focused on staying "on message" that he fails to hear important information that, if properly addressed, could lead to a better result.

The ethics rules allow a lawyer to counsel a client on the social, political, moral, and personal aspects of a matter. A good listener will be able to counsel a client in all relevant aspects of a representation and not focus exclusively on the legal issues.

IV. Focusing on Controlling Law

An area of heightened risk for new lawyers is the common tendency to focus on the compelling facts of their case, and what they perceive as a just cause, without sufficient attention to unfavorable controlling law. It does a client little good for a lawyer to argue to an arbiter that the law "should" result in relief for their client if the rule of law applicable to the case mandates a different outcome. While such "should" arguments may be useful in some appellate litigation, the vast majority of cases are resolved on the basis of what the law is, not what it should be. In such a case, a lawyer could do well to tell a client that it has no case, or if it has one, the case will require them to get the law changed, which can be a long, expensive, and often futile undertaking. Clients have a right to know, as best as can be determined, what the likely outcome of their cases will be.

V. Effective Advocacy

Different skill sets are called upon at different stages as a lawyer advances a client's case. Once a lawyer has acquired a working knowledge of the facts and law applicable to a client's matter, she must determine whether the matter is best handled by discussion, negotiation, mediation or arbitration, or whether it will require litigation, if available.

Effective advocacy encompasses both oral and written communication. Whether the writing is in the form of a brief, a proposal, a client letter, or a transactional document such as a contract, a better-written document will often achieve a better result. Not everyone is a born writer. Some are more relaxed with and suited to oral communication. Most can, however, become better writers with time and effort. There are many excellent books and other materials focusing on sharpening one's writing skills. Continuing to improve throughout one's career is one aspect of the process of learning to be a lawyer.

Complex transactional or litigation matters may require a deep knowledge of all applicable law. These may be "zero-sum" enterprises, with the parties sharing a finite pool of resources, and with one being advantaged only at the cost of another. Such matters typically offer the prospect of an "I win, you lose" scenario (rather than "win-win"), and the process may be very competitive. A lawyer in such a transaction generally is not permitted to alert the opposing party to the fact that the opponent has forgotten an important issue or made a poor choice. It may be ethically inappropriate for a lawyer to share such information if the result would cost the lawyer's client some advantage. Most ethical rules do not prohibit silence in the face of error or inexperience. And most applicable law will not allow a transaction or a court judgment to be reopened because of unilateral mistake by one party. It follows that if a lawyer makes an ill-considered choice in a negotiation, and thereby binds her client to a position that favors her opponent, discovery of that error may not enable the client to later unspool the transaction.

Formal dispute resolution mechanisms such as arbitration or litigation place a large premium on matters of practice and procedure. As it should be, properly framing an arbitration submission or drafting an effective complaint is often the difference between winning and losing a case, or getting a favorable or unfavorable settlement.

As with other aspects of successful practice, the lawyer will first need to soberly assess her skill set and whether she is up to the task of representing the client in a formal proceeding. Sometimes, a lawyer will take a matter through discussion or negotiation with the other party or parties but will collaborate or refer the matter to a different practitioner when it moves to a more complex dispute resolution forum such as arbitration or litigation. It is no sin to seek assistance for complex matters.

VI. Overcoming Inexperience

One challenge for a new lawyer is isolation. Much of the best legal work comes out of collaborative efforts where several lawyers work together to identify issues, find the relevant law, and chart a successful course for their clients. New lawyers who are in solo or small firm environments without peers may lack the richness of such an experience. Somehow, some way, it is imperative for new lawyers, or experienced lawyers entering new fields, to find guidance and support.

Guidance and support can be found in professional organizations, such as local, state, regional, and national bars. A successful new lawyer will have investigated those bars that she is eligible to join or interact with to determine what resources are available and useful to her.

Many bar groups have "young lawyer" sections devoted to the experience of being a newer member of the profession. These groups often offer continuing education geared to the new practitioner. Young lawyer sections and other bar groups, such as solo practitioner sections, often offer valuable technical and substantive resources on getting started in practice. They also are wonderful places to find peer support, to network, and to develop professional friendships and relationships that will last your entire career. Some law schools offer incubator environments for new lawyers, featuring low-cost overhead, reduced-rate legal research, and abundant guidance and support services.

In some large, urban settings, legal aid organizations have developed programs where new lawyers can obtain training or partner with more experienced practitioners to represent people of limited financial means.

Sometimes, the work is done for free (pro bono), while other times, it is done on a sliding scale (sometimes referred to as "low-bono"). These organizations typically take care not to assign matters beyond the skill level of the participating lawyers, and they often provide training, advice, and guidance if a matter involves subject matter or proceedings new to the handling attorney. Working for a good cause in this manner can be a great opportunity for a new lawyer to develop both subject matter competency and client management skills (See Chapter 16, *Pro Bono and Public Service*, by Anthony C. Musto, at page 207.)

Many local and state bars maintain lawyer referral services that pair paying clients with lawyers interested in providing services. Before receiving any client referrals, participating lawyers are first "certified" as experienced and competent in the subject area. Participating on a lawyer referral panel can provide an important source of business for many lawyers as well as an opportunity to grow one's expertise in a practice area.

VII. Specialty Bars

One response to the increased complexity of the law has been the development of "specialty bars" in which lawyers who devote a major portion of their practice to a discrete area of law meet and interact. These groups sometimes exist as stand-alone enterprises. They may be committees or sections of larger bar organizations. Membership may be local, regional, or national. Communication is often aided by list-servs where information is shared, day-to-day questions and issues are floated, and experiences are traded. Considering the complexity of most specialized areas of practice, associating with a specialty bar can offer great advantages, especially for a lawyer new to the field.

With specialty bars, daily interaction on list-servs is commonly supplemented by ongoing continuing legal education courses and classes. Experienced practitioners in the field may also publish articles in monthly newsletters or may compile practice guides or texts. New or developing theories of law, recent case decisions, and pending legislation are all monitored and readily available to members. Experienced lawyers may be identified who can assist with tricky or confusing issues in a particular matter—as long as client confidences are appropriately protected.

The specialty bar experience can be a rich and rewarding one. A common reaction of a new lawyer joining a specialty bar or a practice-focused organization is a sense of awe (or trepidation) as he begins to understand the scope of the field and his own relative lack of knowledge. But few lawyers know everything. Most acknowledge that only out of the collective wisdom of many does a deep and rich understanding of any particular subject matter emerge.

VIII. Financial and Time Issues

In addition to subject-matter competency, a lawyer must assess her financial and time resources to determine whether a particular matter may be ethically undertaken. Areas such a medical malpractice or product liability require the hiring of experts, sometimes as a prerequisite to filing suit. Clients may not have the resources to finance these costs, and a lawyer signing on for such a case may face the prospect of spending tens or hundreds of thousands of dollars to develop the case for trial, on the hope that a contingent fee agreement will ultimately be awarded.

"A Civil Action," the book and movie about a small group of lawyers who took on major corporations and a large law firm, on a contingent-fee basis, in an environmental pollution case in Woburn, Massachusetts, is a good example of what can happen when one of these matters gets out of control. Due to the financial and time requirements of the case, the plaintiff's lawyers lost their property and their practices as they battled the seemingly limitless resources arrayed against them. The tale is a cautionary one.

IX. The Search for Mentors

All new lawyers should seek out mentors to help them build professional competence. Some states and bar groups have formal mentoring programs. In some jurisdictions, new lawyers are required to be in a mentored environment for the first year or longer. Others have mandatory continuing legal education designed to train new lawyers in both substantive and professional areas of the practice. In other instances, less formal but still vibrant mentoring relationships may arise out of networking, professional associations, or friendships (See Chapter 13, *Finding and Getting the Most out of a Mentor*, by Lori L. Keating and Michael P. Maslanka, at page 161).

Lawyers are often surprised how accessible the most experienced lawyers are when asked for assistance. Experienced lawyers understand that new lawyers may be the source of new matters, and will often be very willing to coach, guide, and collaborate with them.

A good mentor can be a friend, a guide, and an advisor. A mentor may be able to assist the new lawyer in making a reasoned appraisal of whether undertaking a particular representation is a wise choice. Remember, in common-law jurisdictions, new law replaces old, yet the old law may still be on the books. Often, experienced mentors can serve the same function as good secondary research resources—they can distill the substantive law, give the new lawyer some perspective, and focus them on the issues that are going to be most relevant while steering them away from blind alleys. An experienced lawyer will be able to point out that though the "winning" case or statute may appear to be the exact answer to the lawyer or client's needs, further research may reveal that is it anything but a safe harbor.

X. The Less Experienced Lawyer Can Carry the Day.

New lawyers sometimes surprise more experienced adversaries by learning the client's case in every detail, thoroughly mastering the law and becoming very well prepared in all respects. The opponent may underestimate the level of preparedness the new lawyer brings to the transaction or case, or the opponent may assume that he can rely on superior knowledge or experience to win the day. But judges and juries have a way of leveling the playing field. While the new lawyer may not know all the nuances of practice, procedure, and protocol, with a bit of coaching a new lawyer often can do quite well for her client.

XI. Time to Breathe, Time to Think

Finally, the importance of taking the time to step back, evaluate, think, and plan cannot be stressed too much. The practice of law can be very demanding. Often decisions are made quickly, while the lawyer is juggling several pressing matters, all of which require immediate attention. Successful lawyers schedule some quiet time every week to allow themselves to decompress, to reflect, and to assess where they are and where they are going. During this time they can dissect problems calmly and logically. They can seek answers to nagging questions and guidance for the future. Problems identified can be rectified before they become overwhelming and incurable.

XII. Conclusion

All lawyers were new lawyers once. The quantity of information new lawyers need to learn and the skills they need to master can seem overwhelming. But the fact that they navigated law school and passed the bar means that they have the tools to do what is needed. Nothing comes quickly or easily. The process of moving from inexperience to competence spans a lawyer's entire career.

MARK A. DUBOIS is an attorney practicing with Geraghty & Bonnano, LLC in New London, CT, where he limits his practice to legal ethics and legal malpractice. From 2003 until 2011, he was Connecticut's Chief Disciplinary Counsel. Mr. Dubois is co-author of *Connecticut Legal Ethics and Malpractice*, Law Tribune Publishing (2012).

Chapter 9

DILIGENCE

DAISY HURST FLOYD AND PAUL A. HASKINS

I. Introduction

Diligence is a virtue, an attitude, a daily resolve, a quality of conduct, an enforceable ethical duty, and a standard of care that applies in lawyers' professional liability litigation. Diligence has many shades of meaning, depending on context, but it always means the steady application of close attention and best efforts to the task at hand. Black's Law Dictionary offers this definition of the adjectival form "Diligent": "Attentive and persistent in doing a thing; steadily applied; active; sedulous; laborious; unremitting; untiring."

The attorney disciplinary rules and legal malpractice law make it clear, albeit from different perspectives, that being diligent on behalf of a client is not just the right way—it's the only way. The rules of conduct obligate a lawyer to represent the client diligently, and malpractice law instructs that where a lack of diligence, or due care, causes a client harm, it will expose a lawyer to liability and damages. There is no middle ground between diligence and negligence—the absence of diligence *is* negligence.

Attorney diligence is a close corollary of attorney competence, but the duties are distinct. If a lawyer possesses the knowledge and skill to be competent in a matter but fails to be diligent, he has failed in his professional duty.

A notion of constancy resides at the core of diligence. The ethics rule on diligence, as well as the diligence standard of care, effectively demands of a lawyer that she conscientiously and in a timely fashion do all that a client's matter requires, every time, for every client, for the duration of the lawyer's career. No filing deadlines blown; no statutes of limitations allowed to lapse. That constant state of compliance, across thousands of discrete acts of diligence over a career, cannot occur in a vacuum. It must be a function of a diligent frame of mind—a deeply ingrained habit of mind that makes diligent actions reflexive and automatic for that lawyer, every time. Diligence means having a professional attitude, and a process, that you can count on to never allow you to "blow it" on a client matter. It is vigilance in action. When you acquire a professional identity as a lawyer, you may just make Diligence your new middle name.

II. Diligence as an Ethical Duty Under Rule 1.3

Among the many professional obligations imposed upon a lawyer, diligence receives relatively little attention in law school or legal ethics scholarship. ABA Model Rule of Professional Conduct 1.3 states, "[a] lawyer shall act with reasonable diligence and promptness in representing a client." Perhaps the rule is rarely discussed because it seems simple and obvious. All would agree that a professional should work hard and be timely in all matters. For many lawyers, however, the concept of diligence has proven to be far more easily mastered in the abstract than in its application. The fact that the diligence rule is neglected in legal teaching and writing does not mean the rule should be regarded as benign or gratuitous. Lawyers who take the diligence rule lightly will soon come to regret it.

Bar disciplinary records reveal that a lack of diligence is among the most common ethics violations generating client complaints and disciplinary action. To stay on the good side of the diligence rule, every lawyer should understand the full scope of the obligation, the types of challenges that may lead to its breach, and the practical solutions to those challenges.

The Scope of Rule 1.3: Diligence

The diligence rule, ABA Model Rule 1.3, is found among the other rules identifying a lawyer's specific obligations to the client, including competence, communication, confidentiality, reasonable fees and avoidance of conflicts of interest.

The comments to Rule 1.3 offer insights into the scope of the diligence duty in the attorney ethics milieu. Comment 1 defines reasonable diligence as encompassing both action taken in pursuit of a matter on behalf of the client and the commitment and zeal to accomplish the client's objectives. The ethical duty to be diligent includes an obligation of advocacy, with Comment 1 noting that the lawyer must act on behalf of a client despite "opposition, obstruction, or personal inconvenience to the lawyer." Comment 2 speaks to the time pressures of modern practice, noting that the lawyer's workload must be controlled "so that each matter can be handled competently."

Comment 3 acknowledges that diligence can be undermined by a lawyer's habit of procrastination, and that lawyer procrastination is a deep source of frustration for clients. A diligent lawyer avoids procrastination and acts promptly. Promptness extends to punctuality—being on time for appointments and court appearances, meeting deadlines, and responding in a timely fashion to correspondence and phone calls.

With its emphasis on promptness and avoiding procrastination, the commentary to Rule 1.3 underscores the point that diligence is an affirmative duty intended to prevent lawyer neglect. Even a single failure of diligence may subject a lawyer to discipline. Further, a failure of diligence may subject an attorney to discipline even when the client is not harmed by that failure. As Comment 3 observes, lack of diligence causes needless anxiety for the client and undermines confidence in a lawyer's trustworthiness. It weakens the client-lawyer relationship and the client's belief in the justice system.

Comment 4 addresses the palpable risk of misunderstanding between lawyer and client over the scope of the client-lawyer relationship. The comment notes that when a lawyer accepts representation, she should continue to work on the matter until its completion or until the lawyer properly withdraws from the representation pursuant to the rules of conduct. Comment 5 suggests a special responsibility on the part of sole practitioners to implement a plan to deal with the lawyer's possible death or disability in a way that protects the lawyer's clients: "[T]he duty of diligence may require that each sole practitioner prepare a plan . . . that designates another competent lawyer to review client files, notify each client of the lawyer's death or disability, and determine whether there is a need for immediate protective action." It is essential to grasp that the duty of diligence is not contingent upon payment of the lawyer's fees. The lawyer may not neglect the client's case even if the client refuses to pay the lawyer's fee. If the client deliberately ignores the obligation to pay the attorney, the attorney may withdraw from the representation in accordance with the rules. Until the attorney properly withdraws, however, she may not neglect the client's case. She must continue to act with promptness and diligence, whether or not the client is current on its fee obligation to the lawyer.

Some examples of conduct that have led to lawyers being sanctioned by disciplinary authorities for lack of diligence are:

- The lawyer provides legal advice without having read the applicable documents supplied by the client.
- The lawyer allows the client to sign a will or other document without the lawyer having read it first.
- The lawyer fails to communicate with the client.
- The lawyer is guilty of "general laxity."
- The lawyer fails to show up for a court proceeding or other important meeting, such as a creditors' meeting in a bankruptcy case.
- The lawyer misses a statute of limitations or other filing deadline.

III. The Relationship of Diligence to Competence

Diligence overlaps with the lawyer's ethical duties of competence. A competent lawyer, however, is not necessarily diligent. For example, even where the lawyer possesses the requisite knowledge and skill in the subject matter, and thus is competent, he fails to act diligently if he does not apply that skill and knowledge to the degree that the representation demands. It is also a failure of diligence for a lawyer to take a matter that the lawyer is unable to handle professionally due to limitations of competence, time, or physical or mental impairment.

The general obligation of competence requires a lawyer to have basic legal knowledge, including knowledge of legal principles and rules, and basic skills, such as research, interviewing and counseling, advocacy, and negotiation. Attaining requisite competence for a specific type of representation can be particularly challenging for new attorneys.

Records of disciplinary violations contain many examples of young lawyers getting into trouble through lack of knowledge, which then becomes a failure of diligence if the attorney fails to correct the lack of knowledge. In one disciplinary case, a young lawyer became "afraid of the file" because of his incompetence to handle the matter. In another, a young lawyer was sanctioned for not thinking that the matter was as complex as it turned out to be, which led to bad judgment.

A lawyer's competence may be limited by more than just his inexperience. Limitations may arise from restraints such as a lack of time or physical or mental impairment of the attorney. Mental impairment encompasses emotional problems, mental illness and substance abuse. Disciplinary records show that the most common violations of professional obligations for attorneys with mental impairment are breaches of duties of diligence and communication.

Diligence relates to the attorney's obligation to plan his workload and client-lawyer relationships so that he has sufficient time and mental and physical resources to represent the client professionally.

Problematic limitations related to workload may be more likely to arise for solo practitioners, as they are not as often able to share responsibilities with colleagues as lawyers practicing in other settings. The majority of respondents to bar disciplinary proceedings are either solo practitioners or small firm practitioners, and the most common violations are those related to diligence. It follows that the solo practitioner may need to take special precautions.

A diligent lawyer can overcome a lack of competence in a variety of ways. She could acquire the missing skill or knowledge through self-study or consultation with experts, such as more experienced attorneys within her geographic or practice community. She could affiliate with competent counsel to jointly handle the case or refer the matter to another lawyer who is competent.

The diligent lawyer may need to explain to the client that his case demands expertise that is beyond the lawyer's experience or training and that the client should consult another lawyer. Many failures of diligence could be avoided if lawyers understood that it is not embarrassing to admit that a case is outside their areas of competence.

The temptation to plunge ahead with a case despite a lack of competence may be particularly strong for a young lawyer, because of financial pressures or insecurities about admitting inexperience. Upon realizing that she has a competence problem, the diligent lawyer will tell the client the truth and seek help immediately. Doing so is not an admission of incompetence. It is just the opposite: admitting that the case exceeds the lawyer's competence and acting appropriately to correct the problem fulfills the related duties of competence and diligence.

IV. The Relationship of Diligence to the Duty of Communication

As noted above, the most common bar disciplinary violations involve neglect of a client matter. Within the area of neglect, the largest complaint is failure to communicate. While failure to communicate is a violation of a separate professional rule, it is also a failure of diligence. A diligent attorney communicates promptly and effectively with clients. Failure to do so potentially subjects the attorney to discipline for violating both the duty of diligence and the duty of communication.

Among the common complaints arising from attorneys' failures to communicate are that a lawyer failed to inform the client of relevant considerations and factors in the decision-making process, and that the lawyer failed to promptly notify the client of the receipt of funds, securities, or other properties of the client. The diligent attorney must ensure that her clients receive timely communication about significant events in their cases.

Additionally, a failure to communicate may occur because the lawyer simply failed to realize that communication is necessary. A diligent attorney will not go long periods without communicating with the client. Although lawyers understand that there can be periods of inactivity during a representation, the client is unlikely to share that understanding. Having a regular schedule of checking in with the client—even if just to explain that nothing is happening with the case and that the period of inactivity is normal—can lessen the client's anxiety and increase satisfaction with the representation. It can also be helpful for establishing client trust and can lead to a more productive client-lawyer relationship and an enhanced ability to counsel the client.

The pairing of diligence and promptness in Rule 1.3 also overlaps with communication. The diligent lawyer should assess the facts and circumstances of each representation at the outset, determine what constitutes reasonable promptness under the circumstances, and communicate with the client about a proposed schedule for completion of the work encompassed within the representation. While it is understood that delays will sometimes occur and that the obligation of diligence does not require that the lawyer refuse requests for reasonable postponements, delay must not prejudice the client's interests.

In today's world, with the expectation of constant availability, it can be difficult to meet client expectations regarding communications. The diligent attorney will set up office procedures that aid effective communication and will be clear with the client about the best ways to communicate with the attorney and others in the office. For example, the attorney may set aside a block of time each day to return that day's phone calls and emails. He will inform clients at the outset of the representation about office procedures for responding to correspondence, phone calls, emails, and texts, and will comply fastidiously with those assurances.

That means that the diligent attorney will set up procedures within the office to make sure that correspondence and messages are received in a timely manner and that office staff clearly understands how to respond to matters when the lawyer is unavailable. Proper law office management is critical to meeting the many challenges of time and expectations in what has been called "the daily grind of law practice."

While it can be effective to delegate at least part of the responsibility for communication, the diligent attorney will be careful about delegation. Some lawyers get into disciplinary trouble for failure to communicate because they over-delegate to office staff who may not realize the importance of communication or understand how to communicate effectively. It is the responsibility of the lawyer to ensure that office staff members are sufficiently trained and properly supervised.

Effective billing practices may help with communication. Sending complete and detailed billing statements is both an obligation and a very effective way to explain what the lawyer has been doing, the reasons for her actions and the amount of time involved.

V. Diligence and Lawyers' Professional Liability

If a failure of diligence is egregious enough, it could result in sanctions rising to a publicly reported suspension or, particularly if part of a pattern of serious neglect, even disbarment. Lawyer discipline, however, is not the only bad consequence potentially confronting the lawyer who fails to act diligently on behalf of a client. An adverse legal malpractice judgment, resulting from a lawyer's failure to meet the appropriate standard of care, of which diligence is a common element, can cost a lawyer significant sums. Even in cases where most damages are covered by a lawyer's liability insurance, the process of defending one's honor, reputation, and professional standing in court can be debilitating. Malpractice claims that settle for a manageable sum, or result in judgment for the defendant, are still a distracting, unpleasant, and emotionally draining experience for the lawyer "accused."

As long as a lawyer has acted in good faith, however, a mere error of judgment or trial tactics will not give rise to malpractice liability.

VI. Conclusion

The professional obligation of diligence lies at the heart of the client-lawyer relationship, which in turn is at the heart of being a lawyer. Its importance to the lawyer's life greatly predates its inclusion in the Model Rules of Professional Conduct. In 1850, Abraham Lincoln underscored the primacy of diligence in his *Notes for a Law Lecture*, touching on the same themes invoked by the modern rule: "The leading rule for the lawyer is diligence. Leave nothing for tomorrow which can be done today. Never let your correspondence fall behind. Whatever piece of business you have in hand, before stopping, do all the labor pertaining to it which can then be done."

This remains good counsel for today's lawyers. Diligence is an immutable rule, a standard of liability and a prominent element of the lawyer's professional identity.

Sources/Reading

Ellen Pansky, *Remedy: Communication and Diligence*, 52 EMORY L.J. 1277 (2003).

RONALD D. ROTUNDA & JOHN S. DZIENKOWSKI, PROFESSIONAL RESPONSIBILITY: A STUDENT'S GUIDE (2012).

Christopher Sabis & Daniel Webert, *Current Development: Understanding the "Knowledge" Requirement of Attorney Competence: A Roadmap for Novice Attorneys*, 15 GEO. J. LEGAL ETHICS 915 (2002).

Stephen E. Schemeneauer, Comment, *What We've Got Here…is a Failure… to Communicate: A Statistical Analysis of the Nation's Most Common Ethical Complaint*, 30 HAMLINE L. REV. 629 (2007).

DAISY HURST FLOYD is University Professor of Law and Ethical Formation at Mercer University School of Law, in Macon, GA, where she served as Dean from 2004 until 2010. She was named a Carnegie Scholar by the Carnegie Foundation for the Advancement of Teaching, in support of her work on American legal education. **PAUL A. HASKINS** is Senior Counsel in the American Bar Association's Center for Professional Responsibility, Lead Counsel for the Standing Committee on Professionalism, and Editor of *Essential Qualities of the Professional Lawyer*.

Chapter 10

HONESTY, INTEGRITY AND LOYALTY

MARK A. DUBOIS

I. Introduction

If asked, most people would say they are honest. That may not be surprising—we all have a tendency to see the best in ourselves and the worst in others. But if asked to describe the top three traits of a lawyer, most people would leave honesty off their list. In fact, studies consistently show that when average citizens think of lawyers, they first think of traits like dishonesty, lack of principles, and the willingness to do anything to win. When the same people are asked what traits they would want in a lawyer representing them, however, they parrot the same or similar traits as those that they found opprobrious—a lack of principle, a willingness to do anything to win, and the ability to find and exploit any weakness or loophole.

Many lawyers initially find this tension to be troubling. Some come to grips with it. Others leave the profession because they can never reconcile their self-image and that which is imposed on them by a disdainful public. A few embrace the worst aspects of the stereotype, reasoning that if the public wants dishonesty, trickiness, and an amoral willingness to win at all costs, then they will provide it. The fact that some are very well compensated for such conduct does little to console the moral and honest lawyer who refuses to bend to the stereotype. But the lawyer with integrity embraces the fact that honesty is more than a virtue, it is a professional imperative. Even so, the reality is that even an honest lawyer's actions may look like something else to a non-lawyer uninitiated in the relativistic nuances of lawyer ethics.

II. Honesty

The ethics rules by which lawyers govern themselves mandate that they be honest—in their dealings with the public, with each other, and with the courts. Of course, honesty may not always advance a client's case. When a judge asks whether there is evidence to support a claim, she expects the lawyer to tell the truth; even if an honest answer means that the client's case will be compromised or lost. A lawyer citing authority to a judge must also disclose on-point contrary authority in the jurisdiction, even if it weakens his argument. A lawyer making material representations in a negotiation may not lie.

The tension between the lawyer's duty to a client and the duty to tell the truth can generate extreme stress. Because lawyers are trained in reasoning and argument, they can often rationalize a way to defend an answer or a position that, to an objective observer, may be completely without merit. And the ethics rules are flexible enough to allow some wiggle room in the grey area where advocacy lapses into affirmative misrepresentation. But finding the line is often a challenge, and if any bright lines exist, they often become visible only in hindsight.

Quite apart from the disciplinary implications of a lack of requisite honesty, many lawyers soon realize that their reputations, for either honesty or trickery, will help or hamper their careers. A lawyer who has a reputation as honest, though a tough and capable advocate, will enjoy professional acceptance and praise. A lawyer pegged as a liar and a cheat will suffer over the long run because his peers, and judges before whom he appears, will not trust him and will not take him at his word for anything.

III. An Inherent Tension

The lawyer's code of conduct sometimes reflects choices rather than moral absolutes. This nuanced reality is often not apparent to the public and, even when explained, it can be easily misunderstood. Take, for example, the issue of confidentiality. The writings and jurisprudence related to confidentiality and privilege all hold this notion to be a foundation of the lawyer-client relationship. Clients must have an unfettered right to tell their lawyers the truth, even if that truth means admitting misconduct. Only with a full knowledge of the facts can a lawyer give competent advice.

Yet what of the instance where a client admits committing a crime? What if another has been accused of the same crime? Or the parents of a victim are being consumed by doubt as to whether their loved one is going to return, and the criminal defendant's lawyer has the answer? Legal lore is replete with instances where lawyers had just such knowledge and withheld it for years or decades because they learned the information as a client confidence. These lawyers have been reviled in the court of public opinion yet praised in legal circles. When asked to explain why they had failed to disclose the fact that their client had confessed to a crime for which another man had spent several years in prison, the lawyers simply said, "We could not ethically do otherwise."

A similar tension can be found in the circumstance where a lawyer has taken on an unpopular client. For instance, the American Civil Liberties Union has represented the American Nazi Party and the Ku Klux Klan in matters regarding their First Amendment right to engage in hateful speech. When this author asked a Jewish lawyer how he could represent the Klan when the materials they wished to distribute contained a picture on the cover of a Jew who had been hanged, with the caption "A Good Start," his answer was, "How can I not represent them?" For that professional, the duty to ensure that principles of free speech were protected overwhelmed his personal distaste for the message. Again, in this instance of principle over popularity, the public's ability to understand choices driving the decision may be limited and may create discomfort for lawyers who live in a larger society.

A third example of the tension between principle and client duty can arise when a party withholds important information, not out of avarice, but simply because the opponent has not asked for it. In the famous case of *Spaulding v. Zimmerman,* 116 N.W.2d 704 (Minn. 1962), lawyers defending an auto accident case learned that the plaintiff had a serious and life-threatening condition of which neither he nor his lawyer had knowledge. Had defense counsel disclosed the injury, it would have allowed the plaintiff to obtain medical treatment, and perhaps saves his life, but doing so also would have increased the value of the case, that is, the amount the defense would likely have paid to settle the case or in damages. The defense lawyers' client prohibited them from disclosing the plaintiff's condition to the plaintiff, and the case was settled.

Later, the injury was discovered and the plaintiff sought to reopen the settlement. The Minnesota supreme court affirmed the lower court's decision to vacate the original settlement, but without finding that defendants' lawyers had violated any ethical duty. The court noted that "no canon of ethics or legal obligation may have required them to inform plaintiff or his counsel with respect thereto, or to advise the court therein." But the supreme court held that the lower court had not abused its discretion in vacating the settlement because the lower court was entitled, when deciding whether to approve the settlement, to learn of plaintiff's condition from defense counsel. The fact that plaintiff's medical condition was detected and remedied before the litigant died did little to insulate the lawyers from criticism that, while they may have acted ethically in not revealing the evidence, they acted immorally.

Forty years after the *Spaulding* decision, in 2002 the ABA ethics rule on confidentiality of information was amended to make clear that a lawyer "may" reveal a client confidence if the lawyer reasonably believes disclosure is necessary to "prevent reasonably certain death or substantial bodily harm" (Model Rules of Professional Conduct, R. 1.6(b)(1)). But note that even now, the rule by its terms is permissive, not mandatory. While ethics rules often, as here, leave room for doubt on the right course to follow, they also make manifest a lawyer's obligation to weigh moral implications before acting. The Preamble to the Model Rules states, in part: "Within the framework of these Rules, however, many difficult issues of professional discretion can arise. Such issues must be resolved through the exercise of sensitive professional and *moral judgment* guided by the basic principles underlying the Rules." [Emphasis added]

On the facts of *Spaulding*, an ethical and moral defense counsel today would do all in her power to persuade her client to allow disclosure of plaintiff-victim's life-threatening condition. Even absent client approval, Rule 1.6(b)(1) suggests counsel may do so anyway in order to potentially save a life.

The popular impression that lawyers as a class are lacking in character may seem to find support in the many accounts, found in the disciplinary digests and reported cases, of serious dishonesty by lawyers. But it is important to note that a relatively small percentage of lawyers ever incur disciplinary sanctions.

IV. Loyalty and its Limits

In addition to the public perception issue, a lawyer's commitment to honesty and integrity may be tested in the context of lawyer-client relations. There, too, walking the fuzzy line between acceptable and improper conduct can at times be challenging. While some duties, such as that of confidentiality, may best be described as owed to "the profession," the duty of honesty in client dealings is squarely owed to that client and should be regarded as inviolate. If there is any place where complete honesty is expected and where sharp tactics and game-playing are never tolerated, it is in dealings with clients. A lawyer's duty of loyalty and honesty mandates that she share all news, good or bad, with the client. There are very rare exceptions to this duty when the immediate transmission of information might cause a client physical or mental harm, but the general rule is that a lawyer may never lie to a client.

Beyond honesty to the client, lawyers involved in litigation have a specific duty of candor and honesty to the court that, on occasion, will even trump their duties of loyalty and confidentiality to their clients. As with other aspects of the lawyers' ethical code, this duty reflects a relativistic sense of the greater good rather than an isolated moral dictate. Why should a lawyer be required to honor a client's confidentiality, even knowing that the client is factually guilty, when defending the client in a criminal case but not be able to offer the same silence in a civil case? Wouldn't it be easier if a lawyer only had to worry about being a capable and loyal advocate and did not have to worry about telling a judge that her client is lying or that the case is without merit? The answer is that social policy values inform the rules. In the criminal context, lawyers are allowed, and indeed required, to make the state prove its case, even if they are aware that the client is guilty. In a civil case, however, a lawyer may not proceed on a case that she knows is frivolous or without a reasonable basis in fact or law. A criminal accused has a constitutional right to a trial, including a right to counsel. There is no concomitant right for civil litigants. In the civil arena, social ends are best served if the interests of any single client are forced to give way to a greater good found in truth-telling. Litigation is a search for the truth, not a private battle between two litigants to be determined by who is the better liar.

Balancing these two competing duties can be one of the most difficult tests a lawyer will face in her career. Consider the lawyer who is asked a question by a judge. An honest answer will result in the client's case being lost. A lie or prevarication might give the lawyer and client time to glean something from the doomed case. What is the proper course? Ethicists will tell you the choice is easy. Battle-tested lawyers will tell you that it is a choice that you will remember for the rest of your career. Part of skilled lawyering, often only learned after many years of experience, is avoiding such situations.

Consider the lawyer who knows that a judge has made a factual mistake. Ethics demand that the lawyer correct the judge's misimpression. The duty of zealous advocacy may argue against doing anything if the mistake advantages the lawyer's client. A closer case may exist when a lawyer knows that her opponent is mistaken as to a fact or as to the law. Correcting this mistake may result in an objectively more just outcome, but it will disadvantage the lawyer's client. How far should the lawyer go as an advocate when he knows that he is taking advantage of inexperience, mistake, or misimpression by his opponent?

In addition to a lawyer's duty of honesty to his client and to a court, there is a duty of honesty in dealing with the public. Many lawyers do not practice in courts. Some spend their days working on transactions. As with litigation, it is easy to imagine how a client's cause might be advantaged by lying about a transactional matter, as in the case of a lawyer who remains silent while a client induces an innocent party into a fraud. Yet the lawyer's code of ethics prohibits it (see Rule 4.1 of the ABA Model Rules of Professional Conduct).

Lawyer dishonesty can take multiple forms. In Illinois, a lawyer was held in criminal contempt in a traffic case for arranging to have a clerical employee of his law firm, who resembled the client defendant, sit at the counsel table during trial, in a seat usually occupied by co-counsel or a party. *People v. Simac*, 603 N.E.2d 97 (Ill. App. 1992). Counsel failed to inform opposing counsel or the court that the person seated next to him was his clerk, not the defendant. The officer who responded to the traffic incident subsequently took the stand and misidentified the lawyer's clerk as the defendant. In affirming the finding of contempt, the appellate court held that counsel had materially deceived the court by his actions, although he had made no verbal representations in court or to opposing counsel suggesting or implying that his clerk was actually the defendant.

V. Testing the Limits

Most cases will not present black or white choices between right and wrong conduct. Case law allows a lawyer to pursue even weak cases for clients if the lawyer has a good-faith legal basis to believe that the matter is supported by fact and law or that a case can be made for a modification or extension of the existing law. Some of our greatest cases were born out of desperate claims that most lawyers would not have thought had any hope of success. For instance, when Clarence Gideon sent a handwritten letter, in pencil and on plain yellow paper, to the U.S. Supreme Court arguing that poor people should be given a lawyer in a criminal trial, many would have dismissed the petition as frivolous. Attorney Abe Fortas (who would later become Chief Justice of the U.S. Supreme Court) believed that, despite the fact that no court had ever held that there was an absolute right to representation in criminal cases, the principle was important enough to be tested at the highest court in the land. *Gideon v. Wainright* forever changed the course of U.S. criminal jurisprudence, establishing that the constitutional right to criminal defense counsel is not contingent upon the defendant's ability to pay counsel fees.

VI. Lawyer Integrity in the Commercial Realm

The rules, interpretive commentary, and decisions recognize many nuances, protocols, conventions, and understandings that reflect the complex realities of actual practice in the commercial realm. Thus, assertions of opinion as to price, value, or a client's settling point are understood to be advocacy that need not reflect absolute truth. Similarly, a fine line is drawn between affirmative misrepresentation, on the one hand, and, on the other, silence in the face of an opponent's ill-informed decision as to whether a particular deal will be advantageous to them.

As with the other aspects of honesty addressed above, finding the right balance between creative advocacy and fraud is something that may be learned through hard lessons. Once a lawyer is branded as dishonest, the taint is often impossible to remove. Anticipating the challenge is often the key to correctly navigating those difficult shoals.

VII. Lawyer as Client Counselor

The lawyers' ethics code recognizes that lawyers are both advocates and counselors. While an advocate advances a client's cause, a counselor helps the client choose the proper course. The traditional allocation of responsibility between client and lawyer was that the client always controlled the objectives of the representation, while the means to the ends belonged to the lawyer. The more modern vision anticipates a more collaborative relationship in both areas.

Clients own their cases, not their lawyers. But often a client will need professional advice as to which objectives are realistic, which make economic sense, and which are likely to do harm as well as good. The rules allow lawyers to counsel clients on all aspects of an undertaking, including social, political, and moral factors that may be involved. And there is no "one size fits all" model for how a lawyer should counsel a client. Sophisticated clients may need advice on the limits of acceptable conduct, and a lawyer, while prohibited from assisting or schooling a client in breaking the law, can point out what conduct is allowed by law and what the possible consequences might be of any particular course of conduct. In doing so, the lawyer should understand that the ultimate decision is the client's, but that a good decision cannot be made without a full understanding of all of the relevant considerations.

VIII. Balancing Client Loyalty and Independent Judgment

In advising clients, lawyers are expected to remain neutral, unemotional, and loyal to their social, professional, and institutional duties. They must also guard against allowing external forces to shade or influence their advice to their clients. Thus, if a lawyer cannot give dispassionate advice to a client because of a personal interest the lawyer may have in the matter, the lawyer should withdraw from the representation. Similarly, the lawyer may not accept payment for the representation of a client if the payment comes with any compromise of the lawyer's independence and ability to counsel the client without outside interference.

Once a client has made an informed choice as to the objectives of a representation, the rules anticipate a similarly collaborative relationship with regard to the means to reach the ends. While the rules allow a criminal client absolute control over decisions as to whether to take a plea offer, whether to try a case to a court or a jury, and whether to testify, all other decisions are collaborative. In a civil case, the client has sole, final authority over whether to settle a case. Certain issues, such as trial strategy, will ordinarily be the lawyer's alone, especially when the exigencies of a trial or other setting make collaboration impossible.

That does not mean that a lawyer, by advancing a client's legitimate interests, is endorsing them. Often, as with the representation of those who wish to engage in hate speech, principled lawyers will advance causes and cases they personally find obnoxious. Because professionals are dispassionate and objective and serve both private and public goals, they can do so without endorsing the client's political, economic, social, or moral views. But if the lawyer realizes that she cannot be loyal because the client's goals are so disconsonant with the lawyer's own moral code, the lawyer should withdraw. Lawyers are not automatons. `robots`

Passionate

After the client identifies the goals of an undertaking, and the lawyer and the client come to an agreement on the means to those ends, the principles of professionalism require the lawyer to be a capable, loyal, and zealous advocate. Thus, the lawyer must possess or acquire adequate skill and knowledge to successfully carry out the representation. She must avoid any conflict of interest, whether arising out of a duty to a present or former client or to a third person, or arising out of the lawyer's own self-interest. And the lawyer must advance the client's goals even in the face of public disapproval.

When asked, experienced criminal lawyers often will explain that guilt or innocence matters little to them. The lawyer's duty is to her client and to the client's right to have each and every element of the case against him tested according to legal principles. Again, this approach reflects choices and values over objective morality. While it may, from a different, non-legal perspective, appear morally improper to aid a guilty person to avoid punishment for a crime, it is understood that the lawyer's only professional choice is to do so.

The duties of competent, loyal and zealous representation do not, however, mean that a lawyer may employ any means to serve the client's ends. Lawyers' personal, professional, social, and institutional duties mandate that they advocate for their clients honestly, without deceit or trickery, and according to accepted legal principles.

Some clients need extra help and guidance through a legal process. The rules reflect an understanding that the range of competence and knowledge among the population of clients is infinite and allow some flexibility on the part of a lawyer representing a client who, because of age, infirmity, or disability, needs help identifying and reaching appropriate goals. Ultimately, though the rules allow lawyers in rare instances to bring in third parties, such as conservators or family members, to help guide impaired or cognitively challenged clients to appropriate ends, the case and its direction remain the client's, not the lawyer's. Clients have the right to make choices that the lawyer may consider unwise or inappropriate. An essential element of lawyer integrity is a willingness to allow that to happen, consistent with rights held by the client.

IX. Fees: An Honest Day's Work

A lawyer's honesty and integrity extend to the obligation not to over-charge clients for legal services. The rules contain a list of non-exclusive factors that can be applied in determining reasonableness, including the nature and scope of the work, the fees typically charged for such work, risk, time, expertise, reputation of the lawyer, and results obtained. Fees may be both fixed and contingent.

There is no simple, universal formula for setting a fee that is reasonable. Context is important. In some states, statutory limits on contingent fees establish the normative fee. In other contexts, many related factors must be considered together to determine whether a particular fee passes muster. Ultimately, arriving at a "good" fee will be a collaborative process between the lawyer and the client. If the lawyer spends large amounts of time on a matter because of his inexperience, it is unfair for him to charge the client for the lawyer's education. Conversely, if the matter was delayed because the opposing side was obstreperous and exploited every delay, it might be unfair to ask the lawyer to bear that cost.

As with other aspects of a good client-lawyer relationship, a good lawyer will guide the client to choices that offer the best return for the investment. It would be unethical to suggest a course of conduct that has little chance of advancing the client's ultimate goals but that might incidentally enrich the lawyer given the time and effort required. If there are reasonable alternatives available, such as mediation, arbitration, or truncated presentations, the ethical lawyer will make certain the client can make an informed choice.

A lawyer's integrity is often in play in those instances compelling a decision on whether to withdraw from representing a particular client. Permissive withdrawal is allowed when the lawyer and client's opinions become so divergent that the lawyer can no longer in good faith endorse the client's course of action, when the lawyer and client reach a point of irreconcilable disagreement on some important point, when the client has stopped paying the lawyer, when continued involvement with the client's matter will financially harm the lawyer, or when other good cause is shown. Such withdrawals must be managed in a way that does not harm the client or the client's case. When continued representation would require the lawyer to breach an ethical duty, the lawyer's physical or mental health mandates ending the relationship, or the client discharges the lawyer, there is no choice.

If a representation involves court appearances or appearance in some other forum, the lawyer may need permission to withdraw. Sometimes, a lawyer may wish to withdraw because he learns the client intends to perjure himself or has otherwise indicated he will engage in conduct requiring the lawyer to report him to the tribunal. Signaling the reason for withdrawal without prejudicing the client's case can be tricky.

Lawyers are expected to maintain an independent professional identity, whether they practice alone, in a partnership, in a corporate setting, in a large firm, or for the government. While the business of lawyering is about providing service to clients, as discussed above, the lawyer's professional and personal duties may, on occasion, require the interests of the client to take a back seat.

These duties also require lawyers to police each other. A lawyer has a duty to report, to the appropriate disciplinary authority, misconduct of another lawyer that raises a substantial question as to that lawyer's honesty, trustworthiness, or fitness. The Comments to ABA Model Rule 8.3 caution, however, "[T]his Rule limits the reporting obligation to those offenses that a self-regulating profession must vigorously endeavor to prevent. A measure of judgment is, therefore, required in complying with the provisions of this rule."

X. Final Thoughts

Lawyers are always both moral and ethical actors. They walk and work in the confines of their own professional world and in the larger world of citizens and members of communities. Most times, the dictates of the lawyer's moral and professional codes will be congruous. However, there may be instances where professional ethics dictate that a lawyer take or refrain from some action when her moral values would require a different result. To successfully navigate such a conflict, a lawyer must fully and truly understand both herself and her profession. Those lawyers who master this balance are the best of us.

MARK A. DUBOIS is an attorney practicing with Geraghty & Bonnano, LLC in New London, CT, where he limits his practice to legal ethics and legal malpractice. From 2003 until 2011, he was Connecticut's Chief Disciplinary Counsel. Mr. Dubois is co-author of *Connecticut Legal Ethics and Malpractice*, Law Tribune Publishing (2012).

Chapter 11

NAVIGATING THE CHARACTER AND FITNESS PROCESS

PATRICIA A. SEXTON

I. Introduction

Every state and at least five United States territories require all applicants for a law license to pass a character and fitness screening. The purpose of the screening is not to punish the applicant, but to protect the public. The separate testing component of admission is important because it establishes whether an applicant has the minimal competency to practice in a respective state or territory. Testing for competency, however, does not measure whether the applicant can reasonably be trusted by clients and the general public. That is where character and fitness screening enters the picture.

If a character and fitness application is denied, the applicant will not receive a law license in that jurisdiction—notwithstanding that he or she has just spent years in school and tens of thousands of dollars on tuition. The process is that critical to one's future. Fortunately, for most applicants the process, while tedious, time consuming, and potentially nerve-wracking, turns out to be a non-event. After researching all of those old college addresses and locating the details of the moving violation received years ago, most applicants submit the required character and fitness documentation and in due time receive notice that the application is successful—they will in fact become licensed lawyers if they pass the testing component.

II. Approaching the Disclosure Process with the Right Mindset

For that minority of applicants that do not sail through the process, however, it is important that they educate themselves on how to navigate the process successfully. A first indicator that an application is not sailing toward routine approval would be a notice of request to supply supplemental information to the board of law examiners ("Board") or to appear in person for a hearing.

Every applicant should approach character and fitness review with the understanding that the disclosures required on most applications are very likely the broadest and most intrusive disclosures they will have made in their lives. In any jurisdiction where one might wish to practice, those personal disclosures are without question much broader than the conduct disclosures required on law school applications. To approach the process with the right mindset, every applicant should acknowledge and accept that personal disclosures and representations made in the application for bar admission are likely to be investigated by one of the Board's employees or by another investigative entity such as the National Conference of Bar Examiners ("NCBE"). In other words, understand that if you represent on a bar application that you have not engaged in any criminal behavior that must be disclosed, such as being arrested or taken into custody, someone is going to verify that representation or determine that it is not accurate. Moreover, how an applicant chooses to describe a disclosed fact or event may be investigated to determine whether the description is accurate. In short, representations of past conduct made on a bar admission application are *not* accepted at face value.

It is important, then, for all applicants to recognize that the fact they have arrived at this point in their lives either without ever disclosing an incident, or having previously disclosed it in a manner favorable to them, *will be of no value* in the character and fitness review process. In fact, it may come back to haunt them if past disclosures are inconsistent with the character and fitness application. Therefore, prior inaccurate disclosures, for example in a law school application, may need to be corrected.

So, the process must be taken seriously, but it also should be emphasized that at the end of the day it is rare for an applicant to be flatly denied admission to the bar on the basis that he or she does not possess the required character and fitness prerequisites. Indeed, the mantra of many Boards is that they do not punish for past conduct but rather are trying to determine if the past conduct is reflective of how an applicant will behave in the future.

It may be most helpful to discuss the character and fitness review process in three parts, with the first two segments applying to all applicants: 1) preparing, and 2) filling out and submitting the application, and 3) the hearing. Of course, no one wants to participate in the third segment. Where an applicant is required to do so, however, it is vitally important to prepare properly and have a solid understanding of what to expect.

III. Preparing to Apply for Bar Admission

Know the rules and requirements of the state or territory where you are applying. This, in part, is another way of saying know the deadlines. The first deadline you need to know is simple, but critical: when is the application due? If you have inhabited a world where you seemingly can always get time extensions, please keep in mind that this is *not* that world. Another due diligence consideration that may be relevant: is there a due date for transferring a score for the Multistate Professional Responsibility Exam ("MPRE")? Some states have a specific deadline for when the MPRE score must be transferred to the state where you are seeking admission. Other states have no such deadline, but only require that the MPRE score be transferred before admission is permitted.

If an applicant has already taken a bar exam in a state that has adopted the Uniform Bar Exam ("UBE") and wants to transfer the score, the applicant must determine the transfer deadline. Moreover, when transferring a UBE score, an applicant must determine the "cut score," or the minimum score required for passing, in the receiving state. Even where the applicant has achieved the minimum UBE score in the sending state, the receiving state's cut score also must be satisfied. (But note that for almost all states that have adopted the UBE, as long as the applicant's score is a passing score in the receiving state, it need not be a passing score in the sending state—as of 2013, only one state followed a policy of declining transferred UBE scores that did not meet or exceed the cut score in the sending state.)

While UBE scores are freely transferable among jurisdictions, different jurisdictions may set different UBE passing scores for bar admissions purposes. (Example: Sending State has a passing UBE score of 260, Receiving State has a passing UBE score of 280, and applicant has scored a 270 on the UBE. Applicant's score has made the cut in Sending State, but will be rejected in Receiving State.) Different jurisdictions may also set different limits on the number of times an applicant may take the UBE before achieving a jurisdiction's cut score.

Beyond ascertaining and meeting all deadlines, to prepare adequately applicants would do well to consider any other variable affecting the admission process, such as whether the state where they are seeking admission has a residency requirement. If the applicant is still a law student, it could be important to know whether law students are eligible to take the bar examination before graduation. In addition, several states consider a felony conviction to be a bar to admission, at least for a certain period of time post-conviction.

Importantly, you should thoroughly review the application in advance of completing it to determine what type of information is requested, where you need to go to obtain it, and how much time your due diligence will require. A complete financial history is a good example of the type of information an applicant likely will be asked to gather.

In light of the tremendous cost of higher education and a difficult economy, it is not surprising many applicants are experiencing financial challenges. They should know that most, if not all, jurisdictions' bar admission applications will ask questions regarding amount of personal debt and whether applicants are current on their debt. In turn, many Boards will run a credit report on applicants. Please know that the existence of debt, *per se*, should not be a singular disqualifier for admission. Many Boards, however, will look at whether an applicant with a high debt load either is keeping payments current or at least has a realistic plan to do so. In short, a Board may consider whether an applicant is managing his or her financial situation. Management of personal finances is viewed as relevant to potential future management of client funds, for example. When applicants see themselves as being in the category where management of debt may be an issue, they should consider running a credit report on themselves to determine whether it is accurate and up to date.

Another preparation imperative: Study the state board of bar examiners' (or law examiners') website. (The National Conference of Bar Examiners' website also has extensive information on the various requirements of each state and territory; the website is www.ncbex.org.) Most of the state websites have a section on frequently asked questions, and for a reason—they reflect a series of questions that are asked time and time again by applicants. As an applicant, you shouldn't hesitate to contact the Board with questions, but make sure you have read all of the rules first. A frequent complaint among Boards is that they receive numerous phone calls for issues covered on their websites. When an applicant contacts the Board, conduct, tone, and attitude matter. Anyone looking to become a licensed professional should act like one. Being demanding, rude, or "giving the air" will not go over well, particularly if there are red flags and other troublesome issues in one's file. While a negative exchange with the Board will not serve as a singular basis for denial, it can cast an application in a negative light. And it is always good to be cautious about email content before hitting "send," particularly when an applicant is upset about an aspect of the process such as processing time or a notice of hearing. It is in an applicant's best interest not to let an emotional communication compound possible problems with the application.

IV. The Application

Adhering to a few first principles will serve you well in the bar application process: Don't procrastinate. Be on time. Do it right the first time. Waiting until the last minute to locate information requested in the application form is an extremely bad idea. Note that many jurisdictions, for example, require applicants to list all moving violations received over the last decade, if not their entire driving careers. If an applicant had a violation in another state that is hard to recall, retrieving the information can be challenging and time consuming.

Moreover, a sloppy or incomplete application makes applicants look unprofessional for certain, and possibly deceitful. Do not fall into the trap of thinking you can submit a half-hearted application and supplement later. Supplementation is not precluded or necessarily frowned upon, but it can carry risk and raise an unnecessary red flag. Prospective lawyers who appear not to take the application process seriously are sending the wrong message. In the same vein, it is good to keep in mind that a practicing lawyer's life is full of deadlines. This is the first one, and not to be taken lightly.

Optimizing one's chances of smoothly sailing through the process also requires a thorough approach to answering questions. Read the question, re-read it and then read it again. Discern *exactly* what the question is asking for. Does it ask if you were ever arrested, or taken into custody, or both, or something else? Many applicants run into trouble by misreading or misinterpreting a question—generally in a light most favorable to themselves. For example, often the question requires an applicant to disclose an incident irrespective of whether it eventually was dismissed or disposed of via a suspended sentence of limited duration.

It should go without saying that, in all events, be honest. A distressingly large number of applicants are called in for hearings because of either failure to disclose an event or misrepresentation of the facts of the event itself. Invariably, the failure to disclose or the action of misrepresentation is worse than the "crime."

Another rule that will serve the applicant well: be consistent. As noted, character and fitness applications contain some of the broadest conduct disclosures imaginable. What you disclose and the manner in which it is described can be compared with the disclosures you made on your college and law school applications. For those who sail through the process and do not disclose any red flag issues, it is likely that their previous disclosures will not be compared with the character and fitness application. "Red flag files," however, often are subjected to comparison with prior disclosures. It is a good idea for applicants to review their previous disclosures, if available, and be prepared to discuss any discrepancies if questioned during a subsequent hearing.

Be accountable. Applicants are responsible for obtaining the required information. This responsibility can be frustrating at times when an applicant is unable to obtain information controlled by someone else, such as traffic records. Applicants need to go into the process "owning" it and accepting responsibility for necessary follow-up, taking into account possible delays beyond their control.

Be sensitive. Applications can ask for certain ADA-approved disclosures of sensitive information regarding mental health, including substance abuse. These conditions raise difficult issues for both the applicants and the Boards. From the Board's perspective, the issue is not the fact that an applicant may have a mental condition but rather whether the condition is being addressed. For example, is the applicant seeking treatment or taking medications as recommended by the appropriate health care provider? Similarly, it is not necessarily an issue that an applicant has a history of substance abuse, but the Board will need assurance that the applicant is managing the condition and receiving appropriate support and treatment. As a general rule, the fact the condition exists is not grounds for denial or an in-person hearing. The issue, rather, is whether the applicant acknowledges that the condition exists and is managing it properly.

V. The Hearing

If an applicant receives notification that a hearing is required, she should determine whether the Board's communication provides notice about the subject areas to be discussed. Often the Board communication will refer to specific areas of inquiry, such as criminal history or financial responsibility, and then include a catch-all along the lines of "and all other issues relevant to the application." Most applicants have a good understanding of the reasons they are being called in for a hearing, and many applicants admit during their hearing that "I was expecting the letter" or "I knew I would be called in for a hearing."

To grasp the essence of character and fitness review, it is crucial to understand that applicants bear the burden to prove that they possess the requisite character and fitness to receive a law license, not the other way around. Fortunately, Boards are not in business to deny applicants; they generally try to work with applicants to address or overcome issues that may otherwise keep them from receiving a license. But the applicant bears the burden. It doesn't fall to the Board to make a record that an applicant is not qualified. Rather, it is the applicant's charge to demonstrate that the past behavior in question is just that: behavior long in the past and not something that is ongoing or that will influence or foreshadow future behavior.

Should you hire a lawyer to represent you, if called to a hearing? This is an important question, and the right answer may be a close call, depending on the facts. Hiring counsel can be beneficial for several reasons. It is helpful for applicants to get a professional opinion on whether they are taking the correct approach to the process and whether their explanations of certain issues pass the "smell test." Hiring counsel, however, can be unhelpful and actually hurt your cause if the approach is to have the hired counsel speak for you or explain the incidents or red flags at issue. It is very unlikely that a lawyer is going to say something that, on its own, will completely explain away problematic behavior. For example, assume an applicant is placed on academic probation during a semester when he or she also received a DUI. It may be reasonable for a Board to inquire as to what was going on in the applicant's life at that time. The applicant needs to provide the explanation or testimony in response, not the lawyer.

Similarly, whether to bring witnesses to the hearing is a judgment call for the applicant and, if one is retained, her lawyer. Many applicants feel more positive about the process and their case if they know someone who can attest to their character and past behavior will appear before the Board. Law professors, past employers, family members, and friends are all fair game in the witness department. If there is a particular incident at issue, such as a criminal arrest or honor code violation, it can be helpful to hear from a witness who can shed more light. For example, it can be compelling if the professor involved in a student plagiarism incident is willing to testify that, while an incident violated an Honor Code, the conduct is not reflective of the applicant's overall character. Calling such a witness also may help if he or she can explain that the applicant handled a bad situation as well as possible under the circumstances.

Many Boards accept affidavits from character witnesses and give the contents of the affidavit the same weight as in-person testimony. In addition, many Boards allow witnesses to testify by phone if they are unavailable to appear in person.

There are circumstances where it may beneficial for an applicant to produce exhibits or additional documentation for hearing. Explanation documents can be helpful, such as a current credit report showing that certain payments have been made, confirmation that outstanding tax bills have been paid, or documentation that probation has been successfully concluded. It is important that applicants determine whether there is a specific rule as to the process for introducing exhibits, such as the number of copies and the deadline for submission. Providing the documents in advance of the hearing, instead of the same day, can aid the applicant's case by giving the Board time to review the information prior to the applicant's appearance.

The best advice to a bar applicant called to hearing may be this: Be a person first and a lawyer second. The hearing is not something to be "gamed." Being combative is rarely productive and can actually weigh against the applicant's cause. Being contrite can obviously serve an applicant well; however, the delivery of the apology is important. An apology is form over substance when it is insincere or is given in an arrogant manner. Remember, boards likely have heard dozens of apologies from applicants in the past. There is a good chance they can distinguish a heartfelt apology from one read from a script.

Finally, applicants at a hearing should be prepared to discuss how and why their behavior is different now than when the concerning incidents occurred. For example, perhaps an applicant did not initially take her college studies seriously or made nightlife a priority over studying. As a result, she was placed on academic probation or received drinking violations. An applicant can demonstrate that he or she has changed by referring to good law school grades or a clean slate, in terms of drinking violations, over a certain period of time. Perhaps the applicant had a habit of procrastinating that ultimately led to a plagiarism charge, but can demonstrate that he subsequently counseled other students on the evils of plagiarism or that he responded to the plagiarism charge in a way that persuades the board it should not be concerned about the applicant's future behavior.

VI. Conclusion

Character and fitness review is a daunting prospect for virtually all seeking entry to the legal profession, but for the vast majority it needn't be. For those who take the process seriously, leaving adequate time to produce the full record requested and being forthright at all times, the process, though demanding, will prove uneventful. For the relative handful of applicants whose record may require explanation or a showing that missteps are well in the past, it is essential to approach the process by the book, bringing appropriate measures of humility and sincerity to any hearing requested. It is good to remember that law examiners are not in business to prove you are unworthy of a law license, but to afford you a full opportunity to show your worthiness.

In the rare instances when an applicant is called to hearing, common sense, in the end, will rule the day. Being professional and courteous is essential. Dressing professionally is important—applicants seeking a professional license should look the part. But being yourself and being honest are the factors that will really make the difference.

PATRICIA A. SEXTON is a Shareholder in Polsinelli Shughart, P.C.'s Kansas City, MO, office. She is the President of the Missouri Board of Law Examiners. Ms. Sexton's article, "When Character and Fitness Disclosures Collide: The Dilemma of Inconsistent Law School and Bar Admission Applications" appeared in the ABA publication *The Professional Lawyer*, Vol. 21, Issue 2 (June 2012). She is a member of the ABA Standing Committee on Professionalism.

Chapter 12

REPUTATION

AVARITA L. HANSON

I. Overview

As we venture down the road in life and in the law, we become more and more of who we are. What is that? What is my reputation? Will it survive me?

Reputable lawyers are known for being competent, conscientious, thorough and effective, of course—but they are known for more than that. They are reputed to be of good character. Most relate well to people of various stations and walks of life. Building and maintaining relationships matters to them. They possess enduring qualities that are easily articulated, timeless, even biblical: the reputable lawyer is good, worthy of respect, and sincere. She does not pursue dishonest gain. She speaks with temperance and is trustworthy in everything she does.

History teaches that most of the great ones have been loved by their families; they helped the needy, not just the greedy; they took on difficult causes; and they reached out whenever they could to those with no seat at the table.

Reputable lawyers know that what counts is not what they do for a living, it is what they do for the living. They perform simple acts of kindness;

they help people they meet at the supermarket; they are not quick to sue for every unpaid fee; and they are a voice of reason for the client who is at a difficult crossroad.

Reputable lawyers are seen by their peers as caring, dependable, and solid. Colleagues are pleased, even honored, to welcome them onto their bar committees, legal teams, charitable boards, judicial review panels, and other collaborations because they can always be counted on to contribute. Just as importantly, they are welcomed because their mere presence reflects well on the undertaking, giving weight to its work and thereby advancing its mission.

A lawyer with an excellent reputation will have worked diligently to build and preserve it. For the new or aspiring lawyer, now is the time to think about an enduring reputation. As Dr. Stephen R. Covey wisely advised, one should "begin with the end in mind." *See* STEPHEN R. COVEY, THE 7 HABITS OF HIGHLY EFFECTIVE PEOPLE: POWERFUL LESSONS IN PERSONAL CHANGE (1989).

A reputation isn't made of hopes and dreams; it consists of deeds done, of established relationships, and of attainment. As Henry Ford put it, "You can't build a reputation on what you are going to do."

A reputation can be good or bad. Neither one is an accident. Both kinds can last a lifetime. The things you do now to distinguish yourself may stay with you until retirement and beyond. A good reputation built over a career can be lost in an indiscreet moment, through a single moral or ethical lapse or a too-public embarrassing incident. When there is a close question about a lawyer's fitness, however, a stellar reputation will often provide the all-important benefit of the doubt.

A lawyer who has a reputation for taking on unpopular causes or challenging the establishment's way of doing things may face disapproval or resistance from some legal quarters. The upstanding lawyer will distinguish the good, even great advocate from a lawyer acting badly. The discerning reputable lawyer will welcome that good lawyer into the fold and defend him in the community.

Reputations are perceptions that may not always reflect reality. They can be fiction as well as fact. If you ever find your reputation materially smeared by insidious falsehoods, you should fight to protect it with every-thing you've got. Your reputation, after all, is all you have in the end.

II. Earned or Manufactured

A reputation can be earned or manufactured. Some believe it takes a life-time to earn a reputation. Others would say that a reputation is earned day by day. For a lawyer, a reputation may begin to emerge from the start of law school, or even earlier. A reputation comes from relationships, experiences, and deeds. In law school, students forge relationships with classmates as well as with law school administrators, professors, and staff. Some of them may be future colleagues, judges on one's cases, opposing counsel, or even clients. Some could be cherished mentors and confidantes. It is never too early to earn an excellent reputation.

A lawyer's reputation begins with friends, family, and other close relationships. For some lawyers, their best referrals come from family and friends. In any event, potential clients would not look favorably on a lawyer whose competency and professionalism are not vouched for by family or friends.

But a lawyer's success depends on reputation-building beyond that cozy inner circle. It depends on outsiders who have heard and believe that the lawyer has the attributes of a high calling as well as a high degree of competency. Substantive excellence should be the target for those striving to make a mark. Beyond competency, the reputable lawyer will be known for going about his work in a *professional* way, by comporting himself civ-illy and in all ways honoring his duties to clients, opposing parties and their counsel, co-counsel, the profession, the public, and our systems of justice. (The duties of a professional lawyer are set forth in a number of states' lawyer creeds, including the Georgia Lawyer's Creed and Aspi-rational Statement, adopted by the Georgia Chief Justice's Commission on Professionalism and incorporated into the governing rules lations of the State Bar of Georgia.)

Lawyers build their reputations through interaction leagues, clients, neighbors, friends, relatives, the ju A lawyer burnishes her reputation by showing and nurturing professional relationships. The interactions with colleagues are important and include the ways a lawyer communicates with colleagues; acknowledges their life milestones (birthdays, anniversaries, family deaths and births, awards, major illnesses); deals with them in the course of representing clients (negotiations, discovery, and communications); and interacts with them in professional, civic and social organization work and at other gatherings and encounters.

A lawyer can strengthen her reputation by demonstrating proficiency before the bar and public. She can make a name by penning legal articles or authoring a legal blog for the legal or broader community. A lawyer may offer legal analysis and commentary online or on television or radio. She can show capable and committed leadership with—and make presentations before—the bench, the bar, the PTA, civic clubs, sororities, fraternities, and faith-based entities. In all that a lawyer does—24/7, near and far—her words and actions should demonstrate competence and professionalism, all serving to enhance her good reputation.

Any involvement by a lawyer outside of law practice or judicial service should reflect the same commitment to competence, excellence, and professionalism that is reflected in her daily work. If a lawyer finds she cannot competently and professionally perform volunteer and community commitments, she should decline or phase out those engagements.

A lawyer's reputation can be manufactured, as well as earned. A lawyer may employ social media, such as LinkedIn, Plaxo, or Facebook to create a snapshot of his professional competencies, relationships, and experiences. A lawyer can use television and Internet advertising with visual images, dialogue, and client testimonials to build a perception of his abilities and track record for legal success (all within the constraints of the jurisdiction's ethics rules on lawyer advertising). A lawyer may use peer ratings services such as AVVO, Martindale-Hubbell, and SuperLawyers, honors that boost one's reputation as perceived by clients, potential clients, lawyers who may refer cases, and the public.

A reputation can be created consciously and deliberately. By employing legal strategies before certain tribunals or with certain clients or types of clients, a lawyer can create a reputation for doing legal work in a specific table way that may be attractive to other potential clients. A lawyer berately stake out certain "trademark" practice strategies or types of clients as his turf, all part and parcel of an emerging and distinctive reputation. *See* Fred C. Zacharias, *Effects of Reputation on the Legal Profession*, 65 Wash. & Lee L. Rev. 173 (2008).

A lawyer's reputation may matter more to clients of greater means and sophistication who may have access to more information about the lawyer. Such clients may seek out a lawyer with a reputation for a particular legal strategy or track record. A client, having researched a lawyer's reputation, may try to use it to advance the client's interests and causes. A high profile lawyer can elevate public awareness of a client's cause. On the other hand, a less sophisticated client or one of modest means may not have the opportunity or the wherewithal to select a lawyer on the basis of reputation or professional attributes. Persons of limited means are more vunerable to less qualified or reputible counsel. In either case, the lawyer's reputation would be relevant to clients.

III. Asset or Liability

A lawyer's reputation can be an asset and a liability—even at the same time. A lawyer's reputation can be positive, negative, or mixed. Reputation matters in all a lawyer does—whether representing clients, performing community and public service activities, or seeking jobs or other positions. Doing a good job for a client may lead to more work for that client and to new clients. Quality of work may be as important to one's reputation as results. Existing clients will evaluate the lawyer on her competence, ethics, and professionalism in handling their matters. A lawyer's reputation will soar when the client is offered faithfulness, competence, diligence, good judgment, and when the lawyer treats the client the way the lawyer herself would want to be treated. In an era when many clients can look up the law on the Internet, a lawyer who effectively counsels the client and employs sound judgment will boost her reputation for competence and professionalism.

When a lawyer seeks a new position and must provide references, he should consider what his references will say about him—his reputation. A job interviewer will evaluate or perhaps have personal knowledge of the lawyer's community service, public service, or bar work, as well as any work in support of a legal reform or social initiative. The evaluator may have observed or have knowledge of how the applicant has treated and spoken with clients, colleagues, and people in the community. In a global practice environment, interviewers increasingly are focused on lawyers' ability to get along with, and adapt to, different types of people and their cultures.

Most lawyers strive to be competent at all times, yet lawyers do make mistakes in their practice, occasionally with the result that they are called on the carpet by disciplinary authorities. When the matter proceeds past the complaint stage and an ethics violation is found, there is an opportunity to consider the lawyer's past acts and reputation before any discipline is imposed. In a disciplinary setting, particularly in a close call, the strength of the lawyer's reputation and the identity of the people who will vouch for the lawyer in question may be decisive.

IV. When Reputation Matters

Whether a lawyer hopes to get or keep a client, to take the lead in an important engagement, to pursue elective office or appointment to a public or private entity, to be named to a significant bar committee, or to be elected or appointed a judge, her reputation is put on display. For high-profile appointments, reputation is usually a paramount consideration, and may be determinative of whether the appointment will be secured.

A lawyer may seek a judicial or other public appointment, or may be sought out. In either case, reputation will be under close review. If that lawyer has a reputation for competence, honesty, trustworthiness, and preparedness, she will gain further support for her application or appointment. A reputable candidate will most likely receive recommendations from colleagues—those in the best position to assess the candidate's abilities, experience, and professionalism. Colleagues evaluating lawyers for judicial or administrative appointment look for some of the same qualities that clients value, but may also consider other factors. Colleagues will consider whether the candidate is known for fairness, probity, integrity, and civility, as well as for seeking reconciliation while working to make dispute resolution dignified.

Lawyers running for public office or seeking appointments face committees comprised of lawyers and lay persons that vet candidate qualifications.

Most but not all lawyers reviewed by these panels will satisfy the objective criteria—factors such as education, years of practice, subject matter knowledge, age, and residency. The threshold question, however, is whether those position seekers will pass the reputation test—that is, what others say about the candidates in their recommendations and appearances before appointing authorities.

When a lawyer needs support in a tough situation, such as when his qualifications or character are questioned, a solid reputation can deliver that support. If negative information about a lawyer is circulating, the professional peers who know him best are likely to speak out. They can attest that the negative (or insufficiently positive) information is uncharacteristic for that lawyer, or that the information appears inaccurate, untrue or doubtful as it relates to that candidate.

Whether a lawyer regularly or sporadically appears before courts or other tribunals, it is important to exhibit attributes that reinforce the lawyer's reputation for professionalism. In dealings with judges, arbitrators, jurors, mediators and others in decision-making positions, a lawyer should at all times show respect, act with candor, and speak with courtesy. When a lawyer's reputation is uniformly good, she almost always receives the benefit of the doubt.

A lawyer's reputation matters to the firm—whether a solo, small, or large practice. A positive or negative reputation will be a firm asset or liability, in the eyes of those both within and outside the firm. It will cast the firm itself in a light more or less favorable, from the perspective of potential clients, judges, and even adversaries. In most communities, there is a lawyer with a reputation for being exceptionally difficult and unprofessional. Accounts of the lawyer's disreputable conduct make their way around the courthouse, to firms, and even to local bar associations, often with the help of courthouse and firm staff. That kind of reputation will do real damage to the lawyer's practice— deservedly so—and to the firm.

A lawyer's reputation may affect fees earned and charged. Because the legal profession is a field in which tangible goods or readily-quantifiable services are not produced, a lawyer's reputation may be factored into his fees. Many judges and lawyers can relate a story about a lawyer in their community who has a reputation for being extremely difficult to deal with, rude, unprepared, scatter-brained, and unnecessarily demanding. When taking on a difficult adversary, opposing counsel may impose a premium fee on their clients—a form of combat pay. While lawyers, judges, and their staffs know him by his reputation, the difficult lawyer is not always avoidable. All should recognize that the reputation of the local bar, and the legal profession itself, is harmed by the disreputable lawyer's bad conduct and tendency to drag out disputes, making litigation more costly for all concerned.

V. Maintaining a Reputation

The era of instant electronic communications, with potentially unlimited distribution of messaging, brings with it an enhanced risk of harm to a lawyer's good reputation. If the lawyer's reputation is substantial enough, it likely will take more than one ill-conceived tweet or regrettable email to do lasting harm. But if the misstep is egregious enough, such as a criminal act or publicized sexual indiscretion, even the lawyer with a large amount of reputation points "in the bank" can quickly go bankrupt. Rebuilding one's reputation after such an event, if even feasible, may be problematic at best.

VI. Conclusion

A lawyer's reputation is an asset, derived from experiences and relationships, that grows into a public persona. A lawyer's reputation is largely about relationships, which can be developed and nurtured, and should always be protected.

As a lawyer proceeds on the journey of her professional life, she should listen to the voices of dissent, which are often the conscience of society, and cultivate an unshakable sense of fairness and commitment to justice, which will inform and grow her good reputation.

A lawyer may consider whether her actions, decisions and life relationships will build a reputation of mediocrity or one that is memorable and important. A lawyer may act in a manner that primarily helps herself, or may pursue a course of action that also betters her community, the nation, and the world. A lawyer can be known for doing well and doing good. Those who do well and good have the best reputations of all.

Sources/Reading

Stephen R. Covey, The 7 Habits of Highly Effective People: Powerful Lessons in Personal Change (1989).

State Bar of Georgia, *Lawyer's Creed and Aspirational Statement on Professionalism*, http://www.gabar.org/aboutthebar/lawrelatedorganizations/cjcp/lawyers-creed.cfm (last viewed April 12, 2013).

Donna Gerson & David Gerson, The Modern Rules of Business Etiquette (2012).

Michael B. Greenstein, *On Being a Lawyer of Good Reputation, and Why That Matters*, Spouse A Louse, (Mar. 17, 2011), http://spousealouse.wordpress.com/2011/03/17/on-being-a-lawyer-of-good-reputation-and-why-that-matters/.

Daniel L. Harris & John V. Acosta, *Conduct Counts: On Professionalism: Professionalism for Litigation and Courtroom Practice*, 67 Or. St. B. Bull. 40 (2007), *available at* http://www.osbar.org/publications/bulletin/07augsep/professionalism.html.

Christopher J. Masoner, *The Importance of Perceptions*, 75 J. Kan. B.A. 7 (Mar. 2006).

Webster's Third New International Dictionary (2002).

Fred C. Zacharias, *Effects of Reputation on the Legal Profession*, 65 Wash. & Lee L. Rev. 173 (2008).

AVARITA L. HANSON is the Executive Director of the Georgia Chief Justice's Commission on Professionalism in Atlanta, Georgia. Ms. Hanson is the 2011–13 Chair of the ABA Consortium on Professionalism Initiatives.

Chapter 13

FINDING AND GETTING THE MOST OUT OF A MENTOR

LORI L. KEATING AND MICHAEL P. MASLANKA

I. Why New Lawyers Need Mentors

To become a lawyer, go to law school. To learn to be a lawyer, get a mentor. To build a successful career, seek out many mentors.

Veteran attorneys know this truth: new lawyers simply "don't know what they don't know" as they begin their legal career. Although the Socratic method used by many law school professors empowers students to "think like lawyers," legal analysis is only one element of the practice of law. To be sure, qualities such as intellect, perseverance, and writing proficiency, which serve the law student well, are prized attributes in legal practice. Yet in the end, success as a student does not directly translate to success as a legal professional, as the worlds of law school and law practice present very different expectations.

As lawyers begin the practice of law, they are confronted with challenges largely absent in law school. They must learn to hold their own against more experienced opposing counsel and to work with difficult clients; to write research memoranda helpful to particular senior attorneys and briefs tailored to the proclivities of various judges; to master the art of courtroom argument or negotiations; and to strike a workable balance between personal and professional life.

Moreover, new lawyers working in a firm or legal department, who may have never held a supervisory position, must learn to work well with experienced administrative assistants and paralegals who often know more about routine aspects of the practice of law than the recently graduated lawyer. New lawyers also must navigate tricky office politics and meet the demands of more senior attorneys and partners.

II. Special Challenges Facing New Solo Practitioners

New lawyers who do not join an existing firm or legal department, but instead boldly hang out their own shingle, face even greater challenges in terms of attaining needed practical knowledge and experience. They are starting a business and managing a law office. New solo lawyers must develop a business plan, create a marketing strategy, choose a business entity, establish an accounting system, decide which IT services to purchase and utilize (e.g., for reception, legal research, and case management, among other things), select an office space (which may be brick and mortar or virtual), acquire appropriate malpractice insurance, and more. Without the guidance of a mentor, the challenges a new lawyer confronts at the start of a solo practice can be overwhelming.

III. Early Attention to Ethical Risk

For new lawyers in firms large and small, sudden immersion in the practice of law carries with it a heightened risk of professional missteps and ethical violations, often related to the notion that what you don't yet know can hurt you. That is the practical reality of law practice.

Having the right mentor can be crucial to advancing the new lawyer's dual mission of becoming more competent as quickly as possible while staying out of trouble long enough to learn how to build an ethically sound practice.

IV. Passing Along Professional Ideals

Mentoring, when done right, has overarching noble objectives. Mentors help transmit the values of the profession—concepts such as civility, the responsibility that comes with being an officer of the court, and the understanding that a client's needs come before a lawyer's interests. A mentor conveys these values by discussing his or her experiences, and by introducing the new lawyer to groups that prize professional ideals. Bar associations, Inns of Court, and pro bono agencies are among the many legal organizations that may guide professional development.

V. The Value of Multiple Mentors

Successful careers are rarely, if ever, built upon the advice of just one mentor. To maximize mentoring potential, seek out multiple mentors. Relying upon one particular attorney too heavily may unduly burden a mentor who would otherwise be happy to help. Moreover, no single mentor will have the best skill-set to tackle every challenge faced by a protégé. Different mentors have different strengths and interests. At the same time, a protégé's needs will mature as skills are mastered and new challenges are encountered. Finally, career paths are not always linear—young lawyers often move their practice area or setting in new directions. It follows that some of the people who were most influential at one stage of a protégé's career may not remain as important at later stages. Relying on the best talents of many different individuals over a course of years is an empowering experience for the protégé.

VI. Engaging and Relating with a Mentor

A. *The Right Approach*

When seeking a mentor, a new lawyer or law student should first set aside the common misconception that senior lawyers will not make the time or the effort to meet. Here is the truth: Most senior lawyers will take a meeting, and perhaps more than one, if approached by a novice lawyer or law student in the right way. They understand that for the protégé, a chance to learn from a mentor is not a right, it is a gift, and nearly all senior lawyers had someone, at some point, give of their time.

If a law student or not-yet-placed new lawyer's goal is just to get a job, and the senior lawyer is viewed simply as the means to an end, then the intent may be viewed as exploitative. No one wants to be an item on someone else's checklist. Rather, the intent should be to set up a meeting for valid informational or educational purposes. The law student or new lawyer should ask herself why she is contacting the senior lawyer. Is the senior lawyer a specialist in a field in which she is interested? Does the senior lawyer write a blog she reads? Perhaps the protégé wants to start blogging and seek advice on how to do so, or have an informal consultation on dealing with difficult opposing counsel or a demanding client.

Whatever the specific reason, it should be stated at the outset; an "I just want to meet you" request is not as likely to succeed in solidifying a mentoring relationship. Generic requests are susceptible to generic rejections. The motives behind the approach to a prospective mentor must be authentic and sincere. If there is not a satisfactory answer to why the student or new attorney would like to meet with a particular attorney, then it is probably best not to pursue the contact. It will likely be a waste of everyone's time.

B. The Meeting

Time is a lawyer's most precious possession. The student or new lawyer seeking a meeting should leave it to the senior lawyer to decide the meeting place, time, and format. Coffee or lunch work well for an initial mentor meeting. Drinks or dinner, however, are not recommended. While the intent of the overwhelming number of experienced lawyers is to sincerely help a protégé, there are the exceptional few who see "mentoring" as a dating opportunity. It isn't.

In advance of a first mentoring meeting, the senior lawyer likely will have glanced at the protégé's résumé, LinkedIn profile, or Twitter stream. The more information conduits used, the better, and the more pertinent information about professional and personal background, the better. The goal is to distinguish oneself from the multitude. Be professional in all social media communications, but also emphasize positive characteristics or perspectives that are unique to you—people will invest their time in a particular person, not a cardboard cut-out. (See Chapter 15, *eProfessionalism*, by Stephanie L. Kimbro, at Page 189, for further discussion of lawyer conduct on social media.)

The new lawyer or law student should come to the initial mentor meeting with questions that he really wants answered, not questions the sole purpose of which is to fill time, like a less than thrilling first date. On the other hand, be cognizant that a meeting with a mentor is not the place to work through a question checklist—one down, twenty more to go. Rather, it is an opportunity to start a dialogue that may result in a mutually beneficial mentoring relationship. Not every meeting will lead to one, but many will. Useful questions are limitless, but may include:

- Would you share with me your thoughts on certain law firms?
- Is there anything I should be doing differently in starting my career—professionally or in business development?
- Are there opportunities for using my law license other than the traditional practice of law? What other possibilities might I consider?
- I know you are busy and I appreciate that you spent time with me. I know your advice will be valuable. I hope you feel the time is well spent for you as well. (This approach may help draw out the mentor on his reasons for mentoring and what he hopes to impart through the process.)
- Would you mind looking at my résumé?

Asking the right questions will both add to the protégé's knowledge and leave a favorable impression with the mentor that may benefit the protégé immediately or in the future.

In addition to asking the right kinds of questions, it is important to ask the right-sized questions. Avoid the big questions, such as "How can I get a job in six months?" or "How can I double my business?" These questions paralyze. As Robert Maurer points out in his book, *The Spirit of Kaizen: Creating Lasting Excellence One Small Step at a Time*, "they trigger a fear response, shutting down the brain." On the other hand, the brain absorbs without panic small questions. Here are some starter questions for protégés to ask:

- What is the *one* small thing I can do to make and/or solidify connections that takes no more than five/three/one minute(s) each day?
- What is the one thing I can do every day that should help me in getting a job or developing business?
- Who do I know *now* who may be a person of influence in twenty years? What small steps I am making *now* to develop a relationship?

There is another cardinal rule to follow in identifying one's legal areas of interest to a mentor or potential mentor: show, don't tell. If a law student or new lawyer professes an interest in employment law, or securities, or general litigation, then she should be prepared to demonstrate that interest by, for example, discussing some of the latest developments in the field, trading information with the senior lawyer on related blogs they each read, or identifying subject-matter specialists on Twitter whom she follows. It is important to do the homework before the meeting. When the protégé asserts strong interest in a subject or issue, senior lawyers may ask themselves, "Does this person have a sincere interest or is she just telling me what I want to hear?" If the interest is not genuine, there will be no connection.

VII. Mentoring Challenges in Today's Legal Practice

In years past, when legal communities were smaller and more homogenous, everyone knew who the new lawyers were when they began to practice, and it was easier to make sure those attorneys had the guidance they needed at the start of their careers. In those days, it was equally true that a new lawyer who was hired by a firm upon graduation could reasonably expect to spend his entire legal career with that firm; firms made a concerted effort to mentor each new lawyer from day one. Now legal communities tend to be much larger and more diverse, with the expectation that lawyers will change employers several times during the course of their professional lives.

Further, more and more new lawyers are graduating from law school and starting practice by going out on their own, without benefit of any mentors. Add to this mix an increase in competition between lawyers (in between and within firms), as well as high demand from many firms for billable hours, and the result is that a significant number of new lawyers are entering the profession without the help of mentors.

VIII. The Ethics of Mentor Communications

For new lawyers already employed in a legal position, certain ethical considerations should be top-of-mind during a mentoring meeting. When a new lawyer from one firm seeks the advice of a more senior lawyer from another firm, that dialogue should be appropriately constrained if arising from an actual case or legal matter. For example, the Oregon Bar Association issued formal ethics opinion No. 2011–184 (March 2011), entitled "Confidentiality, Conflicts of Interest: Consulting Between Lawyers Not in the Same Firm," expressly dealing with lawyers who are in a mentoring relationship.

The opinion notes that legal knowledge is often transferred through informal relationships between lawyers, and that is to be encouraged. For example, a lawyer may ask the name or citation of a recent case on a subject applicable to a client matter or inquire about a general issue of law or procedure that might be present in a client matter. A lawyer may ask questions and seek answers related to actual cases, but safeguards must be in place. For example, framing the issue as a hypothetical is acceptable. That is not a panacea, however, and the new lawyer must take care not to make disclosures to the senior lawyer if, in the words of the Oregon ethics opinion, "the facts provided permit persons outside the lawyer's firm to determine the client's identity. Where the facts are so unique or where other circumstances might reveal the identity of the consulting lawyer's client without even being named, the lawyer must first obtain the client's informed consent for the disclosures."

For more on this issue, see Formal Opinion 98–411, issued by the ABA Standing Committee on Ethics and Professional Responsibility, August 30, 1998.

IX. The Mentoring Movement

Throughout the United States, many bar association, courts, law firms, law schools, and other legal organizations that value mentoring have developed formal mentoring programs to bring law school students and new lawyers into the fold. New lawyer participation in these programs may be mandatory or voluntary, depending upon the administering body's philosophy. The first statewide mandatory mentoring program, Georgia's Transition into Law Practice Program, was created by the State Bar of Georgia in 2005. In 2006, the Supreme Court of Ohio created Lawyer to Lawyer Mentoring, a voluntary statewide program for its new lawyers. With the Georgia and Ohio programs serving as models, statewide mentoring programs now operate in more than twenty jurisdictions.

In formats such as the Supreme Court of Ohio Lawyer to Lawyer Mentoring Program, a mentor and protégé commit to the mentoring process in writing, submit a plan for their mentoring term by choosing activities and topics from a proposed list, read materials in preparation for each meeting, and certify completion of the program to the Court at the end of the term. Mentors and their protégés are required to meet at least six times for a total of nine hours during the term. New mentors receive training about how to be effective in their role during an orientation. Upon completion of the program, participants receive continuing legal education credit. Ohio's program is one of many formal programs that provide structure and accountability, setting the stage for a successful mentoring relationship.

X. Finding Mentors Through Formal Programs or Informal Contacts

In 2011, the National Legal Mentoring Consortium was formed. Its website, http://legalmentoring.org, collects information about mentoring programs throughout the country, including those sponsored by state and local bar associations, with web links to each. There is also a reference library containing articles about mentoring and being mentored. Law students and new lawyers are encouraged to participate in any formal mentoring programs available to them. They should seek informal mentoring relationships as well.

Mentoring connections are stronger and more structured when managed through an established mentoring program using best standards and organizational support (whether school or bar). To be sure, however, demand for mentors exceeds supply provided by structured programs, and some states still lack formal programs that match mentoring pairs and provide standard for their interaction.

Long-term and meaningful mentoring relationships may form after a protégé and mentor introduce themselves at a bar association meeting, a law firm event, a continuing legal education program, a law school alumni function, or any other gathering that brings legal professionals together. Even the most informal meetings between mentor and protégé can be incredibly helpful. And mentors may be found in unexpected places—even opposing counsel (See accompanying text box).

Mike counts opposing counsel among his mentors. As a new staff lawyer at the National Labor Relations Board, Mike was prosecuting a lawsuit in a small town in East Texas. Opposing counsel lived in the town. When the lunch break came, he ambled over and asked Mike to go to lunch. Mike refused, thinking it would be improper for an attorney for the federal government to eat with the other side. Opposing counsel looked at Mike with a mixture of bemusement and pity, saying—in very explicit terms—that in 40 years of practice, encompassing fiercer fights than this one, not one opponent had refused to eat with him. Mike re-thought his position and joined his fellow lawyer for lunch.

XI. Cyberspace and Mentoring: Use Wisely

Some protégés receive guidance through exchanges that occur in cyberspace. LinkedIn Groups and listservs hosted by bar associations or other lawyer groups provide opportunities to seek the wisdom of more experienced legal professionals. Often delineated by practice area, these conversation groups are comprised of experienced practitioners who are happy to respond to a gamut of participant questions, from the very basic to the most sophisticated. Facebook, Twitter, and other social media communities may also offer great opportunities for questions to be asked and answered.

In some ways, social media offers advantages over conventional mentoring. Social media allows for questions to be answered quickly. The time-consuming process of cultivating individual relationships is generally unnecessary online—participation in a social media group instantaneously provides a common connection. Nor is a person's online mentoring opportunity limited by physical proximity. In addition, when these online communities include diverse membership, multiple perspectives regarding a single issue may be generated quickly for the protégé's consideration.

Although this type of exchange has its place, law students or new lawyers who exclusively seek professional advice via social media are greatly disadvantaged. The most experienced attorneys in practice today are members of the Baby Boom Generation and Generation X. These generations highly value in-person conversation and relationships and understand that there is something organic and expansive about in-person conversation that provides a better opportunity to thoroughly consider complex issues. Perhaps most importantly, although questions posed in cyberspace may yield useful information, the end result of the experience is most often the answer itself. In an effective in-person mentoring relationship, the end result of asking questions might not be getting answers but could be something bigger—the beginning of a relationship (or friendship) with a mentor that may last for years to come.

XII. Creating Contact Capital

All the best advice on mentoring relationships supports a singular imperative for every lawyer: create contact capital. Value is derived from a web of professional relationships, not just one or two.

Steve Jobs expressed this idea, albeit in a somewhat different context, in a 1996 interview with *Wired* magazine: "Creativity is connecting things . . . . A lot of people in our industry haven't had very diverse experiences. So they don't have enough dots to connect, and they end up with very linear solutions without a broad perspective to the problem."

The bottom line for new lawyers and law students: The first people you reach as you develop contact capital often will not be the source of a job or business or sought-after knowledge. *But* their contacts, or their contacts' contacts, may be the answer. So, set a goal of creating contact capital, and accomplish that goal. Succeed at the small things, and the rest will follow. If no action is taken, no results will flow.

XIII. The Diagnostic Dozen: Questions to Ensure a Healthy Mentoring Relationship

A solid, positive relationship is essential to mentoring success. A protégé (or mentor) may ask these questions to determine whether the mentoring effort is on track:

Right Track

1. Is the mentoring process providing a candid (but caring) view of the protégé's strengths and weaknesses?
2. Are specific and concrete ideas and suggestions being discussed or are conversations full of gauzy platitudes and empty rhetoric?
3. Does the mentor listen to the protégé's questions and concerns and respond appropriately to both the facts and the feelings expressed?
4. Is the process framing issues as challenges instead of as problems?
5. Is the mentor making suggestions about how the protégé may learn from sources other than him or her? (These resources may include bar associations, Inns of Court, other lawyers, reading materials, or cyberspace exploration.)
6. As a result of the meetings does the protégé feel more independent as a lawyer?
7. Is the protégé more inclined to be a mentor because of the experience?

If the answer to these questions is "yes," then the mentoring relationship is progressing as it should.

Wrong Track

1. Does either the mentor or the protégé feel that the process, for whatever reason, is not productive? (If so, have a candid conversation—better to acknowledge it early than late.)
2. Is the process engaging the mentor to perform work tasks as opposed to offering broader counseling and advice?
3. Is the mentor trying to change the protégé?

4. Are personal issues with no relation to professional development being brought into the process by either the protégé or the mentor?
5. Is the mentor "taking over" aspects of the protégé's practice or a particular case?

If the answer to these questions is "yes" re-evaluate the relationship because it is veering off course.

XIV. Post-Mentorship: Staying in Touch

For unstructured mentoring relationships in particular, but also for structured mentoring programs that formally end on a predetermined date, the burden falls to the student or new lawyer—not the senor lawyer—to preserve the relationship going forward. Yes, it is nice to get a one-time thank you note. But the idea is to maintain effective contact so that you are remembered, not forgotten. Send a holiday card. Follow the lawyer on Twitter. Email a link to an article she may find interesting. Attorneys meet a lot of people—strive to be remembered.

XV. Mentoring as a Career-Long Endeavor

Although the advantages of mentoring are perhaps most obvious at the start of practice, the benefits continue throughout a lawyer's career. No matter what career milestones an attorney achieves, she may still learn from others with different strengths, networks, and perspectives. Lawyers who seek out multiple mentors throughout their career enjoy great rewards.

Just as importantly, as new attorneys gain skills, confidence, and experience, they should seek to mentor others. Even brand new lawyers have knowledge and skills they may share with law school students, paralegals, college students, and others.

Being a mentor has its own benefits. Through mentoring, experienced lawyers recognize and appreciate their own accomplishments and just how far they have come in their careers. Mentors may experience a renewed sense of purpose and enhance their personal satisfaction with the practice of law. Through mentoring, an attorney honors the mentors who have helped him along the way, while fulfilling the obligation of all lawyers to give back to the profession.

For the mentor, the experience often has the effect of enhancing one's own professionalism. A more senior lawyer trying to teach best practices to a protégé may realize that she needs to improve some aspects of her own professional conduct. As Dan Vinovich, president of the Indiana State Bar Association, said of his association's mentoring program, "[i]t really brings out the best in the mentors. When you have the responsibility of teaching a new lawyer, you put your best foot forward." Paul Haskins, *Award-Winning Bar Professionalism Programs Offer Templates for Success*, BAR LEADER, Jan-Feb 2013, *available at* http://www.americanbar.org/publications/bar_leader/2012_13/january_february.html. Mentoring is also a wonderful way to leave a legacy, as a mentor passes along parts of his approach to the practice to others, and sees them succeed. Lawyers may mentor others in the profession who are at similar stages of professional growth, as different people have varying strengths that others can learn from. Good mentors also know when to introduce their protégés to additional mentors, thus expanding the mentor's circle of influence.

XVI. Benefits to Mentors

In the best of relationships, mentoring is a two-way street. Mentors may learn from the protégé. If a protégé is appreciably younger or from a different ethnic group, the experience broadens the mentor's knowledge of how different people think and act, helping the mentor prepare for changes in the profession that a new generation and an increasingly diverse lawyer population are sure to introduce.

For the more senior lawyer, mentoring is the professional thing to do. The word "professional" is derived from the ancient practice of advocates and physicians going to the town square to "profess" (from the Latin "professus") that the needs of the people assembled there would come before their own interests. The concept of professionalism thus rests upon principles of selfless service to others. Attorneys who mentor invest their personal time and resources in serving something greater than themselves: the efficient and fair administration of justice. Whether by showing a protégé how to interact with court staff, how to defuse the impact of a dysfunctional opposing counsel, or by helping a new lawyer deeply reflect on her role in society, a mentor embodies and preserves the legal profession's profound commitment to the greater good.

XVII. Conclusion

Access to mentors and constructive mentoring relationships is essential to new lawyers' professional development, even more so in an era when many of those entering the profession are "on their own" in terms of practice setting and the organized bar as a whole is perhaps less paternalistic and nurturing in its attitude toward new bar admittees than in times past. To find and get the full benefit of mentoring, law students and new lawyers should proactively seek out mentors and strive to build the mentoring relationship strategically and constructively—ever mindful of how to make the best use of the senior lawyer's time, as well as one's own. Those who wish to make the most of a mentoring relationship should take advantage of new program resources such as the National Legal Mentoring Consortium.

For the established lawyer, becoming a mentor is not only the right thing to do, and badly needed by the profession—a shortage of willing lawyer mentors persists across the country—it also can serve as a journey of renewal and self-discovery that helps many lawyers recommit to those professional values that attracted them to the law in the first instance, while helping young lawyers find their way.

Go ahead—join the virtuous circle of mentoring.

LORI L. KEATING is Secretary to the Supreme Court of Ohio Commission on Professionalism and Chair of the National Legal Mentoring Consortium. Ms. Keating oversees the Supreme Court of Ohio Lawyer to Lawyer Mentoring Program.
MICHAEL P. MASLANKA is the Office Head of the Dallas office of Constangy Brooks & Smith, a national labor and employment firm. Mr. Maslanka is the author of "Maslanka's Pocket Guide to Employment Law" (American Lawyer Media 2013), and he writes a blog on employment law, http://www.texaslawyer.typepad.com/work matters.

Chapter 14

HANDLING MONEY

MARTHA MIDDLETON

I. Introduction

Any discussion of lawyers and money should prominently acknowledge the special responsibilities all lawyers assume with respect to the handling of money—their clients', their own, and that of any others whom they serve as fiduciaries. (In this chapter, the words "client money" and like terms will refer to the resources of both clients and others whom the lawyer serves as a fiduciary.) With few exceptions, the goal of a professionally satisfying and materially comfortable life will only be realized by those who make a point of mastering, early on, the rules related to money and then observing those rules each day. Those who learn and execute fiscal responsibility in their lives and practices will benefit by minimizing the sort of oppressive financial stress that can darken one's days and by avoiding the kind of ethical trouble that could derail a career.

On the other hand, those who violate the first commandment of lawyer money-handling—Leave Client Money Alone—will invite serious professional travail that no amount of good intentions, good history, and mitigating circumstances can stave off. As discussed below, that this presumptively inviolate ethical rule is so often violated speaks not only to a stunningly widespread lack of awareness of, or respect for, the duty to keep your hands off client funds, but also to the reality that even otherwise highly principled lawyers will break rules if their financial needs become acute. Problems such as substance abuse, a gambling habit, or a mental health crisis also can compromise a lawyer's good judgment.

Some lawyers, clinging to a moral thread, rationalize that certain clients do not need their funds or would not miss them if the lawyer was to "borrow" from a client account for a time. And the more naive among new lawyers—those whose parents bailed them out of every past financial misstep, for example—may assume that licensing and disciplinary boards will be equally as forgiving should the lawyers fail to handle their own finances wisely or go astray by mishandling or stealing client funds. They should be disabused of such notions as quickly as possible. In the eyes of disciplinary boards, dipping into client funds is the unforgivable sin, never to be ignored or glossed over.

The remainder of this chapter will survey ethics principles and rules pertaining to lawyers' handling of money, explore why and how too many lawyers get derailed in handling finances in their practices, look at factors informing bar-admission decisions on the financial fitness of applicants, and highlight the special danger of financial misconduct posed by substance abuse, gambling problems, and mental health issues.

This book is about professionalism, not business management, and accordingly this chapter does not presume to advise on best business practices for law firms. But the end of the chapter will highlight resources and courses for lawyers, particularly the growing number of new sole practitioners, on law firm management, including some related to financial management.

II. First Principles of Lawyer Financial Responsibility: Rules and Concepts

Every lawyer starting out in practice should already know the ethical rules governing handling client money. And every new lawyer already handling client funds would do well to master those rules, as insurance against financial misconduct. Under the ABA Model Rules of Professional Conduct, specifically Rule 1.15, entitled "Safekeeping Property," lawyers have a duty to keep all money and property entrusted to them safe and separate. The Rule states in pertinent part:

> A lawyer shall hold property of clients or third persons that is in a lawyer's possession in connection with a representation separate from the lawyer's own property. Funds shall be kept in a separate account maintained in the state where the lawyer's office is situated, or elsewhere with the consent of the client or third person. Other property shall be identified as such and appropriately safeguarded. Complete records of such account funds and other property shall be kept by the lawyer and shall be preserved for a period of [five years] after termination of the representation.

The controlling rule thus plainly leaves no leeway or doubt as to a lawyer's duty to segregate in separate accounts funds held on a client's behalf, and to segregate, safeguard, and label any other client property.

In 2010, the ABA adopted the black letter Model Rules for Client Trust Account Records, replacing the previous Model Rule on Financial Record-keeping, to address issues arising from technological advances in the banking industry, particularly its conversion to electronic imaging of checks and electronic fund transfers. These Rules offer lawyers more specific guidelines to ensure that their client trust accounts in banks comply with the "[c]omplete records" requirement of Rule 1.15, especially because today's banking practices often leave lawyers with no paper trail to their transactions.

As the ethics rules spell out, when lawyers receive funds from or for clients or third persons, including prospective clients, they must deposit them into trust accounts, usually a checking or savings account in a financial institution. Lawyers must tell their clients or third parties when funds are received, must provide a full accounting to clients or third persons of their property, and must timely pay out to clients any funds obtained on their behalf.

Handling Client Money by the Book

Under no circumstances may lawyers use any money belonging to a client or third person for business or office expenses or for personal expenses or personal purposes. They cannot take funds from a client trust account to pay their mortgage or the office rent even if they plan (or say they plan) to return it with interest. To cover expenses such as rent, salaries, utility bills, and other overhead items, lawyers must set up and maintain separate office operating accounts.

The Model Rules allow non-lawyer employees under the supervision of a lawyer to authorize transactions on a client trust account, but lawyers are advised to limit employee access and monitor all transactions. If a lawyer grants authorization privileges to nonlawyer employees, the lawyer remains personally and professionally liable for all transactions.

In what are called Interest on Lawyers' Trust Accounts (IOLTA) programs, lawyers and law firms turn over interest from client trust accounts to a public fund that provides legal services for low-income clients. Every state, along with the District of Columbia and the Virgin Islands, operates an IOLTA program.

There can be one IOLTA account into which the funds of all clients or third parties are deposited, although a lawyer may want to set up individual trust accounts for clients whose cases involve large amounts of money. Examples of funds that generally go into a trust account are: escrow funds, client advances for fees until they are actually earned by the lawyer, fees belonging in part to the client and in part to the lawyer, court costs collected from the client, fines collected from the client, real estate conveyance funds, settlement proceeds or awards held for disbursement, and any amounts held in dispute.

When deposits and withdrawals are made from trust accounts, a lawyer must keep careful records and identify the client for which a particular deposit or withdrawal has been made. Records generally must be maintained for five years from the date a client matter is closed.

The most important thing that a lawyer needs to do is read the relevant rules of the jurisdiction in which he or she is licensed and follow its rules to set up and manage the trust account.

Misappropriation, a concept encompassing the different ways a lawyer mishandles client funds or property, is an egregious violation of a lawyer's fiduciary duty. *Black's Law Dictionary* defines misappropriation as "[t]he unauthorized, improper, or unlawful use of funds or other property for purposes other than that for which intended . . . including not only stealing but also unauthorized temporary use for lawyer's own purpose, whether or not he derives any personal gain or benefit therefrom." A lawyer generally will be found to have misappropriated when he or she *intentionally deprives* a client of money by deceit or fraud. Where dishonest intent is established, such a finding will presumptively invoke the harshest disciplinary sanction, disbarment, in almost all cases.

In some jurisdictions, disbarment is a virtually automatic sanction where a dishonest intent to deprive is established. In others, only significant mitigating factors, such as proof of rehabilitation from a substance abuse habit, may reduce the sanction's severity.

It should be noted that a finding of dishonest intent is not necessary to establish a charge of misappropriation. A lawyer who is a sloppy bookkeeper may be found to have misappropriated client funds by failing to conscientiously segregate client accounts, as required. The lawyer's intent comes into play at the time the disciplinary agency considers appropriate sanctions.

Misappropriation includes "conversion," a term commonly defined as a lawyer's making use of the funds of his or her client. *See, e.g.,* 7 Am. Jur. 2d, *Attorneys at Law* § 66 (1997). Conversion occurs when a lawyer uses client or third-party funds permanently or for an indefinite time for a purpose other than that for which they were intended, without the party's consent. Typically, the lawyer is converting funds for his or her own use or for the law firm's use. Examples are paying one client out of money due another, taking an unearned advance fee, keeping unused escrow funds, or applying client funds to the client's bill without permission. In many jurisdictions, conversion of a client's funds, like misappropriation, is grounds for disbarment.

Commingling takes place when client funds are combined with personal funds, that is, when a lawyer deposits his or her personal funds into a client trust account or vice versa. Although commingling is considered a less serious violation than conversion and misappropriation—and sometimes does not even harm a client—the practice still is strictly prohibited.

III. Contingent Fees

Another financial aspect of legal practice that can be ethically challenging is handling of contingent fees. In such arrangements, made between lawyer and client, the client pays a fee only when a case has a successful judgment or settlement. If there is no recovery, the lawyer receives nothing. Under Model Rule 1.5(c), such arrangements must be in writing, signed by the client, and explain the method by which the fee is to be determined, including the percentage or percentages a lawyer will collect in the event of settlement, trial, or appeal. (Many states have adopted permissible maximum fees as a percentage of recovery and other contingent fee and legal cost recovery rules.)

A common ethical breach involving contingent fee arrangements arises when a lawyer turns down an adequate settlement in the hope that it will grow larger as negotiations continue, thereby increasing the lawyer's percentage-based fee. The risk is that giving up the "bird in the hand" could result in no settlement, no subsequent success at trial, and ultimately no recovery whatsoever for the client. To avoid such outcomes, the Model Rules instruct that a lawyer has a duty to always act in the client's best interest, communicate all settlement offers to the client, and abide by the client's decision on whether to accept a settlement offer. It follows that the lawyer should closely and conscientiously examine his or her own motives before advising a client whether to accept or reject a settlement offer.

IV. Forbidden Fruit: Why Some Lawyers Just Can't Leave it Alone

The seriousness of a lawyer's solemn duty to protect client funds is only underscored by the stark historical inability of so many lawyers to honor that duty. You'd think it would be easy but, time and again, some lawyers—even those who entered law school and practice with honorable motives—prove that it isn't. Commingling, conversion, and misappropriation of client money have spawned hundreds of disciplinary cases, many of them the result of greed, irresponsibility, financial struggles, or even of illness. Setting aside knowing wrongdoing, some lawyers lapse into improper fiscal practices due to ignorance, sloppiness, or just inattentiveness. The fact is, people have trouble handling money, and lawyers, as part of the general population, are no exception.

It should be clear that one's standing as a respected legal professional can be placed at risk by a poor financial profile. Even a lawyer's handling of his or her personal checking account is fair game; a lawyer can be disciplined for knowingly issuing non-sufficient-funds checks, for example. And falling behind on such financial obligations as personal credit card debt and mortgage payments or, if running an office, payroll, taxes, and insurance premiums, can trigger a debt cycle only compounded by low credit ratings that lead to unfavorable future credit terms and more debt. That cycle may end badly for a lawyer even when client funds are untouched. Lawyers have a right to avail themselves of all legal relief within the law, such as bankruptcy, but they must be scrupulously honest when doing so.

Some disciplinary bodies and courts, in fact, have imposed discipline on the basis of a nexus between how lawyers handle *their own* finances and the likelihood they will cause harm to clients if allowed to continue practicing. In *Santulli v. Texas Board of Law Examiners*, 2009 WL 961568 (Tex. App. 2009), for example, a Texas court revoked a lawyer's probationary license after he failed to comply with orders that he make suitable arrangements to pay or discharge a substantial amount of student loan and personal debt. The court established a clear and rational connection between the lawyer's financial irresponsibility and the substantial possibility of harm to future clients or the obstruction of justice.

Bar disciplinary authorities and courts reserve the heaviest hammer for those lawyers who abuse client funds, in some states even when a lawyer can point to highly sympathetic facts underlying the misappropriation. In *In re Warhaftig*, 524 A.2d 398 (N.J. 1987), for example, the Supreme Court of New Jersey disbarred a lawyer who took money from clients because of a "gigantic cash flow burden" arising from his wife's treatment for cancer and his son's need for psychiatric treatment, despite no clients suffering any losses. The lawyer had told the ethics committee that, while he believed taking the money was wrong, he was so certain that no one could be hurt "that I didn't feel that I was stealing, certainly not stealing." The court disagreed, concluding that the lawyer's conduct constituted knowing misappropriation. It should be noted that New Jersey is among the states least tolerant of lawyers' dipping into client funds—in any circumstance. The New Jersey rule mandates disbarment for knowing misappropriation of client funds.

Failing to properly handle client funds obviously can have criminal as well as disciplinary consequences. In 2012, a former lawyer with the law firm Crowell & Moring received a four-to-twelve-year prison sentence for stealing more than $10 million from two corporate clients' escrow funds and putting them into bank accounts he controlled. He subsequently was disbarred. *In re Arntsen*, 2013 WL 1110510 (N.Y. App. Div. Mar. 19, 2013). There are hundreds of other examples of cases in which lawyers have experienced similar fates for theft of client funds.

The risk of financial misconduct or mismanagement by lawyers may be exacerbated by the fact that many enter the profession with little or no education or training in business or financial management; some find money management challenging or prefer not to deal with it. But where client funds, contingent fees, and other financial matters covered by the disciplinary rules are concerned, applying sound judgment and practices is not discretionary, irrespective of the lawyer's aptitude or appetite for business management. Absent application of good judgment, even high-earning lawyers can slip into financial misfeasance, or worse.

V. Financial Fitness as a Pre-Requisite for Bar Admission

Today's reality is that many law graduates carry significant student debt that can be paid down over a course of years. It should be emphasized that the mere presence of debt, even substantial student debt, should not be a barrier to bar admissions.

To be sure, financial fitness is a standard element of character and fitness reviews in the course of the bar admission process. (*See supra* Chapter 11, p. 141.) Bar examiners focus not on the presence of debt, but on signs that the applicant is handling credit and debt responsibly and has at least a good-faith plan for retiring personal debt. Those applicants whose records are rife with financial irregularities or evidence of persistent, uncured irresponsibility—what a number of states' bar character and fitness requirements refer to as "a significant deficiency in the honesty, trustworthiness, diligence, or reliability of an applicant"—may face denial of admission to practice even when they have passed the bar exam. Bear in mind, though, that most boards of bar examiners are open to sincere persuasion that past bad habits have been remedied. (*See supra* Chapter 11.)

In one extreme and still rare case, a law school graduate's application to the bar was disapproved because of the large debt load he was carrying. In this closely watched case, *In re Griffin*, 943 N.E.2d 1008 (Ohio 2011), the Supreme Court of Ohio said that the applicant, a graduate of Ohio State University Moritz College of Law, failed to prove he possessed the requisite character, fitness, and moral qualifications for admission to practice because he did not have a feasible plan to take care of his financial obligations, which included nearly $170,000 in student loans and approximately $16,500 in credit card debt. The court concluded that the applicant had neglected his personal financial obligations when, rather than seek full-time employment after law school, he elected to maintain his $12-an-hour part-time position with a county public defender in the hope that it would lead to a legal position at the agency when he passed the bar exam.

It should be emphasized that in the body of bar admission decisional law, the *Griffin* case remains somewhat anomalous, particularly to the extent that the court held that the applicant's failure to pursue a full-time job temporarily precluded his admission to the bar. Still, for applicants anywhere, *Griffin* serves to underscore the importance of being prepared to demonstrate not the absence of debt, but a sound plan to deal with it.

The universal rule to date has been that an applicant's debt, even substantial debt, by itself will not stand in the way of bar admission. But bar examiners require that an applicant show he or she is prepared to deal with debt responsibly. Bankruptcy as a means of eliminating student debt is not a realistic (or responsible) option under federal law. Under section 523(a)(8) of the United States Bankruptcy Code, student loan debt is dischargeable only when the continued obligation to repay will impose an "undue hardship" on the debtor and his or her dependents. Finding such "undue hardship" has been exceptionally difficult to prove under two widely-established tests courts have used in recent years.

In one recently reported case, however, a bankruptcy court judge did rule that a couple's student loans were dischargeable in bankruptcy. In *In re Ackley*, 463 B.R. 146 (Me. 2011), two Chapter 7 debtors, ages sixty and fifty-eight, sought a determination that they were entitled to "undue hardship" discharge of more than $450,000 in student loan debt. After weighing the debtors' past, present, and future financial resources, their reasonable necessary living expenses, and other relevant facts and circumstances, particularly their age and current health issues, the judge said that paying their educational loans posed an undue hardship on them.

VI. Substance Abuse, Gambling, Depression

As any regulation counsel could tell you, lawyers with serious substance abuse, gambling problems, and mental health issues are well represented among those sanctioned for abuse of client funds. The combination of financial desperation and poor judgment may cause the addicted or afflicted to ignore those ethical, moral, and legal stop signs that keep most of us in line. The ABA has estimated that as many as one in five lawyers is a problem drinker—twice the national rate. Substance abuse is a factor in 40 to 60 percent of the country's lawyer discipline cases, according to the ABA; other sources estimate the figure to be even higher—up to 70 percent.

Courts differ in how they discipline lawyers suffering from alcoholism, substance abuse and gambling addictions—some are exacting and mete out serious sanctions while others are more accepting and consider such conditions in mitigation, if there is evidence of rehabilitation. A lawyer with an "uncontrollable gambling habit" whose misconduct included misappropriating client funds was disbarred by the high courts of Iowa and Nebraska. The Nebraska high court, quoting the Iowa court, noted that "[u]nfortunately, [respondent's gambling] is a matter which, although regrettable and cause for sympathy, does not obviate the seriousness of the improper attorney conduct that has occurred." *State ex rel. Counsel for Dis. v. Reilly*, 712 N.W.2d 278 (Neb. 2006) (quoting *Iowa Supreme Court. Atty. Disc. Bd. v. Reilly*, 708 N.W.2d 82, 85 (Iowa 2006)). In contrast, the court in *In re Brown*, 912 A.2d 568 (D.C. 2006), stayed the disbarment of an alcoholic lawyer for misconduct that included misappropriation of client funds. Instead, he was placed on probation for three years "because [the lawyer's] alcohol addiction was the substantial cause of the misconduct and because he is substantially rehabilitated."

In the realm of mental health, it's no secret that lawyers disproportionately suffer from depression and other mental health problems. Commentators have reported that depression is four times more likely for lawyers than for other professional groups in the United States. (See, for example, Connie J.A. Beck, Bruce D. Sales & C. Andrew H. Benjamin, *Lawyer Distress: Alcohol-Related Problems and Other Psychological Concerns Among a Sample of Practicing Lawyers*, 10 J.L. & Health 1 (1996).) Such a propensity has led some courts to take a serious look at that disability as a mitigating factor in sanctioning lawyers for misappropriation. In *In re Mooers*, 910 A.2d 1046 (D.C. 2006), the court disbarred a lawyer whose use of client funds for personal and business expenses was attributed to his depression, but then stayed that disbarment and imposed a three-year probation. The court said the lawyer had candidly admitted and taken full responsibility for his actions and that he was continuing to obtain treatment for his depression, which was significantly improved and did not impair his ability to practice law. The reduced punishment was conditioned on satisfactory reports every ninety days from the lawyer's psychiatrist.

The very good news for lawyers, judges, and even law students suffering from addictions or mental and emotional health issues is that today there is concrete and sustainable help for them, literally a phone call away, at hundreds of state and local bar associations and lawyer assistance programs. On a national level, the ABA Commission on Lawyer Assistance Programs serves as a clearinghouse for educating the profession about such problems and supports the bars and assistance programs in developing and maintaining methods to provide effective recovery. And there are many, many success stories. In *In re Whitworth*, 261 P.3d 1173 (Okla. 2011), for example, a lawyer who had been suspended for misconduct arising out of his addiction to methamphetamine and alcohol was reinstated by the state's high court after he became sober and drug-free. After addiction had destroyed his professional and personal life, the lawyer credited his original disciplinary hearing "[f]or the genesis of my walk through sobriety." (*See infra* Chapter 17, *Health and Wellness,* by Frederic S. Ury & Deborah Garskof, at p. 219.)

Money Management Resources for Solos and Young Lawyers

Money takes on a different dimension for that growing percentage of new lawyers hanging out shingles in solo or small practices. Most young lawyers starting their own firms or a small firm initially have no idea how to go about setting up or managing a firm as a business. In addition to ethics-implicating requirements such as proper accounting for client and third-party funds, self-employed lawyers must think about such matters as liability and health insurance, incorporation and taxes, and employee compensation and benefits.

There are numerous resources for lawyers in solo and small practices, including the ABA's Law Practice Management Section. The section supports new bar admittees in small or solo firms by helping them gain experience and develop skills focusing on such core areas as management, finance, and technology.

Several years ago, the District of Columbia Bar launched a program for solo or small-firm lawyers, especially those newly thrust into such positions due to the recessionary economy. The bar's two-day Basic Training covers such areas as business plans, client selection and issues, employees, and fees and agreements. It also teaches solo and small-firm practitioners about office operations, including file creation and intake. As of December 2012, the program had served nearly 1,600 lawyers.

Law schools increasingly are establishing so-called solo or small practice incubators, which assume a variety of forms but commonly help recent graduates set up and run their practices. Several offer office space in their libraries either free or for rent at low prices, provide technological resources and research materials, and pair new lawyers with seasoned mentors. IIT Chicago-Kent College of Law began a program in 2012 offering such resources, while in return requiring participants to complete just 10 hours of legal work weekly for the school's law clinic. A program at City University of New York School of Law, Community Legal Resource Network, offers the Incubator for Justice in Manhattan project that trains young lawyers in basic business issues such as billing, record-keeping, technology, bookkeeping, and taxes while helping serve the disadvantaged in communities that are underserved by lawyers.

Many law schools now also have begun to offer such "practical" courses to their students, including financial planning to teach them to exist on a budget in school and to set one up as they enter the legal profession. In early 2013, the University of Pennsylvania Law School announced that it was launching a partnership with the business school—The Wharton School—in the form of a management program for law students. Upper-class law students were to have the option to take a semester-long course at Wharton that is specifically designed for them, covering such issues as finance and accounting literacy, leadership and organization design, strategic decision-making and competitive advantage. Those who completed the course were to receive a Wharton Certificate in Management. New York University School of Law has also pursued ways to help its students gain a foothold on their executive and management skills. According to its Strategy Committee, as of 2013 the law school was introducing a module on business and financial literacy in its first-year curriculum. It also planned a course introducing law students to basic concepts in business, statistics, accounting and quantitative analysis.

VIII. Conclusion

Law students and young lawyers would do well both to know the rules on safekeeping client property and to learn from the mistakes of other lawyers, many of whom no doubt viewed themselves as highly principled people before lapsing into misappropriation of client funds. In many instances, the records show, financial misconduct is a function of financial desperation, substance abuse, or illness.

In their personal lives, aspiring and new lawyers should be vigilant about finances. They should also know that the mere existence of substantial personal debt, particularly student loan obligations, almost certainly will not impair their prospects for admission to the bar or lead to lawyer discipline, provided they can articulate a good-faith plan for addressing that debt over time.

MARTHA MIDDLETON is a legal researcher and writer who has reported for the *American Bar Association Journal* and *The National Law Journal*. Ms. Middleton is a graduate of DePaul University College of Law in Chicago.

Chapter 15

*e*PROFESSIONALISM

STEPHANIE L. KIMBRO

I. Overview

In their personal lives, lawyers are engaging in more online social networking activities than ever before. Many are adapting skills learned through interacting with friends and family online to create a web presence. As of 2012, virtually half (49.1 percent) of all lawyers responding to an ABA Legal Technology Resources Center survey were with law firms with a presence on LinkedIn. The firms of nearly a third (30.3 percent) of those lawyer-respondents had a Facebook presence, and only 29 percent of responding lawyers had no presence whatsoever on social networks, either personally or via a law firm.

Some lawyers have turned to the Internet for client and business development, and even more are now using it as a networking tool for engaging with other professionals and building a potential online referral network. Still, most of the lawyers engaging in social media today are doing so as individuals, rather than as a firm. They may find a personal presence more effective and engaging, but preservation of one's professional identity on a personal web page requires the lawyer to carefully balance, and keep separate, the personal and the professional.

The legal profession's headlong dive into social media mimics the trend within the larger public, but unlike the average user, lawyers must take care to conform their online conduct to professional standards and ethical duties. At a time of accelerating change in online culture and capabilities, it is an ongoing struggle for the legal profession to preserve and adapt professional ideals and ethics to the world of Twitter and Facebook.

*e*Professionalism is the term we will use in this chapter to characterize the application of concepts of lawyer professionalism to a lawyer's Internet activities. Other chapters in this book examine different dimensions of lawyer professionalism in practice. This chapter will examine the difference between public and private communications online while providing guidance for a lawyer's online behavior, from a lawyer professionalism and ethics perspective. Different platforms and methods of engaging online will be reviewed, as well as best practices for maintaining *e*professionalism and developing appropriate lawyer "netiquette."

Although *e*professionalism does require a lawyer to be ever conscious of his or her professional identity while online and to draw appropriate boundaries between a professional and personal web presence, it does not require that a lawyer cease to be an engaged friend or family member. The point of social media is to share and to bring the human element into online interactions. It facilitates online conversation and builds trust and relationships. But *e*professionalism does require that the lawyer (1) educate herself regarding the most effective and safe privacy and security settings to protect her profile, (2) monitor her profile on a regular basis by setting up notifications and regularly checking the profile as an administrative function of the practice, and (3) show restraint regarding the posting of personal information that may cross the line and be seen as inappropriate within the larger professional community.

Among the applications used by lawyers as part of their online engagement are LinkedIn, Facebook, Twitter, and Google+. These models represent distinct platforms, each raising its own unique security, privacy, and confidentiality considerations. Many of the companies behind these free applications, with the exception of LinkedIn, initially developed them for use by the general public, rather than for professionals or business use.

The content generated by users of these platforms enables the companies to thrive financially. It follows that the platforms' usage rules are designed to maximize sharing and interaction among users. But the confidentiality, security, privacy, and similar concerns of lawyers registering on these platforms are very much secondary considerations for companies focused on ramping up the user base and resultant revenues. With that in mind, lawyers using social media should take particular care to understand the terms of use and policies of the companies and to maintain best practices of professionalism in the largely uncharted social territory.

As a lawyer increasingly uses online communications methods, it can become more difficult to separate personal use from professional use. A lawyer's ability to conduct himself professionally online will be a function of both his familiarity with the particular platforms and his comfort level with and knowledge of the underlying technology.

Many people know how to use common features of Facebook but may lack a deep appreciation of a technology that, for example, can preserve and spread photos and other personal data across the Internet for an indefinite period, absent adequate front-end controls.

Most law students have family members who are "friends" on Facebook, and they may have a Twitter account or post Instagram pictures of their travels to share with their closest friends. What happens when those law students pass the bar and must comport themselves as "professionals" in the public eye? Do they have to change the way they approach social media? Is it too late to suppress existing online content that does not reflect a professional image or professional values? Should law students consider such concerns long before they take the bar exam, and conduct themselves accordingly online? It would be difficult and some might argue detrimental to suddenly drop all online, personal communication with friends and family upon entering law school or passing the bar exam. But law students should be thinking about where and when to draw the line between the personal and the professional on social media. Moreover, while new law students and lawyers can change their approach to using social media, it may not be as simple to create change in how their "friends" and other online contacts interact with them so as to ensure an aura of professionalism.

Given the difficulty and unnaturalness of separating the professional from the personal in the use of social media applications, why should lawyers bother to engage online at all? It is not within the scope of this chapter to examine all of the benefits of online engagement with the public or describe the growing impact of ecommerce on societal behaviors.

The chapter will, however, accept and proceed from the premise that those lawyers who do not learn how to use social media effectively in their practices, particularly those not in large law firms, may struggle professionally given pervasive, technology-driven change in the legal marketplace. (See, for example, the descriptions of the evolving legal marketplace in RICHARD SUSSKIND, END OF LAWYERS? RETHINKING THE NATURE OF LEGAL SERVICES. (2010).) The public today searches online for legal assistance. Consumers use various online resources to rate and review lawyers. Recent investment in the growth of online legal service companies, such as Rocket Lawyer and LegalZoom, serve as evidence that the public is looking online for information about and delivery of legal services—particularly in certain areas of practice.

Those lawyers who have not developed an online presence will be largely invisible to the majority of their potential client base. Even lawyers who do not like to engage in more aggressive (but ethically permissible) forms of lawyer advertising should come to understand that traditional methods of marketing are no longer the most effective avenues of client development. Engaging online is a smart business decision, and as with any business decision a lawyer makes, it must comply with the rules of professional conduct as well as standards of professionalism.

But what does professionalism look like online? Failing to understand how traditional notions of professionalism transfer to online engagement may pose risks for the lawyer, not only from her own online activity but from that of clients, potential and prospective clients, and other professionals who may reach out to or mention the lawyer or law firm online through a website, forum, blog, tweet, post, or other digital method. Lawyers at every stage of their careers must learn how to behave as professionals when engaging online, or risk potentially serious consequences.

II. Private Versus Public Communications

The first step in analyzing the professionalism of online conduct is identifying the intended audience for the communication. The second step
is deciding whether, in the context of that communication, a particular
platform is an appropriate conduit for the message. If a lawyer is not
familiar with how a certain online platform works, "lurking" might be the
appropriate starting point for understanding how he or she will engage
professionally online. "Lurking," or joining an online community and
watching the engagements of others for a few months without actively
participating, can help lawyers grasp the "culture" of the network and
how others communicate using it.

A good first step for lawyers devising a system to professionally manage their online messaging is knowing when it is appropriate to expose a
given communication to public access, without restriction, versus when
a communication must be or should be private in nature. As a general
proposition, subject to many variables of course, a lawyer's communications are more likely to yield unwanted results—such as a perception of
inappropriateness, or even potential malpractice exposure—if they are
public and therefore visible to anyone with Internet access. Public exposure of a communication can be controlled to a degree if limited to a few
hours duration online, rather than in the form of a permanent public post.

Public communications would include anything posted on a social
media platform or other social networking application where the public
is able to register to create an account. Private communications would
include email, text messaging, private group posting, or any communication where the lawyer is able to limit the transmission of the message
to a specific individual or group of individuals.

To illustrate how a lawyer might conduct himself online, using public
forms of communication, let's look at several of the most popular social
media platforms: LinkedIn, Facebook and Twitter, as well as blogging.
Lawyers should be aware of and conform to the unique culture and community that each application inhabits before creating an online profile to
engage publicly within these online communities.

III. Blogging

Lawyers may blog to communicate online either for their law firms or their personal use. They may also be guest authors for the blogs of other lawyers or law-related organizations or companies. Blogging can create valuable content related to the lawyer's practice area. A blog's target audience may be legal professionals with shared interests, or the lawyer's existing and target client base. The content produced on a blog is typically shared through other social media platforms, such as those discussed below.

Because the majority of the content shared through different forms of social media engagement lead back to the content of the lawyer's original post, sound *e*professional conduct for the blogging lawyer should begin with close attention to the writing, content quality, and accuracy of the original post. Notwithstanding that law bloggers all hope to establish a unique voice and style, a serious blogger's posts will be written in a manner that conveys to the readers that the author is an educated professional. With respect to a law firm blog, the firm should develop a strategy and guidelines for how it will produce and manage the content of its blog to ensure that it is tailored to the intended audience and stays professional in tone. This strategy must also address the treatment of comments added on posts by readers. It reflects badly upon the firm to allow unprofessional comments from others to appear on its site. Only screened and approved comments should appear on the firm's blog page. Individual lawyers who maintain a blog may wish to pre-approve comments submitted by specific individuals or engage openly with readers in the comments section by closely monitoring and promptly responding to activity.

A good rule of thumb for maintaining professionalism when blogging is to think twice about the appropriateness of the content before hitting the publish button. The same standard applies when lawyers publish posts, comments, or responses on the many online legal forums and question-and-answer sites available to the public seeking free online legal assistance. As a rule, if the content is something you would not want to say in public or see splashed across the front page of the Wall Street Journal, and attributed to you, then you should not publish it online.

Blog post topics should cover only general or basic legal information and avoid hypotheticals of real client situations. Disclaimers stating that the information on the blog is only intended to be general in nature, and that readers should consult a lawyer regarding specific personal situations, should be a highly visible fixture on any lawyer's blog. Different jurisdictions may have different rules on necessary and adequate elements of a lawyer's online disclaimers aimed at, among other things, avoiding inadvertent establishment of a client-attorney relationship.

A lawyer's personal profile on a blog should be factually accurate in every detail and should not exaggerate the lawyer's experience or qualifications. It would be wise to check any applicable disciplinary rules on advertising, in that jurisdiction, before posting a profile.

If the blog is a personal one that the lawyer writes on his or her own time, the lawyer presumably does not want that content shared with his or her professional social media contacts. But the lawyer should be aware that anything posted on a public blog has the potential to be found by a client or other party through keywords on a search engine. Even anonymous bloggers have been unmasked through the use of algorithms that search on the basis of writing styles and frequently used syntax of the author to discern the blog author's actual identity. If lawyers wish to have personal blogs that may contain information that would offend colleagues or clients, or not be appropriate for them to read, then the lawyer should consider creating a private blog or writing only within a private or closed community of friends or like-minded individuals. Doing so would permit the lawyer to maintain his or her interests outside of the profession with less risk of having any judgments about those interests extend into his or her professional life.

No matter how overextended lawyers may feel—or perhaps insecure about their own writing facility—they should be cautious about retaining the services of ghostwriters for their professional blogs. The task of maintaining a firm's blog and posting two or three times a week may seem daunting, but the downside of using a ghostwriter, especially one without any legal experience, might not bet worth it. If a lawyer does retain a ghostwriter, whether inside or outside the firm, to write posts under the lawyer's name, the lawyer should give specific, clear guidance before the post is composed, then meticulously review the product before publication.

IV. LinkedIn

Of all of the available social media applications, lawyers are generally most comfortable using LinkedIn because it focuses on professional networking, not the sharing of personal information with friends and family. Founded in 2003, LinkedIn had more than 100 million users ten years later. The 700,000 LinkedIn users in the legal sector comprise the fifth largest community on the network. Lawyers wishing to engage online create a LinkedIn profile that may include their resume, photo, information about the services they offer, and links to their law firm websites, blogs, or other online resources. Lawyers may list "skills and expertise" and receive recommendations from others. After setting up a LinkedIn profile, the lawyer then connects with others to create a list of contacts or "connections."

LinkedIn also hosts many groups under the legal profession umbrella. Many lawyers who join LinkedIn join groups in their practice area or other professional interest area. While the invitation or request to join a specific group might be made privately, the rest of the information a lawyer provides on his or her profile is visible to the general public. Lawyers may make "status updates" and have their most recent blog posts showcased on their profile pages.

Because LinkedIn is firmly focused on professional networking, the engagement of others on the network tends not to cross over into personal comments or areas outside of educational background and work experience. The platform does enable lawyers to comment on any contact's status updates and on posts within groups that the lawyer has joined.

Lawyers may also ask other professionals, colleagues, or former clients to provide professional recommendations of that lawyer that will appear on his or her LinkedIn profile. That practice can be problematic, however, as a number states have rules of professional conduct that limit the use of testimonials.

Lawyers may want to consider how their choice of hobbies or interests outside of the legal profession could be viewed by their colleagues, clients, and potential clients. There may be groups on LinkedIn whose very identity would be offensive to a segment of a lawyer's client base, such as certain political groups. When a lawyer joins such a group, the affiliation shows up on the lawyer's profile that he or she is a member. Even a loose association raises a potential for misunderstanding by someone viewing the lawyer's profile.

To manage and minimize such problems, a lawyer may use the application's privacy settings to specify those items in his or her profile that will be publicly visible. Such settings are a valuable tool for any lawyer who wants to join a group with minimal risk of offending people viewing his profile. Privacy settings are also helpful to shield activity that simply relates more to a lawyer's personal life than his professional life.

LinkedIn may be the easiest of the major social media platforms for lawyers, in terms of ability to assess whether conduct within that community is professional. Some examples of unprofessional behavior on LinkedIn might include:

1. Posting an inappropriate photo on the lawyer's profile page rather than the customary professional headshot as is customary.
2. Posting unprofessional comments on the status updates of others within a group community.
3. Setting up other social media accounts from Twitter or Facebook to cross-post into LinkedIn when the messages posted on those other accounts would not be appropriate for the lawyer's profile page on LinkedIn.

V. Facebook

Facebook was created for sharing personal, largely informal, information between friends and family. Business "fan" pages on Facebook are an option for lawyers and law firms wishing to tap into the 900 million-plus user base of the application as a form of marketing. User content delivered to Facebook through individual profile pages drives the value and use of this application. More personal information shared through the application is visible publicly than the typical Facebook user may suspect, even if she pays careful attention to the security and privacy settings of the user's profile. Moreover, Facebook and other social media applications have a tendency to change their privacy and default settings with little or no notice. For the lawyer with a social media presence, practicing *e*professionalism means keeping up with these changes and adjusting one's page accordingly.

It is also vital for a lawyer with a Facebook presence to ensure that her profile is accurate in all professional aspects and does not contain puffery. Here again, it is a good practice to review the jurisdiction's lawyer advertising rules before posting Facebook content regarding one's work.

Many lawyers opened their current personal Facebook accounts before they attended law school and passed the bar. The "timeline" feature of the application allows "friends" and, potentially, acquaintances of those contacts to view the activities and postings of the user going back a number of years. A viewer may also be able to see who the other friends of a particular user are. Users may be "tagged" in photos identifying them as being present in the posted photo and comments, and status updates may reference the profile of another user and post a duplicate of that post on his or her wall. Accordingly, if the lawyer is not aware of ways to limit others from interacting on his or her profile page or timeline, the lawyer may not realize that his profile page is linked to content she would prefer that clients or others not see—or at least not associate with the lawyer.

For example, if a lawyer has not set the default in the privacy settings so that he or she may not be tagged in a post without his or her permission, a former college buddy could post and tag an old photo of the lawyer from their college days showing the lawyer in an inappropriate situation, perhaps with a rude comment. If the lawyer is tagged, the photo and comment will appear on the lawyer's public profile page for anyone to see. While it is possible for the lawyer to monitor his or her timeline and remove posts that are not professional, any member of the public may have viewed an offending item before the lawyer could detect and remove it. The safer option would be for the lawyer to have the privacy settings in place to prevent anyone from tagging the lawyer in any posted photos without his or her permission. Additionally, a lawyer who has had an account for years before entering the profession may wish to go back and "hide" posts from the public profile that he or she would now deem inappropriate for a professional to show on a public profile.

Law students and lawyers with friends who frequently engage with them via Facebook may wish to send a group message to all their Facebook "friends" advising that any personal messages should be handled through other private online forms of communication—such as private Facebook messaging, chat or email—that will not become public knowledge. Facebook also allows the creation of private groups. Law students and lawyers wanting to maintain friendships with groups of individuals who may wish to discuss and post items that could be seen as unprofessional may wish to create a private group and invite those friends to communicate with each other that way.

Lawyers posting on their personal Facebook pages should be careful not to disclose client confidences or say anything that could be considered advertising of their services or soliciting business. That kind of communication should be done through law firm business pages, where the lawyer should dbe sure to comply with all rules of professional conduct in the set-up and maintenance of the page. Even on a firm web page, the lawyer must make sure that the posted content does not reveal information related to client matters without permission of the client and is related only to legal services the firm offers,,firm news, or general information.

VI. Twitter

Maintaining *e*professionalism on Twitter can be very challenging because of the more rapid and impersonal nature of the platform's culture. Not only must the communication be appropriate, it also must stay within a 140-character limitation. It is easy for comments on Twitter to be taken in the wrong context or misunderstood as a result of the content limit. There are a number of other drawbacks to clear, comprehensible, and responsible communication on Twitter, among them: (1) the message size is too small for a meaningful disclaimer, and links to disclaimers may be ignored; (2) elements of a conversation may not appear in a viewer's public Twitter Stream in chronological order, giving the impression of a disjointed, hard-to-follow dialogue; (3) the absence of friend and group features on Twitter may pose risks for the lawyer user, because anyone may send a message to the account holder using the account holder's handle; (4) it is difficult to formulate a meaningful bio for the Twitter profile, and given a bio size limitation of 160 characters, the bio size restraint discourages use of prudent disclaimers; and (5) there are privacy options on Twitter, but they are minimal: a user can designate her account as private, meaning only authorized followers may view her tweets, and a lawyer user may block an individual, meaning that individual may not direct tweets to the lawyer's user handle or send them direct messages.

Tweets made by the lawyer are retained on his or her account profile page. The lawyer is also able to compose direct messages, to other followers on Twitter. These are sent via email and privately to each user's account.

A heightened risk of unprofessional lawyer behavior on Twitter arises when the lawyer responds to other tweets or posts comments that may represent inappropriate advertising and solicitation. Lawyers wishing to use Twitter for professional networking may want to focus on the following tweeting practices: (1) send out useful law-related blog posts or links to other articles related to the lawyer's practice area; (2) take care not to tweet inappropriate photos from a service like Instagram; (3) retweet comments only from other lawyers or professionals whom the lawyer trusts and knows; (4) follow only those individuals who the lawyer believes would not make inappropriate posts containing the lawyer's handle; (5) avoid engagement on Twitter with other individuals or lawyers who do not conduct themselves in a professional manner; (6) notify clients that communicating online via Twitter is not secure and could be a confidentiality risk; (7) get over strict adherence to grammar and spelling norms—because of the 140-character limitation, abbreviations are part of the culture on this platform; and (8) follow Twitter etiquette, such as crediting the source when retweeting statements and links, or using "HT" (hat tip), "MT" (modified tweet), or sending out "Thx" for retweets. It can also be worthwhile to engage in community trends, such as #followfriday or # for specific legal events.

VII. Email

Email is now the older form of digital communication, but one still preferred and used by most law firms and their clients. As more lawyers have become comfortable with text messaging and other abbreviated communication forms using acronyms and other expressions that are not part of the lawyer's traditional lexicon, a similar informality has made its way into emails. Originally, many externally directed emails were drafted in the same format as a traditional snail mail letter, with a formal heading, body of the communication, formal closing and then the law firm's disclaimer about the potential unsecure method of digital communications and unintended recipients. As firms depend on emails more for workflow as well as formal case-related communications with clients and opposing council, the standard business email format has evolved.

Maintaining professionalism in the use of email begins with a clear comprehension of the recipient or recipients, the professional standing or posture of the sender vis-à-vis the recipient(s), and the nature of what needs to be communicated. If an email is directed to a client to provide a status update on the client's case, the firm would want to use the traditional format. Many firms have a standard formal-email-format office policy. If the email is from one associate to another in the firm and it concerns the status of a deposition that afternoon, it does not require a heading or a closing. If the associates regularly work together and are aware of how each other works, it may be acceptable to use acronyms rather than complete sentences. If the associate is emailing a partner in the firm and knows the partner prefers the more traditional format, the associate will want to defer to the senior lawyer's concept of professionalism in the workplace and write the email with a more formal structure. As more "digital natives" enter the legal workplace, sensitivity to generation gaps in the use of technology and in how we communicate has emerged as a significant element of *e*professionalism. The need for such sensitivity applies to new and more seasoned lawyers when they are working together in a professional environment.

There are some instances when professionalism dictates that email or other forms of online communication would be inappropriate. For example, if the lawyer needs to communicate important news to the client, such as a loss or win in their case, the news is better conveyed through a phone call or in-person visit. The lawyer must make this determination on a case-by-case basis given the personality of his or her client and the nature of the message that needs to be conveyed.

Pretexting—Don't Go There

What if you want to create an anonymous profile to blog and post comments online?

The lawyer should assume that anonymity online does not exist. Always assume that information posted online 1) is public, 2) can be found in a search, 3) will be attributed to you, 4) will be discovered by the person you least want to see it, 5) has the potential to be recirculated across multiple online channels, and 6) will live forever in a digital format.

Pretexting is also not professional online behavior for a lawyer. Pretexting is the creation of an anonymous or fake user account and profile on an online platform for the purpose of "following," "friending," or otherwise connecting with another individual without his or her knowledge of the pretexter's identity. For example, some lawyers may attempt to use pretexting as a way to gain access to private social media account information that might be useful to them in a case. The pretexting lawyer may be concerned that the information would not become available during the discovery process or may be deleted by the user before the lawyer is able to review it for the case. All lawyers should know that pretexting in this manner is unprofessional, and a growing number of jurisdictions have issued ethics opinions that it is a violation of the lawyer's duty of professional conduct.

VIII. Video/Web Conferencing

As more lawyers work remotely, they are relying on video and web conferencing tools to supplement email and voice communication with clients and colleagues. Lawyers who practice in virtual law offices and do not meet with clients face-to-face may find the use of video conferencing necessary to ascertain the competency of a client and to authenticate the client's identity. Many lawyers are also working with virtual paralegals or assistants and using web conferencing to share their desktops remotely for purposes of training these employees on the use of practice management systems or to review and discuss client files in real time. From time to time, lawyers will also use these tools to negotiate and settle cases with opposing counsel.

In each situation, professionalism demands that the lawyer conduct himself as if he were meeting face-to-face with the individual on the other end of the video feed. That not only means appropriate attire and grooming for a meeting of that nature, but ensuring the absence of background noise or other potential distractions. For lawyers working from home, ensuring a distraction-free environment may be a challenge. The visual background for the video should also be professional, allowing the viewer to easily see the speaker without being distracted by clutter or poor lighting. A best practice for using video conferencing would be to use the application's preview video tool before commencing the communication to make sure the image projected will be professional.

IX. Online Marketing Tools

Lawyers must rethink concepts of professionalism as they pertain to new methods of online advertising, including the opportunity for lawyers to work with online marketing tools, such as online Q & A forums, directories, video or real-time chat, and other services delivered directly to consumers by nonlawyer, for-profit companies through various technology platforms. (For example, as of 2013, some of the companies featuring online marketing platforms for lawyers to connect and communicate with the public were: SmartLegalForms.com, LawZam, AttorneyFee.com, LawGives, Lexspot, EagleFee, Law99, LegalSonar, MyLegalBriefCase.com, LawDingo, UpCounsel, LegalForce (Trademarkia), LawGuru, Fizzlaw, LawQA, Pearl.com (formerly JustAnswer),Virtual Law Direct, Yodlelaw. com, LegalReach, Tabulaw, ExpertHub, LegalMatch, MyLawSuit, Jurify, AttorneyBoost, Wirelawyer, Findlaw, Nolo, Total Attorney's Legal Leads, Ravel, Judicata, LawPal, Avvo, Justia, JDSupra, Docracy, Shpoonkle, and ExpertBids.)

While lawyer rules of advertising are clear that false or misleading communications are violations of the rules of professional conduct, the rules do not dictate such subjective factors as taste and quality of the communication. There are different philosophies of marketing a lawyer's services, from more aggressive and direct methods to merely introductory and informative approaches. The method of advertising that the lawyer chooses should depend on the practice area, target client base for the message, and whether that method will appeal to the target audience. For example, personal injury lawyer advertising tends to be more aggressive given the typical immediacy of the prospective clients' legal needs. In contrast, advertising for estate planning practices may be less aggressive and more consistent over a longer period of time because prospective clients for those services are typically not pressed to seek out assistance and may have more time to research and consider their options.

Regardless of the form of online marketing chosen, lawyers should be aware that, just because the method is handled online, it is not different in terms of professional behavior. As the number of online marketing tools grows, lawyers will be instrumental in crafting the tone of professionalism and etiquette required to work with nonprofessionals serving the public online.

X. Conclusion

*e*Professionalism is something lawyers in all stages of their careers are learning to implement in their daily online interactions. Adherence to the following basic guidelines in the context of any online communication will help the lawyer maintain a strong online professional reputation:

1. When in doubt about posting something or how best to use a platform, find mentors, but don't limit it to a single mentor in a single generation. Get the advice of lawyers with years of professional experience and of younger lawyers who may have more experience with the online culture of the individual platforms. Combine the two.
2. Don't copy the behavior of the rogue lawyers you see online. Each online application has a handful of lawyers who have made a name for themselves by behaving in ways that are unprofessional. They may have large followings or fans online, but copying their outlandish behavior is not going to help your client development or ability to network with other professionals.
3. Yes, the First Amendment does apply to your online activities. As servants of the public, however, we lawyers should strive to limit ourselves to expressions that are going to be the most constructive and least harmful. Being professional in your online self-expression means making an intelligent benefit/harm analysis before publishing

and considering more than just the personal impact your message will have.

4. As a standard, if you would not want to see what you wrote splashed across the front page of the Wall Street Journal, do not publish it online.

5. If you would not say it in person, do not say it online.

6. Make an effort to stay updated on new online methods of communication, both from security and cultural standpoints. Stay aware of how *e*Professionalism considerations evolve as lawyers integrate these online methods into their practices, and determine the best strategy for your own legal career.

Sources/Reading

Jared Correia, Twitter for Lawyers in One Hour (2012).

DENNIS KENNEDY & ALLISON C. SHIELDS, FACEBOOK FOR LAWYERS IN ONE HOUR (2012).

Dennis Kennedy & Allison C. Shields, LinkedIn for Lawyers in One Hour (2012).

ERNIE SVENSON, BLOGGING IN ONE HOUR FOR LAWYERS (2012).

Cal. Comm. on Prof'l Responsibility & Conduct, Formal Ethics Op. 2012–186 (2012) (providing specific examples of Facebook postings by lawyers who do not comply with lawyer advertising rules).

STEPHANIE L. KIMBRO is a lawyer with Burton Law LLC and an author, consultant, and lecturer. Ms. Kimbro teaches legal technology and ethics topics as an adjunct professor at several law schools. She provides consultations to law firms and legal technology startups. Ms. Kimbro is the author of *Virtual Law Practice: How to Deliver Legal Services Online* (ABA 2010).

Chapter 16
PRO BONO AND PUBLIC SERVICE

ANTHONY C. MUSTO

I. Introduction

Public service has always been a hallmark of truly professional lawyers. It is woven into the fiber of their careers. It takes many forms. It serves many goals. It helps the poor; it helps society; and, yes, it helps the lawyers themselves. It can provide an extraordinary level of satisfaction, invaluable legal experience, an enhanced professional reputation, and an opportunity for real achievement.

This chapter will reflect on a lawyer's professional duty to deliver pro bono legal services to those in need; define pro bono, distinguishing it from other forms of donated legal services; detail the many benefits to lawyers of pro bono work; speak to the virtues of public sector legal work as a form of public service; discuss forms of service to the legal profession; and survey other types of public service by lawyers, including political service and charitable work.

II. Pro Bono

Any review of the forms of public service delivered by lawyers should begin with the form that is unique to lawyers and that represents a duty of the profession: the provision of pro bono legal services to those who cannot afford legal counsel.

A. *The Duty of the Legal Profession*

With great power comes great responsibility. This familiar adage captures why lawyers must provide legal services to the poor. Lawyers share equally with other occupations society's responsibility to address such social ills as hunger, poverty, and homelessness. When it comes to legal injustices victimizing the poor, however, attorneys stand alone. Others do not share in society's obligation to address those injustices because they *cannot* do so. Society entrusts lawyers, and only lawyers, with the right to solve those problems. Only we can enter the arena. Only we can fight the fight. Only we can right the wrong.

That is truly a great power. As such, it comes with great responsibility. If we as lawyers don't act, no one will. Slumlords will ignore rats. Usurious lenders will repossess cars. Employers will discriminate against persons on the basis of color, background, or gender.

Look at it this way: A group of people is picnicking near a lake. A swimmer calls for help and appears about to drown. All members of the group with sufficient swimming skills share a collective moral obligation to try to save the swimmer, but it doesn't matter which of them does so. If only one member knows how to swim, however, that moral obligation falls squarely on his or her shoulders.

In an era when legal services organizations struggle with emaciated budgets and more and more people find lawyers unaffordable, the need for attorneys to enter the waters of the legal system on behalf of the poor is more acute than ever. Otherwise, justice will only be available to those of means. As observed by United States Supreme Court Justice Stephen Breyer, "No one believes that a democracy's legal system can work effectively while reserving its benefits exclusively for those who are more affluent." Or, as Learned Hand put it, "If we are to keep our democracy, there must be one commandment: Thou shalt not ration justice."

Accordingly, ABA Model Rule of Professional Conduct 6.1 recognizes that "[e]very lawyer has a professional responsibility to provide legal services to those unable to pay." The Comment to the Rule points out that it applies to all lawyers "regardless of professional prominence or professional workload."

Model Rule 6.1 urges every lawyer to donate annually at least 50 hours of legal work, with a "substantial majority" of those 50 hours devoted to pure pro bono work, that is, "to: (1) persons of limited means; or (2) charitable, religious, civic, community, governmental and educational organizations in matters that are designed primarily to address the needs of persons of limited means."

Every year, legions of American lawyers not only accept their pro bono obligation, they embrace it, delivering countless pro bono hours to those in need. Measuring pro bono volume from all lawyers from every firm size is problematic, and there is no central, comprehensive data source on total pro bono hours delivered. But in the context of the biggest firms, according to the Pro Bono Institute, lawyers from about 40 of the largest United States law firms reported donating 2.84 million hours of legal services to persons of limited means in 2010.

Those who answer the call and embrace pro bono will come to see it not as a sacrifice but as a priceless practice enhancement, offering new and sharpened skills, new subject matter expertise, and the kind of profound professional satisfaction that only comes from helping people for one simple reason: they need help, and we lawyers are the answer. We know these benefits will flow to those who do pro bono, because that has always been the case.

B. Defining Pro Bono

Every lawyer should be crystal clear about the distinction between pure pro bono work and other kinds of "public service" or unpaid legal work. Many lawyers are under the misimpression that any legal work for which they are not compensated is pro bono in nature. Sorry, but the attorney handling a niece's DUI case or helping a major client by representing his son in a marijuana possession case is not providing pro bono legal services, even if no payment is received. Neither is the lawyer who writes off a deadbeat client's bill.

Some lawyers believe that they meet their pro bono obligation by volunteering for charities, religious institutions or organizations, schools, civic groups and even political candidates or parties. And, to be sure, those other volunteer activities are admirable, badly needed and richly rewarding forms of public service. But let's be clear: they are not pro bono publico, in the taking-care-of-the-poor's-legal-needs sense. True pro bono is the lawyer's first duty to society.

In adopting an aspirational goal of 20 hours of annual pro bono service for Florida lawyers, that state's supreme court discussed the distinction between the two types of lawyer public service:

> The entire focus of this action has been to address the *legal needs of the poor*. That objective is distinguishable from other types of uncompensated public service activities of the legal profession. . . . Although other public service by the legal profession is important . . . we find that the rules should clearly indicate that their purpose is to . . . motivate the legal profession to provide necessary legal services to the poor. . . . [W]e find that the definition of legal services to the poor should be narrow, expressing simply that Florida lawyers should strive to render (1) pro bono legal services to the poor or (2) to the extent possible, other pro bono service activities that *directly* relate to the legal needs of the poor. It is also our intention that the definition include legal services not only to indigent individuals but also to the "working poor."

Amendments to Rules, 630 So.2d 501, 503 (Fla. 1993). In striving to assume their share of the profession's public responsibility, lawyers should bear this distinction in mind.

Recognizing the fact that legal pro bono work occupies a special place distinct from other donated legal work in no way denigrates other forms of service, many of which are further addressed later in this chapter. Indeed, it is not unusual for codifications of pro bono goals to address such activities in addition to the provision of legal services to the poor.

For instance, the ABA's Model Rule 6.1, the pro bono rule, refers not only to various forms of legal service to persons of limited means, but also to participation in activities for improving the law, the legal system, or the legal profession. In 2012, New York adopted a rule, to take full effect in 2015, requiring as a condition of admission to the bar the provision of 50 hours of pro bono or approved public service work, which will include traditional pro bono as well as work for non-profit organizations, groups promoting access to justice, and public service to the judiciary or state or local governments.

Those other services deliver great value to society and to the cause of justice, but one should always be mindful that the heart of pro bono—the pro bono that lawyers must provide—is legal services to those who need but cannot afford them.

C. Benefits to Lawyers

While the primary purpose of pro bono service is to benefit clients, the justice system, and society, the benefits for lawyers are rich and varied. There is something about pro bono that energizes and fulfills lawyers while reminding them what attracted them to the law initially.

Attorneys can be the only thing standing in the way of disastrous consequences for people who are barely getting by. Without help, they may become homeless, lose the benefits they rely on to survive, or be deprived of their children. When lawyers avoid such outcomes, they are justifiably proud. As noted in an ABA Journal article, they "walk away with stories about the courage of their clients, the changes they helped effect, the lives they've helped reshape—sometimes even their own." Stephanie Francis Ward, *Working for Free*, ABA J., Feb. 2013, p. 28.

Moreover, pro bono cases can give attorneys invaluable courtroom experience, experience otherwise difficult to attain for many young lawyers, who are often relegated to supporting roles at law firms. "When there's not a bill to pay, it's easier for the partner to supervise and let the associate run with the ball," explained Scot Fishman, counsel and pro bono director at Manatt Phelps & Phillips in Los Angeles. "The partner can see whether the associate has good judgment—and if not, it can be a teachable moment." *Id.* at 36. Further, seasoned attorneys with practices that seldom involve in-court matters might welcome the chance to enliven their routines.

Further, lawyers who accept pro bono cases can get valuable guidance from practitioners who are subject-matter experts. Referral agencies and legal services offices, aware that the attorneys taking the cases may have little experience in the subject matter, often make experienced attorneys available for consultation and provide needed training. "You can get out of your comfort zone because almost all of these organizations give you training," said James Hadden, a Philadelphia lawyer who spends about 100 hours a year as a child advocate for abused and neglected children." *Id.* at 33. That training, of course, not only helps in handling of the case but also serves lawyers well in future cases with paying clients.

It also bears mentioning that continuing legal education (CLE) courses often provide training for specific pro bono pursuits while delivering necessary CLE credits to practicing lawyers. (Law student readers should note that CLE is the form of mandatory legal education that goes on *after* law school and for the rest of every lawyer's active career.)

Attorneys can use pro bono work to responsibly explore new areas of practice. Take the lawyer who has always had an interest in family law, but whose career path has led to a criminal law practice. Accepting pro bono divorce or child custody cases would allow that attorney to determine, under proper guidance, if he or she has a real interest in pursuing that area of practice. Attorneys who explore new fields may be inspired to expand or change the focus of their practices. Conversely, attorneys who find the new subject not to their liking can put their minds at ease and move forward without ever regretting not pursuing that alternative path.

A pro bono experience may help a lawyer build needed depth and credentials in a subject matter. The days of lawyers like Atticus Finch—who prepared wills, handled divorces, representd people charged with crimes, draw up contracts, and brought personal injury suits—are largely gone. Many states have adopted board-certification programs, which certify lawyers as specialists in certain legal areas, similar to the approach taken by the medical profession. As young lawyers find themselves settling into their areas of practice, they should note their states' certification requirements. Pro bono work may help them satisfy those requirements.

Handling pro bono cases can also yield valuable professional contacts, the kind that are critical to establishing and pursuing a legal career. Who you know is frequently—some would say usually—more important than what you know. Knowing people can lead to jobs, client referrals, co-counsel opportunities, establishment of references, and connections to people within other lawyers' networks.

Good contacts are particularly important for law students, who, as this chapter is written, face a very difficult job market. Graduating and passing the bar, while important achievements, only make them eligible for consideration for legal jobs. Students need something to make them stand out from the dozens, if not hundreds, of other freshly-minted lawyers applying for positions. Contacts developed from pro bono work can accomplish that goal. When those contacts are impressed with a student's work, they will consider hiring the student. They will also recommend the student to decision-makers in their firms or organizations and to people they know who are hiring. Such recommendations carry great weight and can very easily lead to employment.

Another benefit of pro bono to lawyers is the organized bar's habit of recognizing and publicizing members' exceptional pro bono efforts. Pro bono is honored in highly visible ways because it is a high calling that merits recognition, because that recognition may motivate other lawyers to engage in pro bono work, and because, frankly, it helps elevate the battered image of lawyers in the eyes of the public (although, to be sure, some criticism of the profession is warranted). Whatever the reason, recognition and public attention can only help in terms of establishing a lawyer's reputation and attracting clients. Thus, lawyers grow and gain from their pro bono efforts. As has often been said, "You can do well by doing good."

III. Public Employment

Lawyers working in the public sector, practicing in virtually every area of law, provide non-stop public service—they do it for a living. To advocate on behalf of the United States, a state, or a subdivision thereof, is not merely great service to society. To echo the mission statement of the ABA Government and Public Sector Lawyers Division, there is "No Higher Calling." And as George Waas, a recently retired government lawyer, observed,

"With government, you're seeking a high purpose. You're working for the people and you're doing the people's work." (Gary Blankenship, *Retired ... And Loving It!: There is life after the law books are closed*, FLORIDA BAR NEWS, Dec. 15, 2012, at 19.)

Attorneys who are paid by the government or government-supported entities for representing clients other than the government itself serve that same high calling. Public defenders, for instance, protect the rights of individuals and ensure that the system functions as it should. Legal aid lawyers help meet the legal profession's obligation to people of limited means.

As with pro bono service, government service offers a lawyer many benefits. Surveys show job satisfaction is higher among government lawyers than among private practitioners. Undoubtedly, that fact is due in part to pride taken in doing a job that benefits us all. It is also a function of the camaraderie that develops in the team atmosphere government offices can foster.

Perhaps most significantly, with some exceptions in both sectors, government lawyers just practice law, while attorneys in private practice run, or work for, a business. Private practitioners sell their expertise just as the owner of a deli sells pastrami. As Abraham Lincoln said, "[a] lawyer's time and advice are his stock in trade." The lawyer-as-business-person is concerned with such matters as overhead, attracting and retaining clients, billable hours, setting fees, insurance, and balancing the need for some action against a client's resources. The typical government lawyer blissfully ignores such distractions, while concentrating on legal work for the public good.

Another very significant benefit of government legal work is that government lawyers generally get real practice experience much faster than those who start with firms, especially larger firms. They may try dozens of cases before a classmate in a large firm tries one. In a few years, government lawyers will be involved in major cases, much sooner than that classmate, who will perhaps still be awaiting that first trial.

Note, also, that attorneys drawn to the advantages of government service need not devote their entire careers to it. Many lawyers start out in a government office and move to private practice after a few years. Some start in private firms before moving to the public sector. Some shuttle back and forth in the course of their careers. The power law/lobbying firms of Washington, D.C., are full of good lawyers whose previous executive branch or congressional legal staff work made them attractive to their current firms. Some attorneys in private practice choose to close out their careers in the public sector, particularly on the bench.

Whether as a career, the beginning of a career, a break in a career, or the culmination of a career, government service benefits us all, and it is something every lawyer should consider.

IV. Service to the Profession
A. Bar Service
Lawyers can accomplish much through service to their profession. Bar associations provide opportunities for attorneys to serve on committees, on governing boards, and in various capacities as part of association sections and divisions.

Bar association involvement empowers lawyers to have a meaningful impact on their profession as well as on the justice system through, for example, work on committees developing proposed changes in procedural rules or jury instructions, development of educational programming, and creation or reform of legislation.

In some states, membership in the state bar is a condition of a license to practice law. In others, bar association membership is merely encouraged. Either way, opportunities exist. In addition, there are local bar associations, usually confined to a city or county, as well as organizations—national, statewide and local—comprised of lawyers in specific practice areas or focused on the concerns of particular groups of lawyers. Many associations have sections and divisions relating to practice areas or other interests.

B. Mentoring
Experienced attorneys can provide service to their profession by serving as mentors to young lawyers, either through an organized program, or on a less formal basis. Such efforts should be at least somewhat structured and not left to a "call me if you need me" approach. (For more on

mentoring, see Chapter 13, *Finding and Getting the Most out of a Mentor*, by Lori L. Keating and Michael P. Maslanka, at page 161.).

C. Public Education

The public has many misperceptions about the law and the courts. Lawyers can serve their profession by getting out in the community and helping to educate the public about how the justice system and lawyers really work, and about their critical role in preserving liberty, equality, and justice.

Participating in Law Day activities and speaking to civic organizations, school groups, and other entities are great ways to combat misperceptions. So is writing op-ed pieces or letters to the editor for newspapers or other publications. The range of potential topics is vast. Ballot initiatives are often difficult for the public to understand. Merit retention of judges is a concept that always warrants discussion. When unpopular judicial decisions are unfairly assailed, the profession has a duty to defend judges who are bound by ethical considerations to sit silent. Inaccurate or misleading news accounts of legal matters should be corrected. The list goes on and on.

V. Political Service

There was a time when, to a large extent, it was lawyers who made laws. Seems logical enough: lawyers as legislators. Today, proportionately fewer lawyers serve as elected officials. Whatever the reason for their diminishing presence in state houses, local government councils and Congress, lawyers still bring an important, valued, and unique perspective to public office.

The ability to "think like a lawyer" is a great asset for elected officials. Lawyers are better equipped to comprehend the implications of contemplated actions, foresee potential legal problems and devise ways to avoid them.

Granted, many elected officials, both lawyers and non-lawyers, are more concerned with the political impact of their actions than the legal impact. Even those types, however, would generally prefer to avoid legal problems. Lawyers are capable of identifying ways to reach political goals without incurring legal risks that might not be apparent to non-lawyers.

No doubt many lawyers forsake running for elected office today because they are loath to deal with things like financial disclosure laws and the ugliness that has become a staple of political campaigns. Those who feel that way can provide political service without seeking election. Local governments have boards and committees that offer guidance to elected officials and sometimes have their own authority. Appointment to such a body is a chance to give important service to the community. A lawyer's perspective can greatly augment the entity's collective wisdom and good judgment.

Involvement with a political party is an option that can help elect political officials who share one's philosophy. Putting together, supporting, or opposing ballot initiatives is another way to have an impact.

It is also well worth noting that engagement in political and public policy work can lay the groundwork for actually running for office one day.

VI. Charitable and Other Community Work

In this chapter's discussion of pro bono activities, it was noted that volunteering with charities, religious institutions and organizations, schools, and civic groups does not meet the legal profession's defined pro bono obligation to society. But those activities are no less valuable or worthwhile ways to serve the community.

Charitable work has always been a main conduit of community engagement by lawyers. As in the political sphere, lawyers, by training and experience, are uniquely positioned to advance the work of organized charities via service on boards, committees, councils, and the like. The lawyer is able to advance a charity's cause by helping it recognize and weigh risk, address liability concerns, and pursue legally viable opportunities.

Young lawyers interested in charitable work would be well served by picking a cause or a few causes relatively early and sticking with them, rather than stretching themselves too thin with multiple commitments or moving on from a cause before their contributions have been maximized. An abiding commitment to a charitable cause and organization enables the lawyer to accumulate expertise in the field, build a network of like-minded and allied professionals, and develop the traction needed to climb to a position of leadership and influence within the organization.

VII. Conclusion

In a classic Peanuts comic strip, Snoopy, looking very much the attorney while carrying a briefcase and wearing a bowler hat and a bow tie, walks by Linus, who says, "The lawyer is evermore the leader in society." Snoopy continues walking, stating in the second panel, "I like that," and adding in the third, "I don't understand it, but I like it."

Snoopy's befuddlement aside, Linus's point isn't hard to understand. Attorneys have historically dedicated themselves and their skills to service and, in doing so, they have earned a special position in society.

There is no limit to the ways in which lawyers can provide service. While they must recognize the obligation to provide pro bono legal services to the poor, they should also look for other ways to serve.

What is important is not how they serve, or when they serve, but that they serve. Every lawyer should strive to make service an integral part of his or her professional identity.

ANTHONY C. MUSTO is Director of Community Outreach and Pro Bono Services and Visiting Assistant Professor of Law at St. Thomas University School of Law in Miami Gardens, FL. He teaches criminal law, advanced criminal law, criminal procedure II, advanced criminal procedure, advanced evidence, and appellate practice. He is a member of the ABA Standing Committee on Professionalism and a former member of the Florida Supreme Court Commission on Professionalism.

Chapter 17

HEALTH AND WELLNESS

FREDERIC S. URY AND DEBORAH M. GARSKOF

I. Introduction

Why a chapter on health and wellness in a book about professionalism? The answer is simple: our mental and physical health is closely intertwined with the way we practice law. When a lawyer becomes overwhelmed with stress and strain, not only does career satisfaction suffer, so does his or her ability to perform.

The law is a tough profession. Many who elect to pursue private practice, corporate counsel work, and certain public-sector legal positions are going to work long hours cleaning up other people's problems. You will be dealing with other lawyers and judges who are under a lot of stress, and they will, at times, make your life challenging—sometimes miserable. When you are on trial or working on a large merger or securities deal, you will work even longer hours—that is just the way it is.

The incidence of dissatisfaction in the legal profession can seem daunting, but needn't be defeating. Statistics paint a group portrait of a profession that is tough for many to handle—but you don't have to be part of that picture. By taking control of your professional life and doing everything in moderation—including your work—while making other healthy choices, you can join the countless lawyers who have managed to make the law a rich and satisfying career balanced with a full and fulfilling personal life.

The first step toward building a healthy work-life balance as a lawyer is recognizing that collectively we lawyers *do* have a problem. According to a frequently cited Johns Hopkins University study of more than 100 professions, lawyers were found to have the highest rate of depression. As of 1996, lawyers had the highest suicide rate among the professions, and the American Bar Association ("ABA") estimates that 15 to 20 percent of all lawyers suffer from alcohol or substance abuse. (Tyger Latham, *The Depressed Lawyer*, PSYCHOL. TODAY (May 2, 2011), http://www.psychologytoday.com/blog/therapy-matters/201105/the-depressed-lawyer.)

That said, you can make it your mission to take control of your own physical and psychological well-being while realizing more job satisfaction. By getting (and staying) healthy, getting organized, improving interpersonal relationships, taking breaks, and keeping your life-work priorities in check, you will reduce work-related stress and make life in general more fulfilling. As discussed below, seemingly simple lifestyle adjustments, such as instituting an exercise program, eating healthy, and getting a good night's sleep, will strengthen you for the long haul of a legal career and maximize the prospects of a satisfying professional life. Just know that a career in the law, as with many professions, is a marathon, not a sprint. Plan accordingly, and use this chapter to build a plan.

II. Stress

For lawyers, workplace stress can be hard to avoid. It comes from all directions: dealing with clients who themselves are in stressful situations, managing heavy workloads, tracking and meeting relentless deadlines, being on trial or working on major deals, and working within the adversarial nature of the practice in general. Everyone, lawyer and non-lawyer alike, experiences stress. The question becomes how to recognize, manage, reduce, and deal with stress so that it doesn't overwhelm us. Making smart choices, such as maintaining a healthy lifestyle, exercising, and getting enough sleep, all discussed in Section IV of this chapter, can go surprisingly far toward managing, if not eliminating, the worst effects of stress.

While many lawyers report satisfaction with their career choice, there is evidence of significant dissatisfaction that correlates with job stress. In his law review article, "A Personal Constitution," Michael Serota discusses the prevalence of stress (or, as he calls it, distress) within the profession and suggests ways in which law schools can educate students on stress avoidance and therefore reduce subsequent professional dissatisfaction. (Michael Serota, *A Personal Constitution*, 105 N.W. L. REV. 149 (2010).) Serota points to data showing that only about 55 percent of lawyers report satisfaction with their chosen profession, as opposed to 85 percent of the general population (*id.* at 152 (*quoting* Stephanie Francis Ward, *Pulse*, 93 A.B.A. J. 30, 32 (2007)); and that dissatisfaction has been increasing since the 1980's (Serota (*citing* Susan Diacoff, *Lawyer Be Thyself: An Empirical Investigation of the Relationship Between the Ethic of Care, the Feeling Decision-Making Preference, and Lawyer Wellbeing*, 16 VA. J. SOC. POL'Y & L. 87, 90 n.9 (2008).) In concluding that lawyer dissatisfaction is on the rise, scholars reviewed periodic "State of the Legal Profession" surveys conducted by the ABA Young Lawyers Division between 1984 and 2000. Importantly, Serota notes a correlation between attorney dissatisfaction and distress. (Serota, *supra* at 152 (*citing* Diacoff at 131).) It follows that, by reducing stress and distress in their lives, lawyers may enhance their professional satisfaction.

One way the individual lawyer can manage a stress-inducing professional environment is to try to move away from emphasizing quantity over quality, whenever feasible. With the focus at many law firms on billable hours and "face time," it is easy to see how attorneys fall into the "burn out" trap—a trap that may ultimately result in an inability to continue to work. Studies confirm that long hours spent in the office do not always yield the best work product and, of greater concern, can lead to physical illness. A recent study in the American Journal of Epidemiology, as reported in Forbes (David DiSalvo, contributor, *Why Working More Than 8 Hours A Day Can Kill You*, FORBES, Sept. 12, 2012), found that working in excess of eight hours per day could result in a 40 to 80 percent greater risk of heart disease. Other identified contributing factors included increased levels of the stress hormone cortisol, poor eating habits, and lack of physical activity. *Id.*

The research points to an inescapable conclusion: a lawyer's health and sense of well-being can benefit from less "face time" in the office, with a concurrent commitment to better managing one's time, prioritizing work, and organizing files. (For more on getting organized, See Kelly Lynn Anders, Chapter 19, *The Importance of Personal Organization*, at page 239.)

Effective time management means carving out more time to do other things that promote better health, chief among them being sleep and exercise. Ultimately, becoming more versatile and well-rounded is likely to enhance, not decrease, your productivity and career longevity. In the face of constant demands from clients, co-counsel and partners, the kind of effective time management discipline that leaves room for a well-rounded, good life takes discipline and constant commitment. Even taking time to eat a balanced meal, rather than rushing through junk-food meals, will add immeasurably to one's health and quality of life. Developing good habits early in your career is essential to maintaining a healthy balance.

III. Addiction and Depression

Research suggests that lawyers are at a higher risk of developing substance abuse issues than the population at large. According to a September 2012 research report by the Butler Center for Research at Hazelden, which updated a 1990 study published in the *International Journal of Law and Psychiatry* the rate of problem drinking for attorneys was 18 percent, compared with 10 percent for the population at large. (http://www.hazelden.org/web/public/researchupdates.page.) The study further found that for a significant number of lawyers, excessive drinking begins before they start practicing, with 8 percent of pre-law students reporting problem drinking, 15 percent of first year law students, and 24 percent of third year law students reporting alcohol-related issues. *Id.* According to a 2005 ABA report, one in four lawyers suffers from stress, and the law is ranked as the most depressed profession out of 105 occupations. (Robert A. Stein, *Help is Available*, A.B.A. J. (June 28, 2005, 9:31 A.M.), http://www.aba-journal.com/magazine/article/help_is_available/.) Mary-Anne Enoch and David Goldman, from the National Institute on Alcohol Abuse and Alcoholism, in their 2002 article *Problem Drinking and Alcoholism: Diagnosis and Treatment* defined "problem drinking"or "at-risk alcohol use" as more than fourteen drinks per week/more than four drinks per occasion for men while for women it was more than seven drinks per week/ more than three drinks per occasion. (Am Fam Physician 2002 Feb 1, 65(3) 441-449 http://www.aafp.org/afp/2002.)

A truly insidious aspect of substance abuse and depression is that people are slow to recognize—often the last to recognize—that they have a problem affecting their lives and work. The organized bar, however, for years has recognized the damage done by addiction and has taken steps to help lawyers in need. Lawyer Assistance Programs ("LAPs") operate in almost every state of the country to assist lawyers and law students negatively affected by alcohol, drugs, gambling, or other addictive behaviors. Most LAPs address a wide range of mental health issues and generally offer programming, education, and referral services. The vast majority of these programs offer their services in strict confidence.

In 2010, the ABA, through the Commission on Lawyer Assistance Programs (CoLAP), conducted a Comprehensive Survey of Lawyer Assistance Programs. The study found that the majority of programs operate as agencies within a bar association; others operate as independent agencies or as agencies within the court system. Most if not all of these state-specific programs have websites that provide contact information and content for those interested in further information and/or assistance. In addition, ABA CoLAP has a website listing resource (http://apps.americanbar. org/legalservices/colap/lapdirectory.html) as well as a hotline number 1–866-LAW-LAPS. Most LAP services are available to law students. Moreover, many law schools provide their students with similar services, including counseling.

Beyond LAP services, individuals dealing with addiction may benefit from Twelve Step Programs such as Alcoholics Anonymous. Such programs feature voluntary, self-help groups known for treating various addictions, including but not limited to alcoholism. These groups provide support, structure, goals, and direction to participants while assisting them in their effort to refrain from addictive behaviors. The steps are designed to be worked in order and as a process, a method by which the person rids himself or herself of addictive behaviors. One can find a local Twelve Step Program by visiting the website for the Substance Abuse and Mental Health Services Administration, part of the U.S. Department of Health & Human Services (http://findtreatment.samhsa.gov). The website identifies twelve-step and mental health facilities and programs by state, and then by proximity to an entered address, city, or zip code.

The importance of acknowledging an addiction problem and obtaining help as early as possible is widely known. What may be less evident to those aspiring to a legal career is that substance abuse, addiction, or mental health problems may adversely affect their chances of admission to the bar. All applicants to the bar face an evaluation requiring them to prove good moral character and fitness. The purpose of these evaluations is, ostensibly, to protect the public from potential abuse by compromised lawyers. In many states, bar applications contain questions about an applicant's mental health and/or substance abuse. Of course, with the passage of the Americans with Disabilities Act ("ADA"), there has been much discussion about whether these questions are appropriate and, more specifically, whether they are sufficiently related to behaviors that can affect the applicant's practice of law. (Stuart C. Gauffreau, *The Propriety of Broadly Worded Mental Health Inquiries on Bar Application Forms*, BULL AM. ACAD. PSYCHIATRY LAW, Col. 24, No., 2, 1996, *available at* http://www.jaapl.org/content/24/2/199.full.pdf.) Some states have adopted Conditional Admissions Programs. These programs often allow an applicant to be admitted to the bar, but that admission may be conditioned upon monitoring, treatment, and/or reporting requirements. Whether these programs help or hinder full admissions and whether they promote ADA compliance remains subject to debate. Concerns persist that permitting such questions on applications may deter applicants from seeking treatment. (Stephanie Denzel, *Second-Class Licensure: The Use of Conditional Admission Programs for Bar Applicants with Mental Health and Substance Abuse Histories*, 43 CONN. L. REV. no. 3, Feb. 2011.)

There is good reason that bar examiners are concerned about a history of unresolved substance abuse on the part of an applicant. Unchecked addiction can do great harm to a lawyer's practice. Addictive behaviors can lead to missed deadlines, unauthorized use of client funds, inattention to clients and work, and to other destructive behaviors. That kind of conduct will put a lawyer in the express lane to disciplinary sanctions—particularly where misappropriation of client money is the issue. (For more on the nexus between lawyer substance abuse and lawyer discipline, see See Chapter 14, *Handling Money*, by Martha Middleton, at page 175.)

A number of jurisdictions have observed a clear link between an attorney's impairment from alcoholism and his or her likelihood to be subject to attorney discipline and malpractice claims. (*See* John P. Ratnaswamy, *Substance Abuse and Attorney Discipline*, THE BENCHER, Sept.–Oct. 2011.) In fact, Ratnaswamy cites studies in the U.S. and Canada estimating that some 60 percent of discipline and malpractice actions are tied to lawyer alcohol consumption. (*Id.*) Moreover, Ratnaswamy points to the 2009 Annual Report of the Illinois Attorney Registration & Disciplinary Commission finding a steady increase in the number of disciplined lawyers in that state who either admitted or were suspected of suffering from some sort of substance abuse or mental impairment. (*Id.*) Taken together, these statistics make clear that substance abuse, depression and mental impairment are primary factors leading to attorney discipline and malpractice and that finding ways to stay healthy and avoid excess and abuse will benefit not only individual attorneys but the public at large.

IV. The Healthy Attorney

The healthy attorney is a successful attorney—both professionally and in his or her private life. First and foremost, each person must find the right balance between work and home. An important aspect of the work-life balance is the amount of time a lawyer spends at the office. Finding a time and a place for spiritual expression, physical exercise, and relaxation are all essential to maintaining a healthy body and mind. Finding that happy medium is by no means easy and will naturally change as we progress through our careers and our personal lives. Notwithstanding, it is absolutely worth the effort. Failing to find one's proper place within the home, profession, and community is often part of a destructive pattern that culminates in sickness, addiction, or depression. The phrase "everything in moderation" may be cliché, but it's great advice for a good life.

V. Long Range Planning

In addition to focusing on time management and organization, effective, healthy lawyers do not overlook the importance of long- and short-range planning for home and work. Do you have a short term (2 year), mid-term (5 year), and long term (10 year plus) plan? Have you set goals for your professional development as well as family life? Planning becomes easier when the year is divided into manageable segments. Very importantly, to keep chaos and potential disasters at bay, sound financial planning should be a routine part of every lawyer's life. Financial plans should be changed as you and your family's needs change.

VI. Sleep, Exercise, Nutrition and Time Off

It is very helpful—and healthful—to be mindful of the nexus between one's daily routine and the quality of one's work life. First and foremost, one shouldn't underestimate the need of the body (and mind!) for a good night's sleep. Not only does sufficient sleep aid learning and memory, it helps keep metabolism and weight at consistent levels, improves our moods, and keeps our immune systems and cardiovascular health properly functioning. Press Release, Harvard Health Publications, , Importance of Sleep and Health (Jan. 2006), *available at* http://www.health.harvard.edu/press_releases/importance_of_sleep_and_health.)

Exercise works hand in hand with sufficient sleep to improve health, mood, and energy. Different kinds of exercise are also a fun way to unwind either in a group or individually. (*Exercise, 7 Benefits of Regular Physical Activity*, MAYO CLINIC (July 23, 2011), http://www.mayoclinic.com/health/exercise/HQ01676.) And of course, exercise makes you tired in a good way, inducing needed sleep.

Not that the jokes about lawyers being rats are justified, but interestingly, research on the brains of rats found that physical exercise, over time, appears to cause the brain to better manage other types of stress. (Gretchen Reynolds, *Phys Ed: Why Exercise Makes You Less Anxious*, N.Y. TIMES WELL BLOG (Nov. 18, 2009, 12:01 A.M.), http://well.blogs.nytimes.com/2009/11/18/phys-ed-why-exercise-makes-you-less-anxious/.) Researchers have also found that exercise has both chemical and behavioral effects: it reduces the amounts of stress hormones and can also increase the body's production of endorphins, the body's natural pain-killers. Press Release, Harvard Health Publications, Benefits of Exercise – Reduces Stress, Anxiety and Helps Fight Depression, from Harvard Men's Health Watch (Feb. 2011), *available at* www.health.harvard.edu/press_releases/benefits-of-exercisereduces-stress-anxiety-and-helps-fight-depression.) It also can improve confidence and instill better discipline. *Id.*

One need not be an Olympic athlete to reap the benefits of exercise. Exercising a mere thirty minutes a day, four times a week, has been proven to have a significant beneficial effect. *Id.* According to the Harvard Medical School, moderate physical activity (walking fast, raking leaves) should be undertaken at least 2.5 hours per week and vigorous exercise (running, swimming laps, jumping rope) 1.15 hours per week. For all of these reasons—and for enjoyment—take the time to exercise. In the long run, it will make you look and feel better and work more productively. (*Id.*)

Good nutrition is another factor that figures prominently in the healthy lifestyle. A healthy diet is essential to achieving optimal well-being. It promotes physical and mental vitality, helping to maintain a healthful weight, and fortifying the immune systems to prevent disease. A poor diet, on the other hand, can lead to a number of serious health issues that shorten our lives or make them less enjoyable. Fruits and vegetables, fiber, protein, and unsaturated fats are keys to nutritious eating. (*See, e.g., A Consumer Nutrition Guide*, U.S. NEWS, http://health.usnews.com/health-conditions/heart-health/information-on-nutrition (last visited April 12, 2013).)

On a related point, staying healthy means making regular visits to your primary care physician and any necessary follow-ups with specialists. Dealing with medical situations sooner rather than later promotes both good physical health and, by reducing stress, good mental health.

It may seem counterintuitive to some, but another essential aspect of a healthy work-life balance is planning and taking vacations. Not only can a vacation improve your mental and physical health, it can improve your work. Anticipating an upcoming trip can increase positive emotions and reduce stress. The vacation itself will provide much needed relaxation and stress relief as well as quality time with family and friends.

Perhaps the best evidence of the effect of vacations can be found in the *Framingham Heart Study*, in which scientists looked at 12,000 men over nine years who were at risk for heart disease. Each year the participants were queried about vacations. The conclusion: "The more frequent the vacations, the longer the men lived." (Brenda Wilson, *Relax! Vacations Are Good For You*, NPR, Aug. 17, 2009, http://www.npr.org/templates/story/story.php?storyId=111887591).

VII. Conclusion

The old adage "everything in moderation" is a sensible approach to maintaining a healthy and fulfilled personal and professional life. Put in the extra hours when they are warranted, but take that vacation and make time for activities outside the office. Make time for yourself and especially for your family. There is an old saying that won't go away because it is just too true: nobody on his death bed ever says, "I wish I had spent more time at the office." Not only will the time you invest in organizing and prioritizing your work pay off in better focus and better time management, your personal relationships will benefit and your risk of extreme stress or depression will decrease.

Eat healthy, exercise, and have fun. Make sure you have a life outside of the office. Participate in your local, state, or national bar. Do charitable work. Volunteer for your child's PTA. Take music or foreign language lessons. Go to your child's soccer game. All of this will help make you a well-rounded person—and a better, happier attorney.

FREDERIC S. URY is a Founding Partner of Ury & Moskow, LLC in Fairfield, CT. He concentrates his practice in the areas of civil and criminal litigation, and is listed in Martindale Hubbell's Bar Register of Preeminent Lawyers. Mr. Ury was a member of the ABA Commission on Ethics 20/20 and was 2011–2012 President of the National Conference of Bar Presidents. He is also a former President of the Connecticut Bar Association. Mr. Ury frequently lectures nationally on the subject of the future of the legal profession, and serves as Chair of the ABA Standing Committee on Professionalism.

DEBORAH M. GARSKOF is a member of Ury & Moskow, LLC in Fairfield, CT, where she focuses her practice in the areas of appellate practice, commercial law, employment law, and real estate. Ms. Garskof is a member of the Massachusetts, Connecticut, and New York bars.

Chapter 18

MINDFULNESS AND PROFESSIONALISM

JAN L. JACOBOWITZ

"You are a cheat!" shouted the attorney to his opponent.

"And you are a liar!" bellowed the opposition.

Banging his gavel loudly, the judge interjected, "Now that both attorneys have been identified for the record, let's get on with the case."

—Anonymous

Perhaps it's the grain of truth and the ring of familiarity that make this dusty old chestnut timelessly entertaining. The two lawyers share an acute professionalism problem, and the judge seems to be affirming that, in the case of these two, being unprofessional is part of their professional identity. At the end of the day, behaving unprofessionally is just what they do and who they are.

I. The True Professional: Passion and Reflection in Balance

Many thoughtful scholars, jurists, and lawyers have puzzled over the precise constituent elements of legal professionalism, with much good accomplished through the journey but no consensus reached—or perhaps even possible—on a comprehensive definition of professionalism. It seems fair to suggest, though, that we can all agree on a few foundational elements, such as honesty, civility, loyalty, and a service orientation. Other concise formulations of professionalism seem incontrovertible. For example, Neil Hamilton and Verna Monson have offered this definition, a distillation of extensive research:

> Professionalism is an internalized moral core characterized by a deep responsibility or devotion to others—particularly the client—and some restraint of self-interest in carrying out this responsibility. . . . Professionalism [may also include] these elements: ongoing solicitation of feedback and self-reflection, an internalized standard of excellence at lawyering skills, integrity, honesty, adherence to the ethical codes, public service (especially for the disadvantaged), and independent professional judgment and honest counsel.

However we come to view the pieces of professionalism, it is plain that the words of the two lawyers in the opening dialogue above, and the intemperate and uncivil impulses necessarily underlying them, fall on the opposite end of the spectrum from the acts of a truly professional lawyer. In order to internalize both the reflective and passionate traits of the true professional, lawyers and judges must develop dependable habits that keep them from acting on impulse, out of anger, without careful reflection, or in other ways that undermine and defeat a commitment to civil and professional conduct.

What emerges from the components of professionalism is recognition of an overarching need for ongoing thoughtful discourse, decision-making, and reflection by lawyers and judges on their professional conduct. Whether an individual is confronted with an ethical dilemma, a hostile opposing counsel, a challenging client, or an injustice in the legal system, the individual's response to the situation is governed by his or her unique combination of emotional experience and logical thought process, which yields a final decision as to how to respond. Intense emotions may cause a person to impulsively make a decision that unwisely focuses on the immediate circumstances rather than the impact of the decision on the long-term goal. In fact, an impulsive first reaction tends to be evidence of the individual's failure to effectively collect and process the information necessary to consider the long-term goal before deciding to take action. In other words, a failure to recognize and manage emotions may lead to less than optimal decision-making—the type of decision-making that in turn lacks professionalism.

The lawyers who chose to yell "cheat" and "liar" in the opening dialogue arguably began their emotional outbursts as a consequence of a failure to recognize and modulate their emotions. Perhaps in the heat of battle, each of their focuses narrowed to a short-term goal of aggressively attacking opposing counsel and defending their own integrity rather than considering longer-term goals such as the impact of their conduct upon the judge, upon their likelihood of success in the case, and upon their overall reputations.

II. The Idea of Mindfulness

Presuming for this discussion that these attorneys' reactions stemmed from a lack of mindfulness, let's rewind the exchange to see how it might have differed had at least one of these lawyers engaged in mindful decision-making. It would be good to start the analysis with an explanation of "mindfulness." Jon Kabat-Zinn, the founder of the Mindfulness Based Stress Reduction Program, which is taught throughout the country, defines mindfulness as "paying attention in a particular way, on purpose, in the present moment, and nonjudgmentally."

In other words, the idea of the practice of mindfulness is that it provides a heightened awareness of whatever event is occurring in your life in the present moment, and how you are thinking, feeling and experiencing the event. For example, think about a recent experience that you may have had when a family member, friend, colleague, professor, or even a stranger engaged in behavior that disappointed or offended you. How did you *react or overreact*?

Perhaps you lashed out in anger, cried in disbelief, or internalized your emotions in a way that caused you to ruminate about the unfairness of the situation throughout the day, upset because that person "ruined your day." Any of one of these reactions would certainly not be uncommon, but do you remember what you were thinking, what emotions you experienced, and how the event may have affected your body in that moment? Perhaps you remember thinking about the unfairness of the other person's conduct and feeling so angry that your heart was racing. Maybe you wish you had not said what you did, or conversely that you had spoken rather than felt paralyzed by your emotions.

The idea of mindfulness is to enable you to notice, in the moment, that you are experiencing these thoughts, feelings and bodily sensations so that you may place a *pause* between the event that is occurring and your *response* to the event. It is important to be conscious of the difference between the words *react* and *response* in this context. *Reactivity* is what may occur when a person instantaneously lashes out in anger even though that is not the optimal response to a situation. A person's awareness of the fact that he is experiencing anger may provide the pause necessary to modulate the anger and *respond* in a more productive manner. The non-judgmental aspect of mindfulness suggests that a person should not judge his anger in the moment—just noticing that he is experiencing anger is often enough to positively influence his response.

Now, let's turn back to the attorneys who yelled "cheat" and "liar." What prompted the first attorney to shout "cheat" is unknown, but having been called a cheat in open court in front of a judge, the second attorney, no doubt, experienced a number of thoughts, feelings, and bodily sensations. In mindfulness terms, the shouting of "cheat" is referred to as an "event"—because life, whether in the legal profession or in our personal lives, may be viewed as a series of ongoing events. Imagine that this event—the yelling of the word cheat—has put a spiral in motion. Place on the spiral the likely thoughts, feelings and bodily sensations of the second attorney. He may be thinking, "What a jerk!" "How dare he embarrass me in front of the judge!" Or just, "that's not true!" The accused cheat may be feeling anger, disgust, and humiliation. He may also be experiencing an increased pulse, stomach disturbance, or shaking inside.

As the second attorney's thoughts, feelings, and bodily sensations travel around the spiral, they cause the type of instantaneous reactivity that in turn results in his bellowing the accusation "liar" to the first attorney. Of course the bellowing of "liar" has, no doubt, become an event for which the first attorney now has his own reactive spiral spinning with thoughts, feelings, and bodily sensations. And so, if the judge were not there to bang the gavel, one destructive spiral might continue to lead to another until some other intervening event occurred or one of the attorneys, whether in a belated moment of insight or perhaps mere exhaustion, jumps off of the spiral of reactivity.

III. The Importance of "The Pause"

How might mindfulness make a difference not only in this exchange, but also generally to stem the tide of reactivity that often occurs in interpersonal exchanges? The practice of mindfulness provides a pause between the event and an individual's response. The pause may seem subtle, but it is nonetheless dramatic.

Had the second attorney in our example "paused," he may have been able to abandon or rise above the spiral and avoid overreacting before the judge. The second attorney might have noticed that the first attorney was being highly unprofessional, that being called a cheat in front of judge was causing the second attorney *to think* that the first attorney is a liar, to *feel* extremely angry and to *notice* that his heart is racing. Having had this heightened awareness in the moment, the second attorney might have chosen to respond by simply stating his name for the record and calmly indicating that he was not in agreement with the first attorney's characterization of his character. That response would have likely created quite a different impression before the judge and perhaps diffused or altered the first attorney's state of mind.

The legal profession is replete with adversarial moments—it is the nature of our legal system. Lawyers are expected to zealously advocate for a client whether it is in a courtroom setting, a mediation, or a transactional negotiation. Often emotions run high as a client urges his lawyer to win "at all costs" or demands a "scorched earth" strategy. Opposing counsel may employ unfair tactics or a trial judge may not rule in accordance with the current state of the law. In other words, the practice of law has no shortage of challenging situations in which lawyers may employ mindfulness to engage in professionalism by electing to thoughtfully respond. Alternatively, a lawyer may fall prey to the reactivity that often fuels unproductive and unprofessional behavior by overreacting rather than thoughtfully responding.

The question remains: how does one develop a mindful approach to life's events, and is there any "evidence" that mindfulness really makes a difference? Perhaps, for the mind engaged in legal training, the evidence should be provided before the methodology. Although the contemporary application of mindfulness in the legal profession is often traced to a law and meditation retreat at Yale Law School in 1998, and mindfulness itself stems from teachings that are thousands of years old, the recent popularity of mindfulness in legal communities across the country may partially be the result of research being conducted by neuroscientists on the neurological effects of mindfulness.

In his book, *The Mindful Brain*, Dr. Daniel J. Siegel acknowledges the anecdotal evidence of the effectiveness of mindfulness but moves beyond it to discuss the relevant brain science. In chapter one, *A Mindful Awareness*, Dr. Siegel explains:

> Preliminary research involving brain function hints at the view that mindfulness changes the brain. Why would the way you pay attention in the present moment change your brain? How we pay attention promotes neural plasticity, the change of neural connections in response to experience. What we'll examine [in the book] are the possible mechanisms of how the various dimensions of mindful awareness emerge within the activity of the brain and stimulate the growth of connections in those areas. By diving deeply into direct experience, we will be able to shed some light on why research might reveal left-sided changes, right-sided changes, and global impacts on integrative functioning in the brain as a whole.

Dr. Siegel's book was first published in 2007, and since then additional scientific findings have been reported that further support the impact of mindfulness on the brain. For example, in 2009, Amishi Jha, a neuroscientist conducting research at the University of Pennsylvania, demonstrated that mindfulness practices were associated with changes to working memory and the increased ability to minimize distraction. At UCLA's Laboratory of Neuro Imaging, Eileen Luders and her colleagues have studied the impact of meditation on the brain. In 2009 and 2011, they published the results of studies finding, among people who meditate, increased grey matter, stronger connections between brain regions, and less age-related brain thinning. Then in 2012, the same lab reported findings that mindfulness meditation was associated with larger amounts of gyrification—folding of the cortex—which may allow the brain to process information faster.

While it certainly is not necessary to be a scientist to understand or engage in mindfulness, it may be compelling, for the skeptical mind, to know that early findings from a variety of credible labs and neuroscientists across the country lend themselves to the conclusion that a mindfulness practice may not only assist a person in achieving more effective decision-making—and for the purposes of our discussion, thereby enhance professionalism—but also that mindfulness may literally cause positive changes in a person's brain.

So then how does one engage in a mindfulness practice? Fundamentally, spending a few minutes sitting quietly, lowering, or closing the eyes, and concentrating upon the breath may begin a mindfulness practice. When the mind begins to wander, which it will, just gently bring concentration back to the breath. The process is not about attempting to have the mind go "blank," but rather about noticing thoughts, emotions and bodily sensations, without judgment, and sending them on their way, perhaps to be revisited at a later time, while returning the focus to the breath.

The process is easy to describe, but may be difficult to achieve, and obtaining ultimate benefits requires regular practice. The benefits of mindfulness have been described through its use in diverse contexts. In health care facilities, mindfulness has been employed to assist with managing chronic pain; in schools, mindfulness has helped children with concentration and impulse control; and in large corporations, the goal is to improve creativity and the work environment.

In the professionalism context, mindfulness may be a tool for improved decision-making, which goes hand in hand with becoming not just a lawyer, but also a professional. Being a part of the legal profession means striving to effectively make difficult decisions while maintaining one's personal values and reputation. Mindfulness may provide enhanced clarity, especially in stressful situations, and allow for better decisions. As Phillip Moffitt explains in his book, *Emotional Chaos to Clarity:*

> When you are being mindful, you are better able to clearly see what is happening in each moment of your life. As a result you gain new insights into your experience, which greatly enhances your ability to tolerate difficult situations and to make wiser decisions.

The beauty of mindfulness, and the clarity that it may provide, is that developing a mindfulness practice may be done anywhere, by a single person or in a group, in silence, or with music and a guided meditation. There are many books, websites, recorded guided meditations, classes, workshops, retreats, and community groups available to assist anyone interested in learning more about mindfulness and how to develop a mindfulness practice.

Law schools and legal communities have begun to focus on mindfulness in the context of the legal profession. University of Miami School of Law has a Mindfulness in Law Program and University of California Berkeley School of Law has a Berkeley Initiative for Mindfulness in Law. There are many other schools where professors have integrated mindfulness into their curriculum or where the school has offered mindfulness as an extracurricular program. A number of legal communities have begun mindfulness programming, such as the Miami-Dade Mindfulness in Law Task Force, which is comprised of lawyers, judges, and law students who are interested in both engaging in a mindfulness practice and increasing awareness of mindfulness throughout the legal community.

IV. Conclusion

Mindfulness and professionalism both have many dimensions, and people certainly may disagree about the significance of a particular brain imaging study or the exact definition of legal professionalism. It is difficult to dispute, however, that enhanced decision-making based upon greater mental clarity is a valuable tool for lawyers.

In sum, mindfulness may be a valuable tool to add to your professionalism toolbox. Building a career imbued with mindfulness may naturally lead you—and those who take your cue, to a state of professionalism, which may not only enhance your reputation and success, but also will assist in elevating the stature of the legal profession in our society.

Sources/Reading

Bar Associations Involved in Mindfulness and the Law, MINDFULNESS IN LAW, http://mindfulnessinlaw.org/Bar%20Associations/index.html (last visited April 14, 2013).

Todd Essig, *Google Teaches Employees to 'Search Inside Yourself'*, FORBES (Apr. 30, 2012, 9:42 PM), http://www.forbes.com/sites/toddessig/2012/04/30/google-teaches-employees-to-search-inside-yourself/.

Neil Hamilton & Verna Monson, *Legal Education's Ethical Challenge: Empirical Research on How Most Effectively to Foster Each Student's Professional Formation (Professionalism)*, 9 U. ST. THOMAS L.J. 325 (2011).

Amishi Jha et.al., *Examining the Protective Effects of Mindfulness Training on Working Memory and Affective Experience*, 10 EMOTION 54 (2010), *available at* http://www.mindinsight.co.uk/docs/jha_stanley_etal_emotion_2010.pdf.

JON KABAT-ZINN, WHEREVER YOU GO, THERE YOU ARE: MINDFULNESS MEDITATION IN EVERYDAY LIFE (1994).

Alan Lerner, *Using Our Brains: What Cognitive Science and Social Psychology Teach Us About Teaching Law Students to Make Ethical, Professionally Responsible Choices*, 23 QUINNIPIAC L. REV. 643 (2004).

Eileen Luders & A.W. Toga et al., *The Underlying Anatomical Correlates of Long-term Meditation: Larger Hippocampal and Frontal Volumes of Gray Matter*, 45 NEUROIMAGE 672 (2009), *available at* http://www.ncbi.nlm.nih.gov/pmc/articles/PMC3184843/.

Eileen Luders & Kristi Clark et al., *Enhanced Brain Connectivity in Long-term Meditation Practitioners*, 57 NEUROIMAGE 1308 (2011).

Eileen Luders & Florian Kurth, et al., *The Unique Brain Anatomy of Meditation Practitioners: Alterations in Cortical Gyrification*, 6 FRONTIERS IN HUMAN NEUROSCIENCE 1 (2012).

Mindfulness in the Corporate World: How Businesses are Incorporating the Eastern Practice, HUFFPOST HEALTHY LIVING (Aug. 30, 2012, 12:30 A.M.), http://www.huffingtonpost.com/2012/08/29/mindfulness-businesses-corporate-employees-meditation_n_1840690.html.

PHILLIP MOFFITT, EMOTIONAL CHAOS TO CLARITY: HOW TO LIVE MORE SKILLFULLY, MAKE BETTER DECISIONS, AND FIND PURPOSE IN LIFE (2012).

JENNIFER K. ROBBENNOLT & JEAN R. STERNLIGHT, PSYCHOLOGY FOR LAWYERS: UNDERSTANDING THE HUMAN FACTORS IN NEGOTIATION, LITIGATION, AND DECISION MAKING (2012).

SCOTT L. ROGERS & JAN L. JACOBOWITZ, MINDFULNESS & PROFESSIONAL RESPONSIBILITY: A GUIDEBOOK FOR INTEGRATING MINDFULNESS INTO THE LAW SCHOOL CURRICULUM (2012).

Daniel Schneider, *Mindfulness Helps Soldiers Cope in Iraq*, U.S. DEP'T OF DEF. (Aug. 3, 2012), http://www.defense.gov/news/newsarticle.aspx?id=60294.

DANIEL J. SIEGEL, THE MINDFUL BRAIN: REFLECTION AND ATTUNEMENT IN THE CULTIVATION OF WELL BEING (2007).

Associated Press, *U.S. Marine Corps Members Learn Mindfulness Mediation and Yoga in Pilot Program to Help Reduce Stress*, N.Y. DAILY NEWS (Jan. 23 2012, 11:09 A.M.), http://www.nydailynews.com/life-style/health/u-s-marines-learn-meditate-stress-reduction-program-article-1.1245698.

JAN L. JACOBOWITZ is a Lecturer in Law and the Director of the Professional Responsibility and Ethics Program (PREP) at the University of Miami's School of Law. PREP was a 2012 recipient of the ABA's E. Smythe Gambrell Professionalism Award. Ms. Jacobowitz teaches Mindful Ethics: Professional Responsibility for Lawyers in th Digital Age.

Chapter 19

THE IMPORTANCE OF PERSONAL ORGANIZATION

KELLY LYNN ANDERS

I. Introduction

Disorganization is a common affliction among lawyers. To be sure, some can and do succeed absent a personal organizing principle and system—after all, the lawyer with a hopeless desk, misplaced files, rumpled clothes but a steel-trap mind is an American cultural archetype. For most practitioners, though, getting and staying organized in a busy and complex legal world is essential to success and peace of mind.

Every day the average lawyer takes in an enormous amount of information in various formats. Lawyers themselves generate a large quantity of information. All of it must be managed, used, stored, or discarded. Without a solid toolbox of organizing skills that can be deployed from job to job, and from project to project, work and life can quickly spiral out of control. A lawyer with a chaotic practice may even face disciplinary action, if his or her disorganization negatively affects a client's case.

Practitioners and law students, therefore, would be well served to develop proactive approaches to both preventing disorganization and maintaining organization—two closely connected but still distinct concepts. This chapter will provide an overview of personal organization issues; clarification of how organizational skills can best be developed, maintained, and sharpened; and steps that any legal professional can take to begin the process of conquering clutter.

II. Organization and Information Overload

The practice of law is always demanding and can be overpowering even for those who are highly organized, given a lawyer's relentless responsibilities and constantly competing projects. For those who are not organized, it can be a constant uphill fight. It could be argued that information overload begins before law school, when the first major reading assignments are posted. For many, a common feeling of helplessness in managing large amounts of information continues right through graduation day and beyond.

The rise of technology has played a significant if not primary role in the information overload that law students and practitioners now routinely face in their daily lives. In a modern-day practice, most lawyers are online, connected, and essentially accessible twenty-four hours per day. In today's challenging economic environment, lawyers not only face heightened competition for those jobs that do exist but heightened expectations that, when they are working, they be 100 percent productive, often literally in six-minute billing segments.

And gone are the days when a case resided in a handful of documents, usually paper, stored in only one place. Lawyers now must deal with potentially thousands of documents in multiple formats and multiple locations. Despite this spike in document volume confronting every lawyer, the physical space allocated per lawyer has in many instances decreased. Due to both financial constraints and modern design notions of best use of space, offices are smaller and cubicles have become more common, even for professionals such as lawyers. Less physical space in which to operate places an even greater premium on good habits of organization.

III. How Disorganization Leads to Disciplinary Action

Many lawyers have faced disciplinary action for misconduct traced to disorganization. Examples include unintentional commingling of funds, harm to clients caused by a lawyer's loss of paperwork, failure to respond to clients, and failure to file cases, appeals, and other court documents in a timely manner. Case law shows that disorganized behavior rising to a pattern of conduct prejudicial to client interests will earn stern sanctions from disciplinary authorities—even when the conduct does not rise to misappropriation of client property. One illustrative case concerned a lawyer very well respected among colleagues and clients in his field but also known to have serious organization problems. The lawyer often failed to return telephone calls and had no procedure for new-client intake and no docket management system. Eventually, after the lawyer failed to adequately handle matters related to a will and a medical malpractice action—and after several private reprimands—his state's disciplinary board found that he had violated several rules of professional conduct, including those related to diligence and communication. The board recommended public censure and three years of probation with a practice monitor. (These cases holdings are cited as behavior outcome examples; for purposes of this chapter, case names need not be cited.)

IV. The True Meaning of "Organization"

Organization is directly tied to professionalism in the law because it empowers lawyers to have a stronger command of their work spaces and work flow so that they may work more efficiently in environments that enable them to feel more at peace and in control: qualities that inform performance, client satisfaction, reputations as legal professionals and, indeed, the legal profession as a whole.

One of the greatest misconceptions about organization is that to be organized one is or has to be a cleaning fanatic, and that cleaning itself is the key to organizational success. Cleaning, or perfect neatness, has little to do with it. Anyone can spend long hours cleaning his or her work space (or have someone else do it), but cleaning without a plan is a waste of time. Organization involves devising a personal system that requires daily maintenance and that can be tweaked occasionally as warranted. The focus should be less on idealized notions of how you think an organized lawyer should operate and more on the actual ways you spend your work day, day in and day out. Organization, then, is a highly individualized process of realistically exploring one's natural preferences when working and living among his or her things, and making the sometimes-difficult choices that best address those inclinations. Becoming organized is not "one size fits all."

The organizational process has both visual and conceptual elements, and it is not enough to simply "know where everything is." Many lawyers with disheveled work spaces claim to know where everything is, and they actually may. But because perception still matters in the legal profession, colleagues and clients who see a work space overflowing with clutter, instead of thinking that the lawyer is busy and in demand, may actually question his or her professionalism and ability to handle the caseload and work. So, it is not enough to *be* organized. A lawyer who also *appears to be* organized is likely to receive the greatest benefits from the process and garner the most positive responses from those with whom he or she works and interacts.

V. Elements of "Do It Yourself" Organizing

A lawyer's sense of order comes from personal knowledge of the whereabouts of all of the contents in his or her workspace. A lawyer must develop—and follow—his or her own clear and realistic rules to achieve that sense of order. While colleagues and assistants should be aware of the lawyer's rules, personal-organizing responsibilities cannot be delegated. Assistants and others may follow the rules the lawyer writes, but the lawyer must lead.

It is important to be mindful of small daily activities that should inform organizational choices. What must be pushed aside or searched for when the phone rings? How is the work space left at the end of the day? Are daily "to do" lists used? What is the first thing typically done upon arrival in the morning? Is recycling a personal or firm priority? How heavy is reliance on electronic devices, including the computer? What is taken to meetings, and how are notes recorded before and after interactions with colleagues and clients? If someone needed to find something in the office, how easily could it be located? Is filing an unrealistic expectation on a daily or weekly basis? How much time is spent writing, reading and responding to email? Which tasks are delegable to an assistant? Answering these questions objectively will provide best guidance for development of an effective organizational plan.

It is also important to determine what information stays and what goes. Of the items in the "keep" pile, a good half of them probably can be archived, and some of the other half can be discarded. What is viewed as "historic" or "important" enough to store for safekeeping? Does the firm have rules for archiving clients' files? When and how would these items lose that designation? Each lawyer will have a different answer, and no one's answer will be incorrect, provided he or she is honest about personal proclivities and commits to following the rules.

Times have changed since the days when files consisted entirely of paper documents held in a legal-sized folder, with everyone sharing the same one master copy. Still, there will be paper files, and it takes more than a neat grouping of them to achieve an organized file. For a filing system to work, the name placed on the file should give the lawyer a high degree of certainty that any document on that topic will be found in that file. In developing a personal filing system, a lawyer again must explore and understand how he or she works most efficiently on a daily basis. What's the first file-related task in the morning? Do files leave the office? Besides papers, what other tangible, electronic-media items (e.g., disks) will be placed in files? How often will files be weeded through to keep them clean and well managed, and where will items be archived? Are files left open on the desk? Will they be put away when the lawyer is finished with them, or will they remain stacked on a table or chair? Are there file cabinets in the desk used for that purpose? Here again, an honest assessment of personal tendencies should inform selection of organizing materials and a plan for using them.

In addition to files stored in your desk, in nearby file cabinets, and in other locations, some files may end up on top of the desk because they are the "messy" ones or because they have been set aside as more pressing issues have come up. A bottom of the desktop pile should never become a permanent home for problem files. The lawyer should determine what is atop the desk that could or should be placed in file folders in the interest of privacy, or simply to keep the desktop under control. Color-coding can be an effective tool for organizing personal file systems and personal file colors should differ from the colors used by the firm.

Although some lawyers continue to maintain records in the traditional paper format, and there generally is still one master file for each client, lawyers now also must keep track of countless electronic files. They are often preserved in multiple copies and versions, including updates and revisions that may not match the contents of the paper version. It is crucial to develop reliable methods of maintaining the paper and electronic files in your office, as well as to devise a way to make sure these methods can be readily discerned by others. Any version of a document, whether paper or electronic, that has independent relevance or significance—with a different series of margin notes, for example—must be filed and labeled in a way that signals its significance, and not simply lumped in with other versions or iterations or copies of the same or a similar document.

Electronic files do not occupy as much physical space as paper, but even more than paper files, they must be properly labeled, maintained, and stored. Note that a lawyer may receive hundreds of emails each day. To keep email management from veering out of control, the efficient lawyer will devise—and follow—a system for handling priority emails; managing, responding to, and later retrieving other emails; and deleting unwanted emails. For some lawyers, the better approach is a personal system of classifying all substantive emails by category and moving them into folders. (*See* e.g., *Empty Your Inbox: 4 Ways to Take Control of Your Email*, MICROSOFT AT WORK, http://www.microsoft.com/atwork/productivity/email.aspx#fbid=hrrzPPyMbst (last visited April 4, 2013).) Beyond emails, countless other materials such as documents, images, cases, articles, correspondence and presentations—all in a variety of programs and formats—should be corralled and filed into a system that will enable prompt and easy access.

A luxury of relatively limitless space exists with electronic files—unless one is bound by constraints imposed by employers, equipment, or both. With more storage "space," there's often less pressure to maintain the same disciplined upkeep. Nonetheless, imposing a requirement to spend five minutes per day on electronic upkeep is a wise time investment. That five minutes a day adds up to just over one day per year – and spending just one day a year maintaining electronic files will produce countless dividends every day, regardless of one's position.

VI. Organizing Tips

As in most office environments, law firms and other businesses that employ lawyers tend to have fairly simple and conservative office furniture and layouts. Offices or cubicles generally have a desk, chair, file cabinet, shelving unit, and guest seating. Some spaces will have extra pieces, such as a credenza or a small table and chairs for a conversation area. A window usually completes the picture.

The central and most essential area in one's space is the working surface—the desk top. Strategic use of desk drawers will advantageously free up valuable real estate on the desk's surface. Everything on top of the desk needs to be useful, functional, or decorative—in that order. The top of the desk should hold primary sources, while items stored inside the desk drawers are secondary sources. If there is limited drawer space, those secondary sources will need to be stored in another part of the office, such as on a bookshelf, but close enough to be within easy reach.

Which sources should be classified as primary and which as secondary? What is useful, functional, or decorative? The answers are not written in stone, nor do they depend on the amount of space one has to work with. Rather, they depend on having an established, viable organizational plan that works best for the individual lawyer. Otherwise, anything goes, and everything stays—an approach that the lawyer should recognize is no plan at all.

VII. Conclusion

A final step for a lawyer creating a personal organizational plan should be to type up a master file list, keep it in the "Reference" folder on the desk top and email a copy to collaborating colleagues and assistants. The master should include colors, titles, and locations of all file folders. That way, anyone who might need to locate a file will have a general idea of where to look. Less-organized colleagues might be slightly annoyed (or secretly envious), but even they will appreciate attempts to save valuable time and information. It also may set an example that others will be inspired to emulate.

The decision to become more organized is a personal one that will yield many professional benefits. It takes time and careful thought on the front end, and it requires constant care, commitment, exploration, decision-making, and revision. In the long run, it will pay great dividends in the form of an enhanced sense of control, decreased levels of stress and anxiety, and frankly, a lessened risk of disciplinary violations and legal malpractice.

KELLY LYNN ANDERS is the author of *The Organized Lawyer* (Carolina Academic Press 2009) and *Advocacy to Zealousness: Learning Lawyering Skills from Classic Films* (Carolina Academic Press 2012). She is a member of the ABA Standing Committee on Professionalism.

Chapter 20

THE GLOBALIZATION OF PROFESSIONALISM

ROBERT E. LUTZ

I. Challenges to Conventional Legal Practice and Universal Professionalism

Dynamic forces of global change are revolutionizing the practice of law, and the legal profession is confronting existential questions of how to adapt to a new world economic order while preserving its own core values. In the international-transnational practice context, accelerating globalization and technology innovation are challenging conventional practice approaches and testing ethical and professionalism norms.

These forces increasingly are placing lawyers from countries with established, well-ordered legal and business regimes, such as the United States and Great Britain, on *terra incognita*; that is, either physically or "virtually" inserting them into foreign lands with foreign laws, legal cultures, and business and social customs. Choice-of-law entanglements, a spotty rule of law presence in many nations, and the corrosive impact of corruption on professional ethics and ideals in many corners of the world all emphatically point to the need for a new global professionalism. Only through acceptance of consensual standards can we, as a profession, demystify international-transnational practice and build a global legal system firmly anchored in the rule of law and professionalism principles, rather than uncertainty and at times chaos. More than ever, the role of the lawyer— acting professionally to uphold the core values of honesty, integrity, and civility—will be pre-eminent in suppressing corruption and in essential advocacy of corporate social responsibility in the international system.

For a new generation of U.S.-trained lawyers entering transnational practice, the powerful forces transforming the world present both opportunity and responsibility. A wide-open field awaits those lawyers ready to advance the rule of law across borders and to do the deals, write the policy, and handle the cases that will shape the world's future.

With that opportunity comes the burden of adapting more adroitly than ever to clashing legal cultures by working toward a universal professionalism and ethics lexicon; representing the profession's enduring ideals; urging socially responsible conduct by clients; and taking a stand against corrupt practices that undermine economic stability and foil progress. The road ahead to a global brand of professionalism is long and arduous, but lawyers engaged in transnational practice must find common ground if the legal profession is to remain at the center of social and commercial development globally. The question is not whether the world inhabited by lawyers is undergoing radical change—that is a given. The question, rather, is whether we as a profession will keep up or lose relevance over time.

Encouragingly, recent developments suggest that needed global standards are starting to emerge, especially in the areas of social responsibility and corruption-fighting.

II. Professionalism and Globalization

The legal profession in the United States is conducted via a set of values that guide the provision of legal services by lawyers to serve clients and to uphold a special responsibility to the public for the quality of justice.

At the core of these values is a personal professional commitment to perform with *honesty*, *integrity*, and *civility*. Some have endeavored to give the concept of professionalism more concrete meaning by further reducing it into constituent elements. They find these values manifested in what lawyers do on a daily basis, in the standards to which they hold their fellow lawyers, in the best practices of the profession, and in their compliance with the conduct rules promulgated and enforced by regulatory authorities of the legal profession.

Thus, among lawyers, judges and legal scholars, "professionalism" is a pliable term. For different people, entities, and institutions, "professionalism" suggests different sets of lawyer characteristics, practitioner duties, and behavioral rules. In the United States, the recent focus of lawyer "professionalism" inquiry, however, seems to be an effort to re-generate individual lawyer self-respect among peers and within the bar generally, and to engender public goodwill toward the profession.

A. *The International Practice Context*

But the international practice context presents a very different quality of challenges with respect to what one might call "international practice professionalism." Those challenges are motivating an intensifying search for core understandings of what constitutes "professionalism" in transnational practice.

The context of international-transnational practice differs in significant ways from that of domestic practice (from which our general notions about professionalism are derived). For our purposes, the term "international-transnational practice" refers to the legal practice of lawyers trained and licensed in a "western-style" jurisdiction, such as American or British lawyers, and practicing in an international setting. Today, lawyers in an international-transnational practice engage a wide range of legal-minded participants in a foreign setting (e.g., solo to medium- to large-firm lawyers; in-house and government lawyers (or lawyer equivalents); and non-governmental organization representatives, to name a few). The legal practice activities covered can be divided into three general types: operational (compliance); litigation (which includes other forms of dispute resolution such as arbitration and mediation); and transactional (including consulting, counseling, negotiation, contract-drafting, deal-making, and financing).

Relative to their U.S. lawyer counterparts, lawyers in foreign jurisdictions may function in very different roles with respect to the judicial process and civil society. The profession in foreign lands, for example, may recognize specialized categories of the legal professional, such as barrister and notary, delivering niche legal services not found in the American legal system. The judge-lawyer relationship in court may also be different than in the United States. The credentials and education authorizing one to "practice" law also vary greatly across foreign jurisdictions.

Effective client representation in a multijurisdictional world requires developing appreciation for and sensitivity to other nations' cultures, especially their legal cultures. Those schooled and operating in non-Western cultures may approach legal problems in a very different way.

Choice of law is more a civil procedure than a professionalism area of inquiry, yet one with ethics-rule implications. (But navigating through a morass of choice-of-law questions with adversaries and clients having entirely different legal orientations and business customs can no doubt put a lawyer's professional ideals to the test). Choice of law disputes collectively constitute a major distinction between international-transnational practice and domestic practice. In the international-transnational context, the question of which state's law governs often adds much greater complexity to a representation. It is not unusual for a transnational legal practitioner to discover that several nations' laws control different issues in a transaction. In addition to an amalgam of national laws, international conventions or customs may also govern pieces of a deal or dispute.

B. The Lawyer's Shrinking World

Development of the international legal profession over the last half century is in large measure a function of economic and technological evolution. The impact of that change on many legal practices has been simply astounding. While geography or "place" traditionally was the regulating concept that tied a lawyer to a specific location and subjected her to the regulatory control of that jurisdiction, many lawyers today venture far and wide to serve their clients—often "virtually" through reliance on remarkable communication technologies invented in the last decade. Mobility and trans-jurisdictional virtual and physical "presence" provide access to a world well beyond a law firm desk in the United States.

To a large extent, transnational lawyering is conducted by United States and British law firms, which dominate the worldwide export of legal services with offices located in many of the overseas business centers. Canadian, Australian, and other European firms play a secondary role. When advising, litigating against, or negotiating with lawyers from non-western-legal cultures, they are likely to have different understandings and traditions that color their "professional" behavior. Even in less adversarial contexts—such as cooperative, legal team efforts—there may be marked differences.

C. Some International Professionalism Challenges

In tension with—but also partially a product of—the dynamic forces driving global change, challenges to the rule of law around the world are testing the ability of the private and public sectors to rely on a steady and consistent application of the law. Corruption in both sectors threatens confidence in legal systems' capacity for fairness and justice, and discourages participation in multinational business activity.

Anti-corruption principles continue to gain traction in international compacts, giving lawyers even firmer footing for discouraging clients' corrupt practices, limiting representation of clients with a record of corrupt dealings, or declining representation of them.

In the area of corporate social responsibility as well, new norms are taking hold. For years, states have been reluctant to commit to regulatory regimes that would make corporate enterprises a subject of international responsibility. Yet the international community is beginning to articulate ways in which the responsibilities of business and states may combine to prevent abusive business practices, especially in the human rights area. Lawyers in international-transnational practice play a decisive role in advising and challenging corporate clients to be socially responsible.

1. Resisting Corruption in Rule of Law-Challenged Countries

Corruption, both public and private, is poison to the fair and just operation of a legal system. It infects every aspect of a nation, making it internally dysfunctional and externally handicapped and stigmatized, thus rendering it unable to participate on an equal footing with other states. Corrupt events in the private and public institutions of a society may appear isolated or controllable at first, but then evolve into a culture of corruption that is extremely difficult to eradicate. It can eat away at the very fabric of civil society, inflicting devastating damage on the innocent and unprotected non-participants who become the ultimate victims. It diverts funds intended for development and undermines a government's ability to provide basic services, feeds inequality and injustice, and discourages foreign investment and aid.

Most significantly, corrupt legal institutions and their participants destroy the relationship between government and the governed—the essential ingredients of a healthy and vibrant society governed by the rule of law. Globalized professionalism prohibits corrupt action. It abhors it and incites active opposition to it. Nothing short of a rule of law-centric regime will constitute a cure to corruption.

In the efforts to define professionalism in the international sphere, there is unambiguous condemnation of both public and private corruption. While historically the focus was on bribery of governmental officials, other forms of corruption have also been addressed (*e.g.,* corporate espionage, intellectual property piracy). The global attitude toward corruption has substantially evolved since the United States enacted the first legislation outlawing bribery of foreign public officials by private actors in the mid-1970s. Despite the plaintive cries of multinational corporations that the anti-bribery law placed them at a competitive disadvantage, foreign government claims that the United States was interfering with their sovereign affairs, and accusations that the United States was engaged in economic imperialism and the export of a unique, if not strange, moral code, the U.S. stood firm.

As a direct consequence, today the major international conventions embrace a responsibility to resist and oppose private and public corruption. Those conventions include: the United Nations Convention Against

Corruption; the Organization for Economic Co-operation and Development's (OECD) Convention on Combating Bribery of Foreign Public Officials in International Business Transactions; and the Inter-American Convention Against Corruption. Similar moves have been made by international organizations (*e.g.*, the World Bank) and many countries (*e.g.*, the United Kingdom Bribery Act, the U.S. Foreign Corrupt Practices Act of 1977). Moreover, anti-corruption principles will necessarily inform broader international legal professionalism standards as they emerge.

However strong the emerging paper proscriptions against corrupt practices, defeating corruption will in many instances come down to interactions among lawyers, clients and adversaries. The legal profession, with its core values of honesty, integrity, and civility, is uniquely positioned to deter and combat public-private corruption, and to adopt socially responsible, non-exploitative policies. Lawyers have tremendous influence over their clients' conduct, whether in the public or private sector. They have the ability to encourage clients to conduct transactions in an ethical and principled manner.

The proposition that lawyers may not engage in corrupt client conduct such as bribery without impermissibly tainting themselves is evidenced by the presence of the anti-bribery principle in many instruments adopted over the past 40 years. An American lawyer's professional obligations in that regard are also covered by the lawyer's professional responsibility code (*see, e.g.*, ABA Model Rules of Professional Conduct, Rules 1.2, 3.5(a), 4.1(a), 8.4). Although many lawyers practicing transnationally confront situations where opportunities for corrupt practices present themselves and may be enticing economically, lawyers should find comfort and support in the knowledge that the international legal community is gradually constructing a professional norm that makes it unethical, unprofessional and increasingly illegal (under municipal legal regimes) to engage in such behavior.

2. Role of Lawyers in Advancing Human Rights

Corporate social responsibility principles have occupied an important place in international law discussions and in the work of international organizations for some time. But the idea of binding international norms applied directly to corporate enterprise activities was generally rejected by the international community during the 1970s and 1980s (*see e.g.*, U.N. Centre on Transnational Corporations, the International Labour Organization, and OECD Guidelines for Multinational Corporations). During the 1990s, a partial shift in attitude occurred as part of the impetus to facilitate foreign investment in many parts of the world. Notwithstanding the corporate world's increasing receptivity in that period to the notion of social responsibility policies, international consternation followed revelations of human rights abuses associated with major multinational corporations' activities in foreign lands.

It was not until the last several years that the international community agreed to an approach and substantive principles for dealing with business activities in the international system. Professor John Ruggie, Special Representative to the United Nations' Secretary-General, was assigned, first in 2005, the task of clarifying the responsibilities of business related to human rights. In 2008, he was assigned to develop "Guiding Principles" to implement the duties he previously described as: (1) the duty to protect human rights (principally focused on states); (2) the duty to respect them (focused on both business and states); and (3) the duty to remedy violations (primarily focused on states, but also contains references to non-judicial remedies that can implemented by business).

The Guiding Principles gained endorsement of the United Nations Council of Human Rights in June 2011, and of the American Bar Association in February 2012. As a document, it elevates corporate/business responsibility to a global standard of expected conduct for all business enterprises, above and beyond the responsibility to comply with national laws and regulations protecting human rights.

For the "business" of legal services, it guides lawyers and law firms on the need to establish principles, at the level of professional standards, to protect and respect human rights and to remedy human rights violations. To paraphrase in summary form, the Guiding Principles document calls upon all businesses to: (1) adopt, communicate and embed a high-level commitment to respect human rights; (2) employ a human rights due diligence process to assess, integrate, track, and communicate about actual and potential human rights impacts; and (3) remediate negative human rights impacts that business contributed to or caused.

Applied as a professional standard to the work of lawyers and the business of law firms, this emerging professionalism standard would extend to law firm employment of lawyers and staff. It also can cover all human rights impacts in the supply chain of legal services with which the law firm is involved. By its terms, the Guiding Principles also establish professionalism standards for lawyers and law firms, making lawyers responsible for identifying and addressing how a client's activities might affect human rights. This new lawyer obligation arguably imposes a duty to investigate the human rights impacts of the client before committing to represent it; to establish a high-level law firm policy to address such issues with clients; and—consistent with such other professional standards as those calling for zealous, faithful, and confidential representation—to withdraw from representation if necessary to avoid aiding and abetting human rights violations of the business.

While currently viewed as a "soft-law" instrument, the Guiding Principles (and their application to all businesses including law schools) are gaining momentum as a standard of conduct expected of those engaged in business activities. Much like environmental impact assessment standards, which initially lacked broad acceptance, the Guiding Principles seem well positioned to crystalize over time as standards of conduct for the legal profession. By adopting these standards as a profession and applying them to clients worldwide, lawyers as a profession will be poised to lead the way on adherence to human rights values.

D. The Heightened Need for Conflict Avoidance in Transnational Practice

New professionalism standards for international legal practice will blend aspirational ideals with ethics and some procedural rules, as in the case of conflict resolution. Legal representation of clients depends on competent, zealous and conflict-free lawyering. In the transnational setting, however, representation often necessitates associating with other lawyers from countries that may have different, even conflicting, professional and ethical responsibilities. For example, assume the attorney ethics code in

Nation A would allow counsel to represent both parties in a certain trans-actional circumstance, but the code of Nation B would put co-counsel from that country in a conflict in the identical situation, forcing one of the parties to find new counsel. Where there is a prospect that conflicts related to the lawyers' respective professional responsibilities will arise (as posited above), one solution might be to agree at the time of engage-ment to a choice of ethics rule to apply to all lawyer participants, with the informed consent of the client. Much like a choice-of-law provision in a contract, such a "choice-of-rule" agreement would be a demonstration of the intentions of the lawyers and parties. As a private agreement between the parties, it would not necessarily bind the court in the instance of a challenge, but it could be used to guide it, and serve to provide important predictability in such situations.

E. Responding to Globalizing Impacts on Professionalism Wrought by Social Media, Technology, and Global Outsourcing

The new social media presents lawyers with an open forum as well as communication access to potential markets of legal services worldwide. It offers a means to convey information easily, cheaply, and expeditiously. At the same time, the use of social media in international lawyering also introduces greater risk of conflicting with the social norms, sensibilities and cultures of other societies. Note, for example, that some regimes have prohibitions against lawyer advertising; others restrict the transmission of "private" information under strict privacy laws (for example, the Euro-pean Union). Thus, lawyers operating within the Internet environment, and its vast range of applications, need to appreciate the demands that professionalism and ethics impose with respect to the confidentiality of communications involving clients and the ways in which certain profes-sional uses of social media might run the risk of offending or violating foreign country rules.

The outsourcing by United States lawyers of legal processing services (e.g., e-discovery) and other legal work (e.g., drafting of motions and briefs) to foreign nations and persons who reside there and who, in many instances, are not licensed to practice law in the United States or the foreign jurisdiction, poses ethical questions about competency, confidentiality, and conflicts of interest—all matters relevant to "professional" representation. U.S. firms under increasing pressure to hold down litigation discovery costs, in an era of burgeoning e-discovery, have made outsourcing in places like India, the Philippines, and Northern Ireland a vibrant industry. To maintain a professional approach to foreign outsourcing (or what has been referred to as "offshoring"), lawyers managing the engagement should have a reasonable belief that the other lawyers' services will contribute to the competent and ethical representation of the client. The hiring firm should also be mindful that non-lawyers often are involved in outsourced work. The professional lawyer, in sum, must make reasonable efforts to ensure that the non-lawyers' services are provided in a manner that is compatible with the lawyer's ethical and other professional obligations.

III. "Professionalizing" International-Transnational Practice

Standards of transnational professionalism are gradually being developed, built upon the foundation of shared values. "Professionalizing" transnational practice will necessitate agreement on a broad set of standards representing an amalgam of professional ideals, ethics rules, and procedural conventions (see choice-of-rule discussion above). Effective transnational practice norms will go well beyond, but will certainly encompass, the discrete anti-corruption and social responsibility guidelines promulgated to date.

One approach to development of a complete global professionalism code would be to try to identify shared values of professionalism from a variety of legal cultures, and to attempt to find commonality among them. Another might be the listing of aspirational standards dealing with professionalism in different legal cultures and different contexts. Still another approach might involve the simple listing of best practices based on domestic law practice in the United States.

In the accompanying text box, various existing professionalism codes and guidelines are reviewed, some in paraphrased form, as examples of possible starting points of the discussion of global professionalism standards development.

Examples of Professionalism Codes

A listing of the objectives and virtues of professionalism is offered by the 1990 Florida Bar adoption of the "Ideals and Goals of Professionalism." In that document, paraphrased here, professionalism is identified as including:

1. a commitment to serve others;
2. dedication to the proper use of one's knowledge to promote a fair and just result;
3. enhancing one's knowledge and skills;
4. ensuring that concern for results does not subvert fairness, honesty, respect, and courtesy for others;
5. contributing one's skill, knowledge, and influence to serve others and promote the public good (including providing equal access to the judicial system);
6. educating the public about capabilities and limits of the profession; and
7. accountability for one's professional conduct.

An effort to internationalize professionalism, by identifying the shared professional values of international law practice, was undertaken a few years ago by the association of law firms known as Lex Mundi. (*See* Terrell, 23 Emory International Law Review 472 (2009).) The author cited six common professional values that are shared by member firms of that association. They are paraphrased here:

1. Ethic of excellence (providing the client with best possible legal assistance);
2. Ethic of integrity—the responsibility to reject giving assistance to a client inconsistent with professional values;
3. Respect for the legal system and the rule of law;
4. Respect for other lawyers and their work;
5. Commitment to accountability to clients and the public; and
6. Responsibility for the adequate distribution of legal services to all.

The American Board of Trial Advocates (ABOTA) has also composed and is actively promoting a "Code of Professionalism." The ABOTA Code is similar to those described above in some, but not all, respects. The ABOTA Code states: "As a member of the American Board of Trial Advocates, I shall:

- Always remember that the practice of law is first and foremost a profession.
- Encourage respect for the law, the courts, and the right to trial by jury.
- Always remember that my word is my bond and honor my responsibilities to serve as an officer of the court and protector of individual rights.
- Contribute time and resources to public service, public education, charitable, and pro bono activities in my community.
- Work with the other members of the bar, including judges, opposing counsel, and those whose practices are different from mine, to make our system of justice more accessible and responsive.
- Resolve matters and disputes expeditiously, without unnecessary expense, and through negotiation whenever possible.
- Keep my clients well-informed and involved in making decisions affecting them.
- Achieve and maintain proficiency in my practice and continue to expand my knowledge of the law.
- Be respectful in my conduct toward my adversaries.
- Honor the spirit and intent, as well as the requirements of applicable rules or codes of professional conduct and shall encourage others to do so."

While achieving consensus on a global legal professionalism code will be difficult, the alternative of forcing lawyers engaged in transnational practice to continue to cope with a kaleidoscopic global legal system would inflict lasting harm on the legal profession and the rule of law. What might have been a clear understanding of the ethics and professional conduct rules, as well as standards of professionalism, at home in the United States, too often becomes confused, conflicted, and highly problematic in an international setting. Multiple jurisdictions' legal cultures, national customs and regulatory regimes often impose very different and conflicting standards.

IV. Evolving Global Legal Practice and the Future of Legal Professionalism

Legal practice in an international context is subject to rapidly evolving communication and information technologies that both facilitate and complicate the delivery of legal services. Clients of varying sizes, wealth, and business forms present international-transnational lawyers with a remarkable complexity of multijurisdictional issues.

The dynamic state of flux and uncertainty that characterizes international practice will only intensify going forward, absent development and adoption of global legal professionalism norms. Responses to the challenges of technology and globalization have offered new clarifications about lawyers' conduct and capacity to effectively, consistently operate with the values of honesty and integrity in a changing global environment.

The difficulties of practicing in countries beset by corruption pose substantial obstacles, but they are not insurmountable, even when the playing field is not level. The anti-corruption movement, assisted by international legal support in the form of multilateral conventions and stronger national enforcement, has slowly created a global rejection (in principle) of bribery. The national acculturation of anti-corruption attitudes and rejection of corrupt practices by clients at the urging of counsel are a major advancement for the international legal profession. Professionalism will demand that the legal profession, in dealings with clients, assist in making respect for human rights standard business policy and practice.

While no universal body is available to pronounce or enforce professionalism norms for the international and transnational lawyer, important norms of conduct are emerging that will serve to guide practitioners in the future. Without the support and guidance of such norms, the legal profession's vital interest in preserving professional ideals will be at risk. The next generation of international-transnational lawyers will play a pivotal role in moderating that risk and preserving timeless professional values.

Sources/Reading

Ronald A. Brand, *Professional Responsibility in a Transnational Transactions Practice*, 17 J.L. & Com. 301 (1998).

Ethan S. Burger, *International Legal Malpractice: Not Only Will the Dog Eventually Bark, It Will Also Bite*, 38 St. Mary's L.J. 1025 (2007).

Laurence Etherington & Robert Lee, *Ethical Codes and Cultural Context: Ensuring Legal Ethics in the Global Law Firm*, 14 Ind. J. Global Legal Stud. 95 (2007).

John Flood, *Transnational Lawyering: Clients, Ethics, and Regulation, in* Lawyers in Practice: Ethical Decision Making in Context 176–96 (Leslie C. Levin & Lynn Mather eds., 2012).

Stephen Gillers, *A Profession, If You Can Keep It: How Information Technology and Fading Borders Are Reshaping the Law Marketplace and What We Should Do About It*, 63 Hastings L.J. 953 (2012).

Jonathan Goldsmith, *The Core Values of the Legal Profession for Lawyers Today and Tomorrow*, 28 Nw. J. Int'l. L. & Bus. 441 (2008).

Vivien Holmes & Simon Rice, *Our Common Future: The Imperative For Contextual Ethics in a Connected World, in* Alternative Perspectives on Lawyers and Legal Ethics: Reimagining the Profession 56–84 (Francesca Bartlett, Reid Mortensen & Kieran Tranter eds., 2011).

Robert E. Lutz, *American Perspectives on the Duty of Competence: Special Problems and Risks in Advising on Foreign Law, in* Rights, Liability, and Ethics in International Legal Practice 81–109 (Mary C. Daly & Roger J. Goebel, eds., 1995).

Robert E. Lutz, *An Essay Concerning the Changing International Legal Profession*, 18 Sw. J. Int'l L. 215 (2011).

Robert E. Lutz, *On Combating the Culture of Corruption*, 10 Sw. J.L. & Trade Am. 263 (2004).

Robert E. Lutz, *Reforming Approaches to Educating Transnational Lawyers: Observations from America*, 61 J. Legal Educ. 449 (2012).

JAMES MOLITERNO & GEORGE HARRIS, GLOBAL ISSUES IN LEGAL ETHICS (2007).

Report of the Special Rep. of the Secretary-General on the Issue of Human Rights and Transnational Corporations and Other Business Enterprises, *Guiding Principles on Business and Human Rights: Implementing the United Nations 'Protect, Respect and Remedy' Framework*, Human Rights Council, Doc. A/HRC/17/31 (Mar. 21, 2011) (by John Ruggie), *available at* http://www.terna.it/LinkClick.aspx?fileticket=RrU6uaHqL8I%3D&tabid=5399.

Timothy P. Terrell, *Professionalism on an International Scale: The Lex Mundi Project to Identify the Fundamental Shared Values of Law Practice*, 23 EMORY INT'L L. REV. 469 (2009).

Timothy P. Terrell & James H. Wildman, *Rethinking 'Professionalism'*, 41 EMORY L.J. 403 (1992).

Detlev Vagts, *Transnational Litigation and Professional Ethics*, *in* INTERNATIONAL LITIGATION STRATEGIES AND PRACTICE 25–31 (Barton Legum ed., 2005).

ROBERT E. LUTZ is a Professor of Law at Southwestern Law School in Los Angeles, CA. Professor Lutz is past Chair of the ABA Section of International Law and of the ABA Task Force on International Trade in Legal Services, and is Co-chair of the Indo-U.S. Trade Policy Forum's Working Group on Legal Services. Professor Lutz was an active contributor to the work of the ABA Commission on Ethics 20/20 on issues related to globalization of elegal services.

INDEX